Down on the Island, Up on the Main

A Recollected History of South Bristol, Maine

Compiled and Annotated by Ellen Vincent

Tilbury House, Publishers • Gardiner, Maine
The South Bristol Historical Society

Down on the Island, Up on the Main

A Recollected History of South Bristol, Maine

Tilbury House, Publishers
2 Mechanic Street
Gardiner, ME 04345
800-582-1899 • www.tilburyhouse.com

South Bristol Historical Society
2124 State Route 129
PO Box 229
South Bristol, ME 04568

First Edition May 2003

10 9 8 7 6 5 4 3 2 1

Library of Congress Cataloging-in-Publication Data

Down on the island, up on the main : a recollected history of South Bristol, Maine / compiled and annotated by Ellen Vincent.
p. cm.
Includes bibliographical references and index.
ISBN 0-88448-250-2 (alk. paper)
1. South Bristol (Me.)—History. 2. South Bristol (Me.)—Biography.
I. Vincent, Ellen, 1949-. II. South Bristol Historical Society (South Bristol, Me.)

F29.S673 D69 2003
974.1'57—dc21

2002151870

Cover and text designed on Crummett Mountain by Edith Allard, Somerville, Maine.
Editorial services by Jennifer Bunting and Barbara Diamond.
Layout by Nina DeGraff, Basil Hill Graphics, Somerville, Maine.
Scans by Integrated Composition Systems, Spokane, Washington.
Covers printed by the John P. Pow Company, South Boston, Massachusetts.
Text printing and binding by Maple Vail, Kirkwood, New York.

For the good people of South Bristol,
whose story this is

And for J. Douglas Thompson,
home at last.

Contents

Foreword

THIS IS A WORK of collective memory, an art of people. When Ellen Vincent first told me about this idea in 1993, neither of us knew what it would grow into, nor of the long journey she was embarking upon with the good people of South Bristol, Maine. As the summers passed, and they took her into their homes and hearts, this work took on a life of its own. All of her considerable creative energies were focused on teasing out and bringing together these images and memories, and preserving them for the town. What began as a personal art project became a community work.

When the time came for the exhibition of photographs, stories, and artifacts to open in Damariscotta in October 1998 I was fascinated to see how she would put it all together, and how the townspeople would react to it. When my wife asked me what it was going to be I realized that, even after talking with Ellen about it for all these years, I couldn't really describe it. So I said: first, the community has grown to love her and she them, so it will be very good, and second, it will be very good because Ellen makes things that are very good.

Even then I didn't know *how* good. It wasn't an art show, it was a day of wonder. We took our time there, drifting around reading and re-reading and listening, and I'd say I've never been to an event "about" Mainers at which I saw so many Mainers attending. Such a comfort, to drift around and hear all about me the sounds of my childhood.

I can't tell you what a fine thing she has done here, nor how much she is appreciated and loved and honored for doing it. They have become a community again, all those generations of South Bristol, and it was Ellen that began it, by her curiosity and caring and love.

Good art connects us to each other. She has taken "art" out of the paws of the few and given it back to where it came from, and I'm proud to have witnessed that work: bless her for helping us all with this.

Gordon Bok
Camden, Maine

Introduction

I'm not a folklorist, nor do I pretend to be a historian. I had been a professional photographer and sculptor for twenty years when, in 1993, I stumbled on to South Bristol—little knowing that I had found the place that I would come to think of as home, and that would change the entire direction of my creative energies.

The genesis of this undertaking came about during a studio residency at Watershed Center for the Ceramic Arts in Newcastle, Maine. It began with nineteenth-century portrait photographs and tintypes that I had started to find in local flea markets and secondhand shops. There, piled in shoeboxes and scattered on shelves, were the remnants of nameless families: someone's heritage, sold up for a dime. Somber faces, faces of determination and of strength, pensive faces of hollow-eyed children—they leveled their gazes at me and I couldn't resist. I brought stacks of them back to my studio, and as I gradually assembled groupings of the portraits on the wall, began to see correlations between them and the drawings and photographs on which I'd already been working. As I continued to work in their presence they seemed to demand that their story be told, or at the least that they be part of a story I would tell. The composition on the wall grew with the addition of household and maritime artifacts, old pictures of the locale, and faded scraps of handwriting from century-old postcards. I started thinking about piecing together these seemingly random fragments of time to construct a fictional history.

At that juncture, I moved out of the studio to try and get a sense of the local history and the lives of the people there. I began poring through the history collections of small mid-coast town libraries, exploring old graveyards, developing contacts in the nearby village historical societies, meeting and talking to life-long residents of the local communities. As I did this, it struck me that rather than carry through with my original intention of creating a fictional history, it would be far more worthwhile to document the story of a living, breathing place. The focus of my explorations shifted into finding a community to involve myself with: ideally, to find a place that was still a working town, a place where the families and traditions were part of a generations-old continuum. South Bristol was just such a place, and in the short time remaining for me that summer, I began to meet and speak with some of its people: members of the old families whose memories and stories predated modern ways on the peninsula. With the help of town librarian Ellen Shew, I made arrangements to call on the first two of the tradition bearers I was to meet: Margaret House and Billy Kelsey. I went to each of them with the intention of making just a short visit to introduce myself and the notion of the project, but these kind people greeted me at their doors with smiles and armfuls of old photographs; they welcomed me into their homes with quiet grace, and spent hours sharing old tales, photo albums, and family mementos. I knew that I had found my town.

After that year I returned to South Bristol each summer, and as my relationships with the people there deepened, it became clear to me that a major part of the project, a significant installation, should be for them and for the community as a whole: for the children and their parents, and for the older generations whose direct memories would be the bricks and mortar of the story. Even for the youngest generations, vital aspects of life in South Bristol are merely contemporary forms of the old traditions. By engaging them in the process of putting the project together, as well as by telling the history in an informal and visual manner, I hoped to connect them with the rich heritage that has shaped their lives—and that is so important to their parents and grandparents.

In 1997, while on a teaching sabbatical from the Milwaukee Institute of Art and Design, I lived for three months on Rutherford Island, the heart of South Bristol. I concentrated on collecting materials for the installation and working on various aspects of community involvement with the preservation of the town's heritage. During that time, I collected more than 70 hours of oral histories from the town's tradition bearers and made copy negatives of nearly 500 vintage photographs, postcards, and documents from family collections and albums. I also worked with the South Bristol School seventh and eighth graders to help them in undertaking an oral history project of their own. That fall, I brought in Dr. Pauleena MacDougall of the Maine Folklife Center to work with community members interested in organizing a viable historical society. By the end of December we held the first meeting of the South Bristol Historical Society; less than a year and a half later, we had 90 members, a growing archive and genealogy center, and a village building to house the collection.

The first "memory wall" installation opened in October 1998 at Round Top Center for the Arts in Damariscotta. After nearly a week of 12-hour days of arranging and hanging, it topped out at 550 wall pieces—text and photographs—and about 30 artifacts. The opening was wonderful—it far exceeded my expectations, and exactly what I wanted to happen, did: mixed-generation groups of people clustered around the photos and stories, touching them, talking and laughing and teary-eyed. Many wrote down their own memories, and pinned them up on the walls, as I'd hoped; those notes have become part of the history as well.

Since that time, interest and a justifiable pride in South Bristol history has continued to grow. I still visit, correspond with, and interview residents, many of whom have become dear friends. I make copies of vintage photos and documents when they're offered, and still seek out old stories and new storytellers. This book is merely a stage in a work-in-progress, carried on by all of us in the South Bristol Historical Society. It is my fondest hope that the work will continue, and that it will serve as an inspiration for other communities to preserve their own unique histories.

This is truly a collective memory of place, spoken in the words of its people. Their strength of character and unflagging humor have carried them through many decades, and it shows through in the cadence of these tales. Idyllic at times, at other times laden with hardship, this was a place where self-sufficiency was a virtue and neighbors were as family. It has been my great good fortune to have been entrusted with gathering and assembling these recollections, and to now have the opportunity of sharing them in this book. In these pages I hope to share some of my good fortune with the reader. Through the images and rich memories, and with the words of these remarkable people, I hope to take you back in time to a place called South Bristol—back to those days of grace on the coast of Maine.

Ellen Vincent
Whitefish Bay, Wisconsin

Acknowledgments

First and foremost, I am indebted to the tradition bearers of South Bristol who have been so generous in sharing their stories and spending so many hours with me over the years. My gratitude also goes to all of the folks who dug out mounds of old photographs, postcards, and documents for me, many of which are reproduced in this book. The extent of their contributions, along with their names, can be seen in these pages. In South Bristol, I'd also like to thank Dave Andrews for his many contributions to the effort and his unstoppable enthusiasm for South Bristol history; Betsy Andrews for culinary support; Yvonne Chapman for her invaluable work as the South Bristol Historical Society's first president; Jackie Kelsey for making me feel part of the "neighborhood"; and Ellen Wells, whose persistance and diligent efforts on many fronts have helped make this book a reality.

I would also like to acknowledge the support of the Virginia Center for the Creative Arts for the residency fellowship where I plotted out this project; the Milwaukee Institute of Art and Design for providing grants and the sabbatical leave that helped me complete the work; the Watershed Center for the Ceramic Arts residency program, where it all began; and the Maine Humanities Council and Maine Arts Commission for grants making the exhibition of the "memory wall" possible. For their generous publication grants I would like to thank the Timberhead Foundation, the Davis Family Foundation, the Tripod Fund and the Margaret McNally McFarland Fund of the Maine Community Foundation, the Drukker Foundation, and the private contributors who helped fund the production of this book.

My heartfelt thanks, also, to: Gordon Bok, who first put Maine in my heart and believed in my work even when I didn't; Bobby Pearl, whose generosity first brought me to South Bristol; M. E. and Mame Warren for *Bringing Back the Bay*, their inspiring book about my home place; Juris Ubans, University of Southern Maine, for helping me get the project off the ground; Pauleena MacDougall of the Maine Folklife Center, for advice and encouragement; Peter Bartis of the American Folklife Center, for technical advice and notions about community history projects; Phil Hayward and Deane Nesbitt for their editorial wisdom; Joe Herring, National Endowment for the Humanities, for his insights and steadfast encouragement all these years; Jennifer Bunting for her vision, unflagging enthusiasm, and skill in transforming cartons of texts and pictures into a finely crafted book; in Pemaquid, Margo Hope, for her good works and her May baskets; Nancy Freeman and the Round Top Center for the Arts for giving me my first opportunity to show this material to the South Bristol community; Christina Bertoni and Sherrill Edwards Hunnibell, who were with me from the start and added clarity every step of the way; Captain Tim Paegelow, for putting up with my anxieties and my absences and keeping the home fires burning; and, of course, my family, whose loving support makes all things possible.

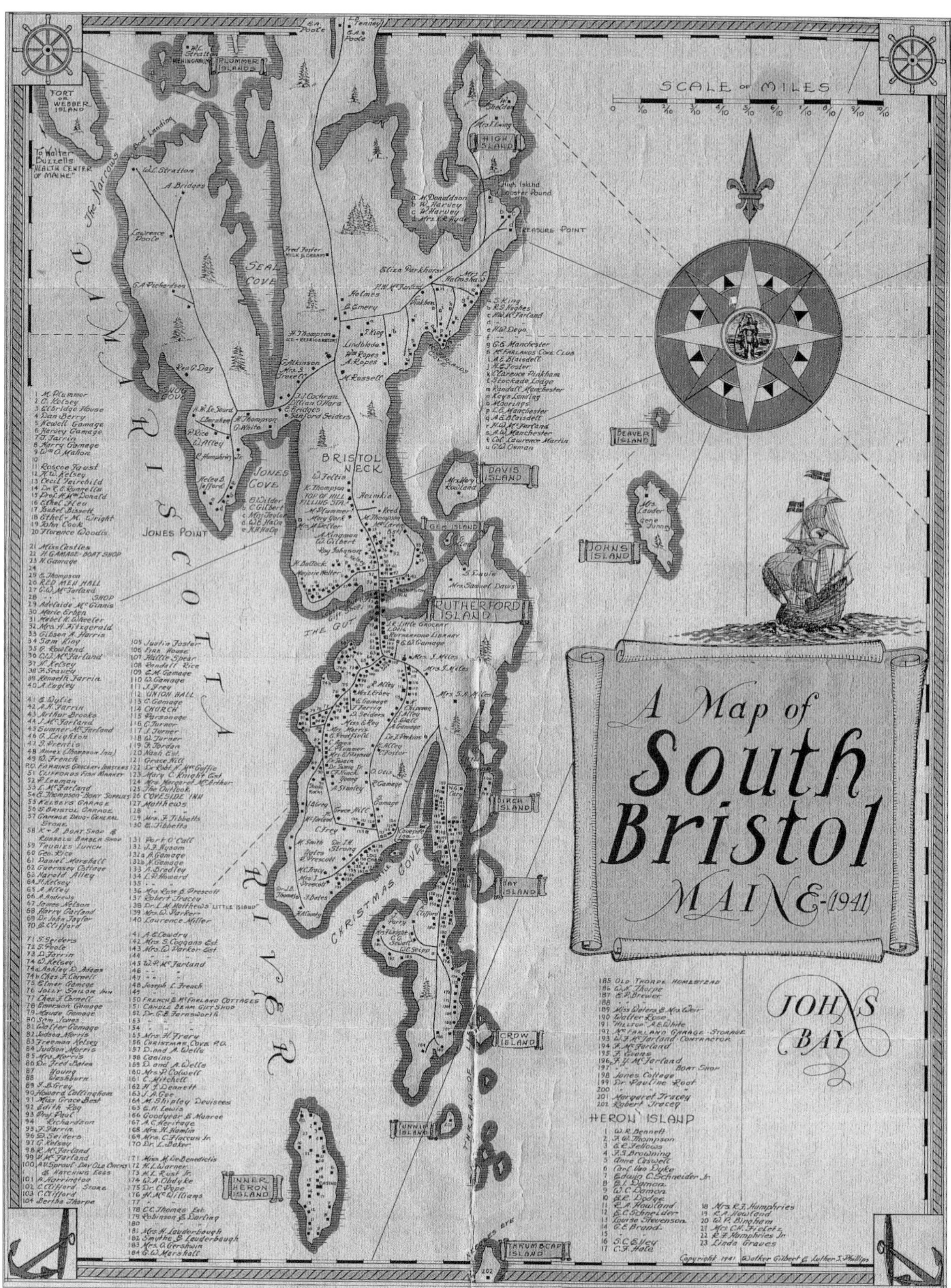

MAP COURTESY OF DAVID W. ANDREWS.

Down on the Island, Up on the Main

A Recollected History of South Bristol, Maine

Those were the days when there were plenty of fish. —Doug Thompson

Afton Farrin, Jr., mans the oars in a dory full of mackerel and bottomfish, along with Alva and Mel Farrin, c. 1960s. Afton H. Farrin, Jr.

Afton, Ted, and Mel Farrin untangle the nets of a mackerel trap near Pemaquid Point, c. 1965. Afton H. Farrin, Jr.

I could look out *from where I lived, right there in that little house—I could see what they were doing. I could see, the night that they shut that whole cove right off—sardines.*

I heard Roy say, "Well, I made three thousand dollars last night." Henry Jones, he was fishing with Henry Jones, and they would do that. Oh, they worked—long hours and hard work, but they did make good money. —Beatrice Plummer Rice

Damariscove Island Coast Guard Station.
AUTHOR PHOTO, 2001

Setting a trap off Pemaquid Point. LYNNE DRISKO

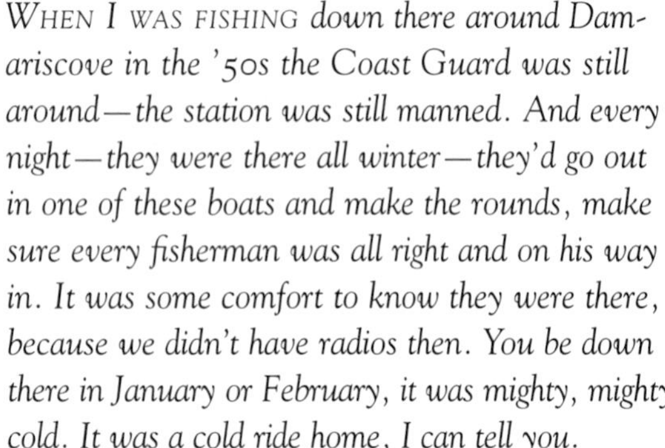

WHEN I WAS FISHING down there around Damariscove in the '50s the Coast Guard was still around—the station was still manned. And every night—they were there all winter—they'd go out in one of these boats and make the rounds, make sure every fisherman was all right and on his way in. It was some comfort to know they were there, because we didn't have radios then. You be down there in January or February, it was mighty, mighty cold. It was a cold ride home, I can tell you.

—Bill Kelsey

AT THAT TIME we were catching whiting. There were plants in Portland; they just were open in the summer. They depended on high school kids for their labor so they usually started after the Fourth of July, really, and went until the kids went back to school in September, so it was a short season. So at that time, when I first started, we were receiving the great price of a cent and a half a pound. So if you caught ten thousand pounds, you got a hundred and fifty dollars. We had to catch a lot of fish because they paid us so little for 'em. You had to catch an unreasonable amount of fish to make a living. The only way a fisherman could survive was to catch more. Always catching more, catching more. —Ralph Norwood

AT THE TIME, all these carriers were in the harbor. They had over thirty thousand bushel of fish over here outside of Witch Island in the nets—in the pockets. Over thirty thousand bushel. They made a hundred dollars a day for thirty days, and that was way back in the '50s. That was big money—they were making a killing. It was an awful raft of fish. All sardines—it was an awful raft of 'em. They went out that one night—and they were stop seining, trying to catch herring all the time—but that one particular night, my Jesus Christ, that area from Witch's Island to McFarland's Cove filled right full. And they just ran the nets out, stopped up any escape holes.... You run the nets out, and in the morning you put the pockets on them and let the fish swim in. The fish go in and they just swim round and round and round—happy fish. —Bill Kelsey

South Bristol fishermen. Ted Farrin, in a brimmed hat, handles the nets. CATHERINE JORDON WALKER

Net reel on Farrin's Wharf. LYNNE DRISKO

THOSE NETS, *you stretch them out they'd reach a mile. They could run one out in five minutes. Got towing one of these dories behind one of them boats, and the net going out over the stern—you want to keep your toes pointed backward all of the time, keep your toes pointed at the aft end of the dory; you got 'em going ahead, you're going to get set with a net.* —Bill Kelsey

THEY HAD TO DRY THEM *because they were cotton—that's why they're on those reels. If they used 'em they'd have to dry them out, resalt them, salt them back in the boat, three or four times a summer. If they got some hard use they'd have to bring them out and dry them, 'cause they'd get slimy. The ocean would make a slimy growth on them, so they'd pull them with the dories, wind them up and dry them, and when they're dry, they'd run them back in the dories and salt them. Put the salt to 'em to get rid of the slimy stuff and preserve the twine.*

—Bill Kelsey

THE NETS *had to be dried. On the wharves were these huge reels: reels large enough so they could accommodate the full width of the net, which might be eight or ten feet. We boys, on Saturdays and during vacations, we'd reel those nets onto the reels and mend them and untangle them. They really got tangled up at times. Pick all the old debris—seaweed and so forth—out of them and reel them onto the reels and they would dry—and later in the day, after they dried, they would be put back into the boxes they were stored in. They were stored in oblong rectangular wooden boxes with sloping ends on them which facilitated the removal or the setting of them when they took them back out into the ocean. We were paid so much a box to reel those and then also store them back into the boxes.*

—Doug Thompson

Fishermen Take Notice!
The Best Menhaden and Mackerel
PURSE SEINES,
And all other varieties of **Fish Nettings** are manufactured at the factory of
United States Net and Twine Company.
Office: 219 Fulton St., New York City.
Please let us know your wants, that we may send ESTIMATES, Quotations & Somples
6m028

Advertisement from the *Pemaquid Messenger*, late 1880s.

TANGLEFIN
GILL NETTING

REAL GENUINE SEA
ISLAND COTTON

LINEN
LONG STAPLE COTTON

Factory to You—No Middlemen

National Net & Twine Co., Inc.
EAST HADDAM, CONN.

WOODBERRY
Seine Twine

STANDARD IN ALL MARKETS
MT. VERNON WOODBERRY MILLS, INC.
BALTIMORE, MD.
TURNER, HALSEY COMPANY
62 Leonard Street
New York
Sole Selling Agents

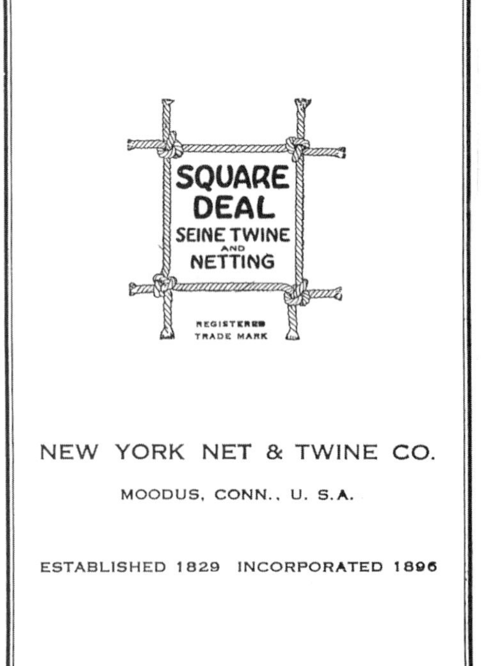

Advertisements from *Atlantic Fisherman* magazine, 1924.

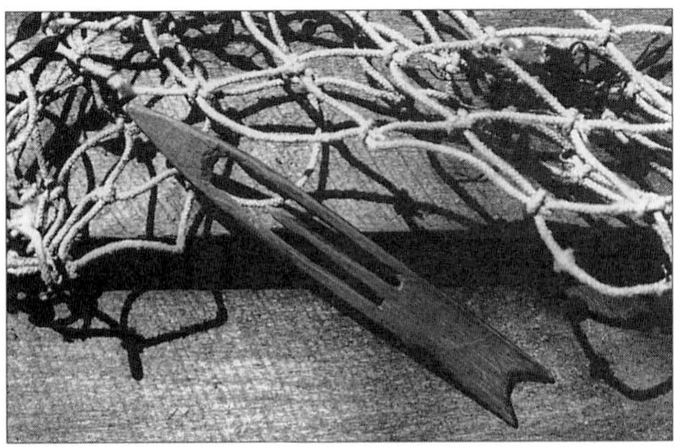

Handmade wooden knitting needle. Needles come in a variety of sizes and proportions, handmade and "boughten," and are used both to repair nets and to knit lobster pot heads. AUTHOR PHOTO

We'd use 'em on stop seines, purse seines, fish traps, and all. On a stop seine you'd use it for hanging a net, we'd call it; you gotta hang the corks on it, you know, you go up over and tie it. It holds the line to attach the leads and corks and nets. Fill it right up same as you would any needle for sewing, I guess. Fill it up and then you make a tie for putting the corks on the net. You make hitches here, then you go 'round the cork the other side; same way with the leads. You usually had about three or four leads to a foot, something like that—hitches right along. The net is kind of a diamond shape, you have to go through the mesh, poke it through and go around the line that holds the cork. —Afton Farrin, Jr.

When you have a tear you have to run it up, we called it, or if it's a bad one you have to put a piece of twine right in. You cut out the square, maybe, tie the net together, fill the hole—patching, we called it. Cut out a piece the same size and tie it in there if you happened to tear it while you were working. After you catch a bunch of fish, if you damaged it in any way, you'd have to take it out and overhaul the whole net. Quite a little job, usually. Now we have power blocks and you can take them out in no time at all, but when we did it by hand it really was hard work. Pull it in over a dory, and as you pulled it in you patched what you could see coming—pull maybe two or three fathoms in. If you see any holes you patch 'em, and pull some more. —Afton Farrin, Jr.

Afton Farrin, Jr., left, and Anthony Eugley repair one section of net while Edison "Ted" Farrin works on another. LYNNE DRISKO

Frank Jordon in a skiff. Catherine Jordon Walker

My father in a skiff. He didn't row a skiff, he sculled it with one oar, standing up.
—Catherine Jordon Walker

Well, that goes way back I think, sculling. Use your wrist, you know, to propel yourself along. Dory, too—you can scull 'em. There's a little trick to it. You only go a short ways, out to the mooring or something. You can get there if you sit down in the boat and row it, but I think you'd be there quicker if you scull it, depending on the distance. You can stand there and see where you're going. See where you're going, and move around the traps and so forth. 'Course if it's blowing and stormy you probably have to row.

You use just one oar when you scull. You notice on dories they always have cut out a little round U-shaped place in the stern to put the oar, to scull by. Way back they used to use a couple of pins, thole pins that would go down into the wood of the boat, the rail of the boat, two on this side. You put the oar down the stern of the boat—use a certain motion to propel you. Gosh, you can go fast. Quite a trick to it—it takes a while. But after you get to do it, it's some easy. It comes natural. I used to like to—oh, you can really go. —Afton Farrin, Jr.

FISH HAWK IV, one of Henry Jones's fishing boats.
WILLIAM A. KELSEY

OF COURSE *there always were guys who seemed to catch more, because they did know more. They'd been fishing longer, and they'd learned more, and their gear might have been a little bit better.*

My friend Henry Jones caught probably more fish than anybody in South Bristol over the years—you know, in the sardine business. He grew up on Damariscove Island, and he didn't have much education. When he was in the seventh grade he stopped going to school and went fishing. If you went fishing with him as one of his crew he never said too much, but his brain was full of fishing, you know. In the sardine business you have to set one seine around in a circle and then make the ends together to keep your fish in—they call it a pocket. And then the trick to getting the herring out is that you've got to set a little purse seine inside of that where the herring are, and there can't be any hang-ups or rocky bottom in there because your seine has to go right to bottom, see. The seine is deeper than the water is. So this Henry, he'd been going so many years he had in his mind all the land-marks, to these places where the bottom was good and he knew he could seine the fish out, but he never said anything. So when he was setting the seine he'd be looking north and south and east and west or wherever he had the marks to, and of course you use trees, houses, and anything else that you remember—you have to line up this house with that tree to be in exactly the same place. So he wouldn't say anything, but every time he set a pocket and then of course set the seine around the circle, and drew up the ends so it's solid; then set four anchors on it to make it square so it'd stay there, y'know, and then seine inside of it.

Herring, of course, are the number one fish in the world for volume. They catch more millions of tons than anything else. So as far as weight goes Henry caught more fish than anybody. And then of course when he went into anything else he always did well. He'd catch lobsters well, and—he just did well. —Ralph Norwood

Irving Clifford at his fish market. WILLIAM A. KELSEY

THERE WAS A good fish market there. You could always find almost anything. Irving Clifford was the fish man, and lived upstairs. He was like the town drunk, more or less—he always drank—but he was a good person and everybody liked him.

I remember he raised beautiful dahlias in front of his fish market. He had this garden on each side of his door: he had wooden planks that he built up and filled in with soil. He had this flower garden, and his dahlias were bigger and brighter than anyone else's because he used some of the fish heads for fertilizer, and seaweed, too.

—Catherine Walker

IRVING USED TO dive for fifty-cent pieces and we'd see his carpet slippers come floating up.

—Annie Louise Alley Farrin

HE'D GET DRUNK and roll around the wharf all day long. He was a happy-go-lucky fella. Never wore anything but carpet slippers—I never seen him without slippers on. —Bill Kelsey

Fishing boat docked at Irving Clifford's wharf.
WILLIAM A. KELSEY

ON THE *Fourth of July, Mother sent me to South Bristol to buy salmon. Irving Clifford, deep in his cups and wearing carpet slippers as usual, grunted at me. I asked for my two pounds of salmon. He whetted a knife, peered at the fish, cut and put it on the scale: two pounds exactly. Pleased with himself, he not only gave me the two pounds but threw in the rest of the fish and lumbered out.*

—Floyd Humphries

HENRY JONES, HE'D COME *in to the wharf—they'd go trawling in the winter, or longlining, or whatever, and in the summer there'd be several boats; they were catching fish one way or the other all the time. Irving would go down to the boats, and he'd stand and look over the side and say, "I w-w-want that one and that one and that one, that one, and that one." He'd pick out the fish and they'd put it in the basket for him. I don't reckon he ever paid for them. It was his wharf, they used it, he was entitled to a fish once in a while.*

In the back of that building, if you went through that door right there, you walked into a great big cooler up against the wall, and right along it was a huge ice chest, and there'd always be a ton, two tons of crushed ice in it and he'd pack fish in it, right in the ice. So he kept a good fish—and they were all cleaned and skinned. And these summer people would come in, and if he didn't like them, they'd say, "Irving, I'd like to have a nice, fresh haddock," and he would say, "Uh, uh, uh, God, I ain't got one." If he didn't like you, he wouldn't sell you one. I cleaned fish for the old buzzard, and he'd pile the top of that ice chest full of hake; and then somebody'd come in, "Irving, I need a nice codfish, about like that," and he'd say, "By God, I've g-g-got just the thing," he'd say, and he'd reach in that ice chest and haul out a hake. They didn't know the difference—there wasn't no skin on it. He didn't give a damn; if he didn't like you he wouldn't sell you one.

You walked out behind that building, I'll tell you, if he was out there cleaning fish—'cause he'd clean up forty or fifty head all the time—man, if he was ripping the skin off of one of the fish, you didn't want to be walking around that corner—you were going to get it right in the side of the head—the crap was flying everywhere. He didn't give a damn. He'd say, "D-d-don't rip 'em, boys. D-d-don't rip 'em...." —Bill Kelsey

George Leighton's fish house on the Eastern Gut, c. 1997. AUTHOR PHOTO

ACROSS THE entrance to the Eastern Gut was a fish house where George Leighton used to make his headquarters for his lobsterfishing; also, he had a smokehouse over there for smoking alewives and herring. —Doug Thompson

George Leighton's Gem Island herring factory, about 1904. J. Douglas Thompson

In the early 1800s the Scotch method of smoking herring became popular, and smokehouses appeared all along the shore. By the end of the century nearly 6 million pounds a year were processed this way, and another 2.5 million pounds were pickled for food or bait; over 70 million were preserved by freezing or canned as sardines.

The herring factory of George Leighton ... it was on Gem Island, turn of the century or pretty close to it. George Leighton used to tell the story about driving a scythe into a whale's back and riding it quite a distance. Nobody ever put too much stock in it. —Doug Thompson

A rare view of one of South Bristol's pogy factories—Fowler, Foote, & Co. The building may have been located about where the Fisherman's Co-Op now stands, on the Eastern Gut.
MARGARET FARRIN HOUSE

THERE WERE pogy factories, too. There was one out around the point from Gem Island, out on Davis's Point. The stonework is still there. And I think there were some on Witch Island, too. The process was, they only used the oil. They cooked them and extracted the oil, and the rest went into fertilizer, or just chum, they called it. I guess it had a great smell. —Doug Thompson

MENHADEN, often called pogys, had long been used for bait along the Maine coast, and at first a modest oil business was carried on by small fishermen, catching the pogys in nets and trying out the oil with small presses. In his 1873 *History of Bristol and Bremen*, John Johnston relates the opposition, at first, to the expansion of the "porgie" fishery. Fishermen feared that their bait would be consumed, and riots were threatened. One factory may even have been destroyed by the old fishermen.

As the Civil War progressed, however, a rich market was created by the increased demand for fish oil. Pogy oil, which brought only 25 cents a gallon in 1863, skyrocketed to $1.25 later in the war; it was used for everything that linseed oil was used for, and the scrap replaced guano as a source of fertilizer. Pogys appeared off the coast in huge numbers at this time, and oil factories were built on an ambitious scale.

The first large enterprise in South Bristol was W. A. Wells & Company, established in 1864. W. A. Wells was the first of four pogy factories in South Bristol; by 1870 these were valued at tens of thousands of dollars and employed hundreds of men. Each factory had several vessels, such as the Wells Company's WILLIAM A. WELLS, a 51-ton steamer built right in South Bristol by A. & M. Gamage. The fishery changed quickly from small seine boats fishing just offshore, to schooners with fleets of small boats attached, and finally to steamers—forty-eight from Lincoln County alone. By 1876 over two million gallons of oil were produced along the Lincoln County shore. The fish were cooked by steam, the oil extracted by hydraulic pressure, and the waste product was used by fertilizer factories which were built alongside the oil works. The prosperity was short-lived, however—by 1878 the pogy was all but fished out, and by the year 1879 came no more.

Vestiges of the business remained for a few years; in the early 1890s the *Maine Register* still lists the Virginia Oil & Guano Company, "E. T. Foote, agent, oil & guano." A paragraph in the December 18, 1887, *Pemaquid Messenger*, however, signals the final demise of the once prosperous W. A. Wells & Company:

> Wm. Sawyer who bought the Wells' & Cos. property here, has removed all the buildings, excepting the cook-house, and has cleared the beautiful grove of all underbrush and intends to make picnic grounds of it another season. It is the finest grove for that purpose in Me. There is a good wharf for steamers to land and a good carriage road leading to it. There is a fine lot for base ball or lawn tennis connected with it, and a spring of never-failing water. He thinks to fit the cook-house up so as to furnish dinners for parties who wish to come to the grove and have a good time. No doubt it will become very popular when people find out what a lovely place it is. COLONEL E.

The WILLIAM A. WELLS, 51-ton pogy steamer built for W. A. Wells & Co. in the South Bristol shipyard of A. & M. Gamage; launched 1873. MAINE MARITIME MUSEUM

When a community makes its living from the sea, tales of adventure and tragedy are sure to abound.

EVEN WITH today's technological advances, commercial fishing is still the most dangerous occupation in the nation. Imagine the days when seafarers had nothing to depend on but their courage, their skill, and their vessel.

In 1903 two vessels came to grief on Pemaquid Point in the same violent September storm. One was the SADIE AND LILLIE, the other a 140-ton schooner captained by a South Bristol mariner, Willard Poole. In 1974, at the age of eighty-eight, Mertie Knipe Curtis gave this account of that memorable night:

WHILE WE WAS WAITING, this awful storm come up—it was terrible. It took all the chimleys and windows out—Oh, it was a terrible storm. I'll never, ever want to see something like that again. I never, never will forget it. It was between twelve o'clock and two at night, somewheres in there, and there was two shipwrecks on the end of Pemaquid Point, the GEORGE S. EDMUNDS and the SADIE AND LILLIE. The EDMUNDS was a mackerel seiner. It had four or five dories and had a big seine boat and they carried sixteen men—and there was fourteen, yes, there were thirteen or fourteen of them lost. You know how the Point makes out like this? Well, the mackerel seiner went onto them flat ledges right in front of the Howard girls' house.

One of the men from the EDMUNDS—there's five of them got in a dory, and the dory swamped and he hung on, and the next sea that come, he was throwed out, and he held on a rock, and when the sea went out, he crawled up, and he kept crawling until he touched land. The ground. And he said that he laid right there and cried. And then he kept crawling along and crawling along, he come up into the road, and he stuck to the bare track the wheels had made, so he kept crawling along on that, and when he got up a

The wreck of the coasting schooner SADIE AND LILLIE on the ledges at Pemaquid Point.
LALEAH CONDON KENNEDY, EUGENE B. SPROUL FARM

ways, he saw this light, and it was the light in the Pemaquid Hotel. And so they heard a noise for help, and Will Elliott went out and he found this man on the steps of the hotel. Well, they got him into the house, and they got some dry clothes on him, and they were just kind of working over him, and getting things—hot drinks—into him, and it wasn't very long before there was another call for help, and Will went out again, and there was another man there.

And Will Elliott told my father, "I don't think I ever saw anything so touching in my life as I did when them two men met." He said they clung to each other, and they kissed and hugged each other, and they cried like babies, because they were so pleased they were saved.

The captain, they got a rope to him and everything, and he got it round his waist for them to haul him ashore, and the sounding line or something—he got his foot tangled up in and he couldn't get clear—it was on a rock, and he couldn't get clear, so he drowned.

They got all the bodies from the mackerel seiner but the captain—Captain Poole from South Bristol—they couldn't find him. And the next spring, they'd be somebody go down 'most every day to look around the shore to see if they could find his body. And finally, in the spring, somebody was hauling pots, and they happened to go on Haddock Island up here, and they found him froze in a great big cake of ice.

Most of all the boys they took and put them in H. H. Chamberlain's cottage at the Point. Sadie and I—that's my husband's youngest sister—it was in September, and the goldenrod was beautiful, and we went and took armfuls of that, and we asked if we could put them on the casket. And everybody give us ribbon, and we tied bows of ribbon and put them on the caskets.

—Mertie Knipe Curtis

Captain Willard Poole, 1839–1903. The Vital Statistics of the town records of Bristol notes: "Drowned at Pemaquid Point Sept. 17th, 1903; body recovered in summer of 1904 down Franklin way." KATHERINE POOLE NORWOOD

Mary Pierce, 1812–1901. Annie May Farrin remembered how all the kids would go to visit "Aunt" Mary in her later years. She would give them candy, and they'd play games; she loved to have them, and they loved to visit her. MARGARET FARRIN HOUSE

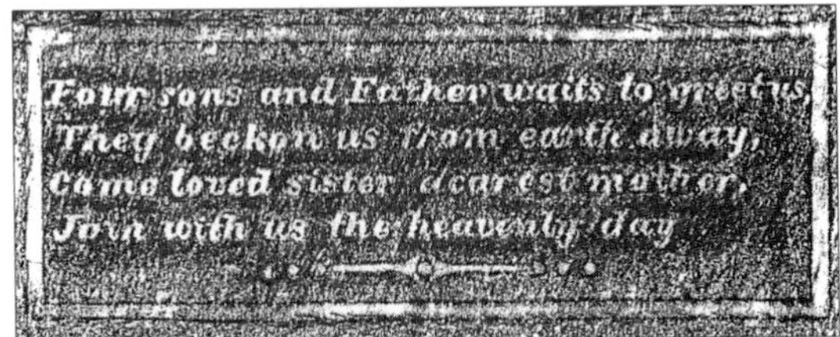

Rubbing of an inscription on the Pierce tombstone in the Rutherford Island cemetery:

Four sons and Father waits to meet us,
They beckon us from earth away,
Come loved sister dearest mother,
Join with us the heavenly day.

TO LOOK AT South Bristol, its beautiful location removed from the rush and turmoil of the busy town and city, we would almost be led to believe that sorrow or trouble would never enter its bounds, yet many homes have been saddened by the loss of dear ones that have gone down to the sea in ships never to return … tragic events I will mention brought more sorrow to South Bristol than any one event or blow of the Civil War which struck South Bristol, as all of the country, hard, and have been felt more than half a century.

The loss of the Schooner GLIDE, a packet running between Boston and Damariscotta, foundered November 24, 1852, a short distance from and in sight of Southport, Maine, with Captain John Pierce and his two sons, Jonathan and James. Mrs. Pierce, with two sons and one daughter, survived: Elliot, Eliphalet, and Martha. Elliot entered the service on the breaking out of the Civil War, and was shot and died at Spotsylvania, Va., member of the 32nd Massachusetts Volunteers. Eliphalet was lost at sea, March 17, 1864. Martha died at her home, April 14, 1870. Mrs. Pierce lived to be more than ninety years old, and although passing through this terrible affliction, she bore it with Christian fortitude and lived and labored for others. —Nelson Gamage, *A Short History of South Bristol, Maine*

THE GLIDE was nearly home when she went down off of Southport Island. Mary's son James was only sixteen years old in that year of 1854; Jonathan was eighteen. None of her five children survived beyond the age of twenty-two.

Captain Marshall M. Wells, 1828–72.
ARLETTA THORPE RICE

CAPTAIN MARSHALL M. WELLS, born in 1828, was only in his thirties when he was master of the bark LAURAETTA, captured and burned in 1862 by the infamous Raphael Semmes and his British privateer ALABAMA. Wells died a young man at the age of forty-three, just a few years after the close of the Civil War.

IT WAS OCTOBER 28, 1862. The sky was overcast and the sea moved in long slow leaden swells under a light breeze. As the LAURAETTA moved ponderously along, a strange ship was seen off the port bow. She was bearing down on them with smoke pouring out of her single funnel. She looked like and was a warship, sleek and new, a ship soon to be dreaded all over the seven seas. It was the British privateer ALABAMA.

Under the bristling guns of the ALABAMA Captain Wells hove to and was boarded by the British sailors. The LAURAETTA's officers and crew were taken to the ALABAMA with nothing but the clothes they were standing in. They were all put in irons and placed in an area between two coal bunkers, deep in the ship.

All the provisions on board the LAURAETTA were transferred to the ALABAMA, for her base of supplies was the ships that she captured. Then the LAURAETTA was set on fire and completely destroyed.

When spring arrived the ALABAMA was back once more in the North Atlantic. One day Captain Semmes gave Grandpa his freedom. The ALABAMA was off the Massachusetts coast near Boston. Grandpa said, "He gave me a dory and a pair of oars. We were nine miles out and I rowed into Boston Harbor wearing only a shirt and pair of pants…."

—Cleveland Poole, *Capture at Sea*

The bark LAURAETTA, entering the harbor at Leghorn, Italy. A. STANTON WELLS

IN AN UNDATED ACCOUNT, a Bristol seaman describes the capture of the LAURAETTA:

On Sept. 1862 I joined the Bark LAURAETTA, Capt. Wells, at Damariscotta, Me. Our crew was all from Bristol, Me., nine in number—they're all dead except two. After getting ready for sea we sailed for New York. There was nothing important occurred during our passage to New York.

Shortly after arriving we commenced loading for Palermo, Sicily. Our cargo was principally flour, which took a week or ten days to load. After that we took steam and towed down to Sandy Hook. All that day we were employed getting ready for sea. The next morning we weighed anchor and started, little thinking we should be back again so soon. The next night after leaving port it commenced to blow a gale from the North West, which lasted about thirty-six hours. On the morning of the third day out from port, which proved to be our last day on board, the wind commenced to moderate. I was at the wheel from eight to ten A.M. The rest of the crew were engaged setting sail when I was relieved from the wheel at ten o'clock. I was sent aloft to set the main royal, being elevated about seventy feet above sea level. I discovered a sail in the distant horizon and according to custom at sea I reported it. The Capt. answered where away—about two points on the port bow. Dir[ectly] after reaching the deck I was asked what the sail appeared to be. I told him it was Bark rig and heading across our bow. In a short time the sail was visible off deck. The Capt. appeared around using his glass often. It now became evident that it was a ship of war and we soon found out by the discharge of a large gun. Our Capt. understood what that meant. I remember well how he looked when he gave orders to put the helm hard down and back the main topsail. Poor man, it was the last order he ever gave on that Bark. Shortly a boat came pulling toward us. When reaching us the officer in charge came on board. He sent our Capt. on board their ship with his papers. The officer remained with us until the boat returned and brought his orders, which was to burn the Bark. We were then told to get ready and leave. There was quite a sea running from the gale we had experienced the day before, which made it very difficult about leaving our vessel and also boarding the other ship, but finally we reached the deck of the famous privateer ALABAMA. We were soon put in irons and in an hour's time the Bark was on fire.

No 1
on Sept 1862 I joined the
Bark Lauretta Capt Wells
at Damariscotta Me our crew
was all from Bristol Me
nine in number their all
dead except two. after geting
ready for sea we sailed
for New York there was
nothing important occured
during our passage to New
York. Shortly after arriving
we commenced loading for
Palermo Sicily our cargo was
principally flour which
took a week or ten days to
load after that we took
steam and towed down to
Sandy hook all that day
we were employed geting ready

First page of the eyewitness account of the capture of the LAURAETTA, written by Bristol seaman William Knipe. Although undated, this was evidently written some time later, since he states that all but two of the crew are dead, and none were known to have been lost in the encounter with the ALABAMA.
BRISTOL AREA LIBRARY

Captain Wells's little daughter, Nellie, accompanied him on one of his voyages and was given a doll to play with during the long weeks at sea. Nellie's granddaughter, Arletta Thorpe Rice, still has that doll, "Little Nell." The photograph behind the doll shows Arletta sitting on the lap of her "Uncle Dud," Albert C. Thorpe.

Nellie Wells's doll "Little Nell," photographed in the Christmas Cove home of Nellie's granddaughter, Arletta Thorpe Rice. Author photo, 1996

A Brave Deed
Rescue of five men from a watery grave
By the heroic acts of three men from
Christmas Cove

Last Thursday morning schooner Ocean Belle, Captain Ruggles, of Digby, N.S., to which place she was bound from Boston, with a cargo of general merchandise, was wrecked on the Thread of Life ledges in John's Bay, Bristol. The schooner sailed from Boston Tuesday afternoon.

At about 12:20 o'clock Thursday morning, when two miles off to the southard of Monhegan, the gale struck them from the east, and after vainly trying to keep their course, they were compelled to run for Boothbay Harbor. At daylight, with the wind almost a hurricane, thick sheets of rain obscuring everything, they somehow lost their reckoning and found themselves among the breakers. Both anchors were put out, but the chains snapped asunder, and she soon struck on the ledges.

About seven o'clock in the morning, Capt. Manley Brewer, Anson Marden, and Loring Thorpe discovered the wreck, mounted a dory on wheels, and carrying it to the eastern shore of the island, launched it in a small cove and pulled off. It was so rough they could not reach the vessel, but landed on the back side of the ledges, and went to the front where the vessel lay, about one hundred and fifty yards off the ledge on a sunken rock.

The men on board, with the sea making a clean break over the vessel, made a piece of plank fast to a rope, and payed it out until it struck the rock where the rescuers were. After great effort, it was secured from the breakers, the rescuers nearly losing their lives in the act, and they hauled the rope in with a second line bent on to it till both were on shore. Here they made a large one fast to a rock, and then, with the second line secured to the men under their arms, they pulled five of the crew through the one hundred and fifty yards to the rocks.

One of the crew, Benjamin Wintzell, did not want to leave the vessel, but after all had gone, he made the attempt. In fastening the noose around the hawser, he constructed a knot that slipped, and when about halfway in, it tightened, and the running line could not be pulled, and so the unfortunate man was drowned.

Captain Manley S. Brewer, 1840–1924.
ARLETTA THORPE RICE

The vessel rolled over and went down in less than half an hour after the crew had left her. Taking two of the men, who were the lightest clad, in the dory, the rescuing party made a successful landing and returned for the captain, mate, and seamen. When they got most to the rock they found, however, that the sea had made so fast, that it was simply impossible to reach them. The breakers had arisen with fearful violence, even on the landward side. The brave fellows, loath to give up, kept watch through the blinding rain, hoping the sea would run down, but at dark they were compelled to leave and trust that the sea would not wash off the poor fellows, nor the cold freeze them before morning.

At daylight Friday morning, the sea had so abated that they were rescued, fearfully chilled, after thirty hours on the barren rock, and the body of the drowned sailor was recovered. He was buried at the Cove Sunday. The crew were hospitably cared for by the generous people of the place.

A large amount of the cargo, flour, beef, etc. has been picked up along the shore for several miles.

The wreck of this vessel brings to mind the disasters of past years. Only about ten years since the CHARLIE BELL of St. John, N.B., went ashore on Thrumcap Island, four men were lost and only one saved, while only a few years previous to that, a vessel went ashore near the scene of the present disaster, and one man died of exposure.

There is no lifesaving station between Popham Beach and White Head, and it seems there ought to be one on the Bristol coast or some of the islands off shore.

BRAVERY REWARDED

IT IS WITH pride that we copy the following concerning the three brave men who risked their lives to save others.

The Canadian government has recognized their heroism and rewards them for their courageous conduct.

Ottawa, Ontario, Jan. 8, 1890. Hon. C. H. Tucker, Canadian Minister of Marine, is sending through President Harrison to each of the three fishermen of South Bristol, Maine, named respectively Brewer, Marden, and Thorp, a gold watch suitably inscribed as a token of their courageous conduct in saving the lives of five of the crew of the schooner OCEAN BELLE of Digby, N.S., on the 28th of November, last, under circumstances of unusual bravery.

Crow Island and the Thread of Life on a November day, the same time of year that OCEAN BELLE foundered.
AUTHOR PHOTO, 1997

THE LONE SURVIVOR

SOMETIME BETWEEN 1895 and 1900 a small fisherman took refuge behind the "Thread of Life" or "Thrumcap," just off Christmas Cove, from a strong gale and storm. The sea ran high and the tempest increased. As they lay there in the lee, enough of the ground swell and waves got around the shelter to cause their little ship to toss violently and at times hit the bottom.

As they lay there riding out the storm, a Nova Scotia fisherman came in on the windward side of the ledges and was wrecked. This wrecked ship had about twenty men on board and the captain's wife. Those on the other ship were powerless to assist them in any way. As they watched the wreckage over the shallow rocks, they noticed a great wave lift the little ship. As it did, the boom swung around and with one great sweep caught the captain's wife and literally tossed her far up in the woods. She was scantily clad and the temperature was very low and yet there was no way she could be rescued. She remained there all night and was rescued in the morning nearly frozen but she survived while all others on the little ship perished. —Harold Castner, "The Castner Papers"

MY FRIEND *Henry Jones grew up on Damariscove Island and when he was just a kid, before they had engines, this schooner was caught in a storm and the skipper anchored her off Southport, over near the Cuckolds Light. She dragged her anchor enough so that her stern went ashore on the bluff shore over there, and when the tide went down, when her bow went down she filled with water and she was a total wreck. Except for, that the stern was still up on the shore so far that the captain's cabin didn't get water in it. So the kids from Damariscove went over, rowed over to see what was going on—they could look right over and see it—and the captain saw them rowing around. He was still aboard the vessel. And he invited these kids aboard, opened up this big trunk, and it was full of chocolates. And he gave these chocolates—fancy chocolates—to these kids on Damariscove. And Henry never forgot. He said he'd never forget that, when he opened up that trunk and there was all these chocolates. 'Course, they'd never seen boughten chocolates before, you know, living on the island.* —Ralph Norwood

Two Fishermen Lose Gamble with Storm

Gerald Fossett, 36, and Roland LaBrie, 18, who were paid record prices here for New Year's Day hake and cusk, today were believed to be the only victims of Southern Maine's howling weekend storm. The wreckage of their 40-foot gillnetter was found ashore in the Ocean Park section of Old Orchard Beach in the wake of a 63-m.p.h. gale.

Known for their enterprising spirit, Fossett, a WWII naval chief bosun's mate, and his youthful companion, had taken to sea New Year's, while most of the fleet was idle, in the hopes of obtaining higher prices. Despite 30-m.p.h. winds, luck was with them, and they landed here a 2,275-pound catch.

In their recent ill-fated voyage, the pair had left New Harbor Saturday night, planning to fish near New Ledge, about 35 miles south of Seguin. When they failed to return Sunday night, Coast Guardsmen were called in to search. The wreckage was sighted in Old Orchard Beach by Harvey Bunker. No trace of the bodies was found.

The stern of the gillnetter Pemaquid II washed ashore at the outlet of Goose Fair Brook near Saco, giving mute testimony that Gerald Fossett and Roland LaBrie perished in the storm which lashed the Maine coast Sunday night. A portion of the craft bearing its name was found driven into the sand 35 feet above the ordinary high water mark.

—*Portland Evening Express*, March 4, 1947

Fisherman Found

The body of Gerald Fossett, washed ashore today at Old Orchard Beach, a short distance from where the wreckage of his fishing boat was found Monday, will be returned to the sea somewhere near the spot where the boat was believed capsized. It had been Fossett's request that should he lose his life at sea, that his body be buried somewhere near the spot where he died. Born in 1911, death occurred on his birthday, March 2. —*Portland Evening Express*, March 5, 1947

We had a couple of friends, they were older than we young people, but they were great friends. They were fishermen, and they made South Bristol a base of operations. Their names were Harold and Gerald Fossett. Harold married one of Sumner McFarland's daughters, and Gerald—we always called him Donk—he was considered a real good fisherman at the time.

Donk Fossett had a boat built there by Sumner McFarland—it was considered a good size boat at that time—and he fished out of that. They didn't build houses on the boats then, they just had a spray hood, a canvas spray hood. Donk had no fear of the ocean, and it led to his tragic death. He was a good fisherman, and he used to go offshore setting his gillnets. He left one afternoon, and in those days the weather reports were scanty, and not too detailed—it was pretty much determined by signs and the air. He left for offshore fishing and never returned. The boat was later found way down near the New Hampshire border, southwestern Maine. —Doug Thompson

THERE WAS THREE *Fossett boys. The older one, his name was Gerald, he drowned; got a kid right with him. This was in March, and they had plenty of warning, on the radio and everything—a storm, big storm, southeast storm. That's when the old Miles tower that was up there was blowed over. Same storm. In March—snowstorm, and rain and snow together, and blowing southeast something terrible. He had plenty of warning, I don't know why—his boat warn't that big—but they went off, you know, and then 'course nobody knows exactly what happened, but evidently he seen he wasn't going to make it, or it was getting too rough for him and he went with the wind and he ended up, they found that boat at the state park beach there; just beyond there they found the pieces of boat.*

They found him, but they never found the other one, they never did. Evidently it got so rough he couldn't come back in this way, so he run tail to it and tried to outrun it, but he didn't make it. Evidently that boat must've got pretty close, 'cause they found where she come ashore and they found one body there, so it kinda proves that he tried to run with the wind and go in somewhere, but he didn't make it.

Oh, it was a hell of a storm, it snowed much a foot—heavy, wet snow. Boy, it blowed something terrible. —Mervin Rice

Gerald Fossett, right, and Roland LaBrie. Gerald "Donk" Fossett fished out of South Bristol, and was also legendary there for his prowess at clamdigging. The youngster Roland LaBrie lived with Walter Gilbert, who owned PEMAQUID II.
PEMAQUID HISTORICAL ASSOCIATION

I'll tell you a lobster story . . .

—Ralph Norwood

A 29-pound lobster pictured in a 1929 issue of *Atlantic Fisherman* magazine. AUTHOR'S COLLECTION

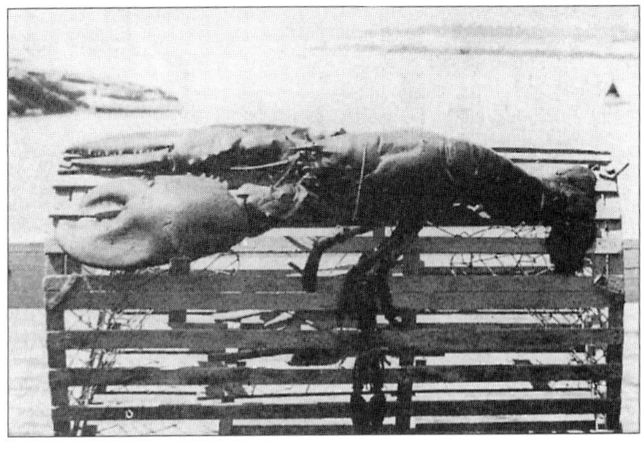

. . . MY NEPHEW, *when he was a teenager, he had a few traps out in the bay here. After school he'd go haul his traps. It was legal to drag lobsters when I first started dragging lobsters; that's why I went. After I dragged 'em a while they made a law—the only way you could take a lobster was out of a trap. It was aimed at skin-divers and also draggers.*

So I was dragging lobsters in the fall, September or October, and I caught this great big, oh, awful big one. I guess he weighed twenty-five pounds or thirty pounds, I mean he was huge. So I was coming up the bay that night and I had him and didn't know what to do with him, so I hauled one of my nephew's lobster traps and stuffed him in there. It was impossible for him to get in the hoops because the funnel hoop in the heads wasn't big enough for him to go through—so the boy should have known that it was a plant, you know. And so he went out and he hauled his traps. When he came in he was stuttering so bad nobody could understand what he was talking about. He had this great big lobster that he caught. She didn't have a pan big enough to cook it. They used a roaster pan—they did well to get it into any kind of a pan.

—Ralph Norwood

THEY TELL SOME *wild stories about lobsters and lobster wardens. In the old days it was illegal to sell big lobsters in Maine but it wasn't in New Hampshire, so the guys would save 'em up, and when they'd get enough they'd run 'em through by boat to New Hampshire to sell them—the big ones. There's a story told over New Harbor how this fella had a whole boatload—big vessel, decked vessel—so he's headed for New Hampshire, when these two wardens, seems though they were in a harbor, 'cause the wardens come aboard the boat and the fella cast off his line, and started the engine, and locked the pilothouse door, and headed for New Hampshire—and they had to make the whole trip on deck. They claim that's a true story. That was before, when laws was slack. Now you'd go to jail forever for doing that.*

—Ralph Norwood

Lobster fisherman, on the way to set out his traps: wooden traps, wooden boat. NORMAN HAMLIN

THOSE WERE *the days of wooden traps. 'Most everyone built their own traps and sometimes they were made of all oak, square traps. Others were oval top traps and they would cut spruce boughs and bend them, and put the ends of the spruce bough into the wood that served as the base of the trap. The heads of the traps were knit by the fishermen's wives or perhaps the fishermen themselves. They were knit out of cotton, and then they were tarred so that they would last longer. They would weight them down when they first put them in the water with rocks or bricks and then after the trap got soaked up good they could remove the weights and they wouldn't float up. Lobsters probably at most times were ten to fifteen cents a pound. There were lots of them, but these fishermen hauled those traps all by hand, no power, and they fished maybe sixty. A hundred traps would have been a lot, would have been a large gang.*

—Doug Thompson

YOU'VE SEEN IT ALL *your life and you just do what the other people are doing. You build some traps, and go ahead. In those days, they used to go into the woods and cut spruce limbs and bend them into bows, we called 'em, and nail the laths over. You knit the heads yourself, did the whole thing natural. That's before they had all the synthetic fibers, you know. Couldn't handle more than sixty or eighty traps 'cause the heads wouldn't last. Natural fibers just didn't last, and it kept fishermen from having these huge number of traps.*

You'd have to bring them out, dry 'em out; and the worms'd eat them. They'd have to dry about a week, then put 'em back in. You'd have to treat the heads, which would prolong the life a little bit. Coal tar or whatever, heat it up and dip the heads in. It'd make them last a little bit longer. But they were pretty limited in those days. I guess it was during the World War that they came out with synthetic fibers and kind of changed the whole picture.

We'd use herring, mostly, and flounders. We'd catch our own bait. You'd go around and you could see them on bottom, and take a spear; "spudging" we called it, you'd get anything you could see on bottom. Sculpin and flounders, spear 'em, use 'em for bait. And they had the hoop nets; they'd put that down and bait it with herring and the fish would swim in over it, pull it up. Get baits that way. Pulled it up quick, and you'd have it. Put it right on fresh. If you got too much you'd salt it.

But there's none of that stuff to catch now. There used to be a lot of flounders before the "shags"—cormorants. They got established here on the coast and they started eating up all the little flounders and everything on bottom. So that spoiled that, and now you very rarely see a flounder or sculpin. —Afton Farrin, Jr.

HOOK LOBSTER POUND *was operated for many years in the narrow passage between Birch Island and the east shore of Rutherford Island. One year a dam broke, freeing the lobsters. Fishermen had a field day setting traps to catch the escaped multitude.* —Edward Myers

ALSO DOWN *in there were a couple of men, I guess you could almost call them recluses. They lived by themselves, went lobstering, and of course these people either rowed in a dory or they had a*

Hook Lobster Pound, opposite Birch Island. NORMAN HAMLIN

small boat with a one-cylinder engine in it. These two men were Mel Upham and Asa Lane.
—Doug Thompson

MEL UPHAM ... *they used to call him "old swivel-head" because he'd row along and swivel his head back and forth, back and forth, to see where he was going.* —Afton Farrin, Jr.

"AMONG the early risers is Mr. Mel Upham. He may be seen pulling in his lobster cars every morning at 5:00 if you care to see him."

YOU HAVE TO *know him to know what that means because he was the craziest person ever lived. That time of the morning he probably wouldn't even be worth seeing! And he lived over where the lobster pound is now.* —Kathleen Thorpe, during a 1972 interview, commenting on an excerpt from a pre-World War I edition of *The Clamdigger*

JULY, 1924

Lobsters are skurce and few and far between; bait is skurce locally but obtainable by long distance searches at a dollar per bushel. Much fog and storm have hindered the lobstermen. The price of lobsters has risen a bit; the smacks are now paying thirty-seven cents a pound. Most of the lobsters are about ready to shed. Some of the lobstermen have hauled out their traps and have gone to haking.

Excerpt from *Atlantic Fisherman* magazine, July 1924. AUTHOR'S COLLECTION

Capt. E. D. Gamage of Sloop Smack Superior arrived from Portland last Sunday and Capt. G. R. Gamage of Schr. Smack Kingfisher arrived Saturday night and they report the lobster and market very dull at 3 cts. per piece.

Excerpt from the *Pemaquid Messenger*, October 1887. E. D. Gamage, referred to in the first clipping, is the same Captain Davis Gamage who was swept overboard and drowned in 1888.

A lobster fisherman pushes by the Tripod in Christmas Cove harbor. NORMAN HAMLIN

ALL THE TIME *that my father used to go back and forth to Heron Island, when he went by any of the lobstermen—he knew them all—they just used to throw him a pail full of lobsters to take home or sometimes he had a stove down there in the back of the store where he could boil a few for his lunch.* —Catherine Jordon Walker

SARAH EMERY *used to tell the story how they'd go to King's Cove, and you could just pick up lobsters underneath the seaweed and get a bushel basket full any time.* —Katherine Poole Norwood

I REMEMBER *lobstermen off Heron Island at four o'clock in the morning, upright in dories, rowing by pushing forward on creaking sweeps in the thole pins. Lobsters sold three for a quarter then.* —Floyd Humphries

THERE WERE QUITE *a few lobstermen in town. 'Course, they didn't have pot haulers in those days, they hauled by hand. Some of them rowed for their traps in dories or skiffs and others who did have boats, they were torpedo-stern boats with one-cylinder engines. Among the fishermen that were considered* real *lobster fishermen were Herman Kelsey, John Andrews, Adoniram Andrews, Freeman Kelsey, Oscar Otis, Sam Jones, Norman Gamage, Orris McFarland, and a little later Ted Farrin, and Afton Farrin's son, Kenneth.*

John Andrews was my grandmother Thompson's brother. He was a lobster fisherman. One day the wardens came alongside his boat to check his catch, and when they hit the boat, he fell, and hit his head—killed him. It was taken as a matter of fact, an accident. No investigation to any degree as there would be now. —Doug Thompson

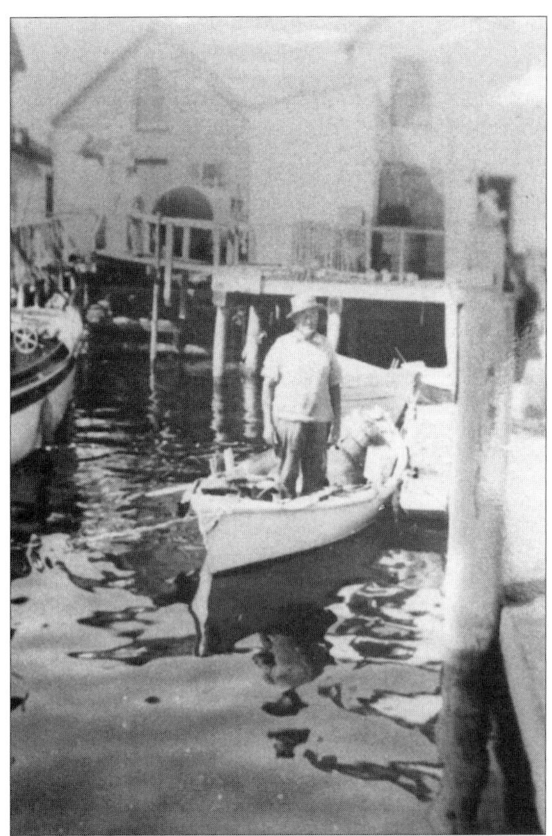

Bainbridge Young, 1866–1957, standing in his double-ender behind Farrin's Lobster Pound.
MARGARET FARRIN HOUSE

FRANK EMERY'S wife Charlotte had a brother who came to live with her in later life, and his name was Bain Young. He was quite a character. He had about twenty-five lobster traps and he was in his nineties when he was still lobstering, and he lobstered out of a rowboat. It was a skiff, as we called them, a long and wide skiff, pretty seaworthy, and he did all of his rowing and hauling of his lobster traps by hand. —Doug Thompson

I REMEMBER him well. He was a real interesting old fella. The late '40s he was still lobstering. He used to have a little double-ender that Will Alley built over on the river, and he was always pushing it so he could see where he was going. I think he stood up and pushed it and then he sat down and pushed it, too.

Uncle Bain Young lived on Matinicus Island and he used to tell the story about how when he first moved there they were all lobstering—and they didn't have any engines then; it was rowing, sailing—so he went out one morning early, and some of his lobster buoys were drifting around. Somebody'd cut 'em in the night. And Uncle Bain, the next morning he went out before daylight—he told me this story himself—he said, "I cut about fifty of 'em, cut the buoys right off. Tied 'em all to the stern of my peapod, then I rowed into the harbor, tied up to where they buy the lobsters up at the wharf." The guys gathered around; he had all these buoys floating astern of his peapod. And Uncle Bain says, "Now looka here," he says, "look at all these buoys I found driftin' out there this morning. Somebody's been cutting traps; I've lost quite a few." He said he never had any more trouble with anybody ever cut him after that. Oh, he was a funny old fella. —Ralph Norwood

Clam factory at Pemaquid Harbor. This stood on the shore where the Fort William Henry restoration park is now. PEMAQUID HISTORICAL ASSOCIATION

IN THOSE DAYS, we boys there in town went clamming to pick up some little spending money, and it was a little, too, because we used to dig clams and then save them up for a while. We'd gather up all of our clams and put them in a dory. Then Afton Farrin, Sr., who had a boat, he would tow them across the bay over to the clam factory. That clam factory was where the restoration now is. We'd take our clams over there and I can remember we got as little as twenty-five cents a bushel. In this factory, I can still see what looked like piles and piles of clams being put into boilers in the shell and then being shucked out and they were canned right there on the spot. —Doug Thompson

WHEN WE WENT clamming we dug for the clam factories. There was a clam factory in Back Narrows, another one in Pemaquid Beach. We got forty-five cents a bushel; at Back Narrows we got thirty-five cents. Took 'em over to Pemaquid we got forty-five, but still, it was a long ways. We'd dig six or seven bushel to a tide; some guys could dig ten bushel. I never could dig ten bushel, but I'd dig six, seven bushel, no sweat. But you couldn't do it today. —Mervin Rice

GERALD [FOSSETT] was a great clamdigger. Boy, he could turn out the clams like nobody I ever saw. I went clamming with him up the Damariscotta River one day, and in one tide he turned out—dug—nine bushel of clams. I think I got three bushel, which was pretty good. Back in those days you turned over an area of flats, two or three forkfuls, then you'd scoop them up with both hands.

—Doug Thompson

WHEN WE WENT clamming, come first of June the clam factories shut down. We didn't dig no clams in the summer. And they'd open up a little while in the fall, September and October, and that was it, they'd shut down again. —Mervin Rice

Rutherford Cook Book

Soups

"Spare your breath to cool your porridge."

CLAM STEW

One pint clams boiled 10 minutes in 1 cup water saved from the clams. Add 1 quart milk scalding hot, a generous piece of butter, pepper to taste.—*Mrs. O. T. Gamage.*

CLAM CHOWDER

1 quart clams
1½ quarts milk
3 potatoes
3 slices salt pork
Eutter half size of egg

Fry out pork, add clams chopped slightly, potatoes sliced thin, a little pepper and boiling water to just cover clams and potatoes. Boil till potatoes are done, then add milk and butter.—*Mrs. O. T. Gamage.*

Recipes from the *South Bristol Cook Book*, originally published by the Ladies' Aid of the South Bristol Union Church, 1930, and reprinted in 1998 as part of the church's centennial commemoration.

BATTER FOR OYSTERS OR CLAMS

2 eggs
½ teaspoon salt
⅛ teaspoon pepper
¾ cup milk
1 cup bread flour

Beat eggs, add milk, flour, salt and pepper.—*Josephine Berry.*

CLAM FRITTERS

2 eggs
⅓ cup milk
1⅓ cups flour
½ pint chopped clams
½ teaspoon soda
1 teaspoon cream tartar
Salt

Fry in deep lard.—*Mrs. O. T. G.*

CLAMS ON TOAST

Drain 1 quart clams, separate the stomach from the rims, chop the rims and heads very fine, add stomachs and season with piece of butter size of an egg, pepper and salt. Heat in double boiler and serve on buttered toast cut in neat shapes.—*E. G. M.*

STEAMED CLAMS

Thoroughly wash ½ peck clams, put in kettle and add 1 quart boiling water. Steam until shells open well.—*Mrs. May Jones.*

EVERYBODY always had a basket of clams in their cellar. There were many, many very delightful, delectable dishes that could be prepared from clams.

—Doug Thompson

From Life's Harvest—An Appreciation

When dread depression stalked abroad
With threat of hunger-pain,
From wide and far came kith and kin
Home to the shores of Maine

Whose orchard trees are fruitful,
Whose balsamed woods are sweet,
Whose fields are broad and fertile
With harvest store, a treat.

But give to me her largesse
Of ocean's briny deep:
Her tomcods, scallops, mussels, crabs,
And lobsters—What a heap!

Though king, queen, kingfish, what-have-you,
I'd title that which am
Her crowning gem of lusciousness,
Maine's gift of God—the clam.

Through summer's heat and winter's chill
The clam lies at her door,
With never falter in demand,
No limit to the store.

Like mushrooms in their speedy growth
Clams seem to spring o'er night;
One never wearies of their taste,
Nor tires of their sight.

To turn them out from under rocks
To glean them from the mud,
To (gloating) pile them in the hod
To know you are no dud.

What though your back may rend in twain—
Or feel that way? by jing!
So long as you are storing up
Fit treasure for a king!

Clam chowder bubbling in the pot
With aroma divine,
Dispels the blues, drives care away
And makes the sun to shine.

There is no limit to the spiel,
No end to the refrain
But that of time when native bard
Extols the clams of Maine.

So we'll not quail what'er befalls
The wheat, the corn, the ham,
So long as Nature spares to us
Her masterpiece—the clam.

—"County Contributor,"
Lincoln County News, 1935

The old-timers told some interesting true stories about weather . . .

—Ralph Norwood

Bar Cottage, Christmas Cove, January 1933. The view faces northeast, with Birch Island in the left background.
WILLIAM A. KELSEY

. . . IF THEY were fishing offshore and catching—hake is especially the fish that they noticed did this—when you were dressing, gutting your hake, slitting the gut and pulling the guts out, if you noticed little rocks in their intestines then you'd know that there was a storm coming because they'd ballast—took on little round rocks as ballast to hold themselves steady because they knew that a storm was coming. And the old-timers swear it's true, and I believe them. I've seen 'em in them. The old-timers when they saw the fish with rocks in 'em, they got their gear aboard and headed home as fast as they could, and they usually ended up being right.

—Ralph Norwood

PERSON GROWING up on the coast, you kinda get used to certain patterns. You have a feel. I think it starts way back when people used their dories more. They'd row off when it's more calm in the morning. They'd row offshore just a few miles then. They'd be pretty sure the wind was coming up southerly and blow 'em back. After they did their fishing they'd depend on the wind to bring 'em back. They seemed to sense that it was going to blow in the south. They'd pick days that was fairly calm in the morning; usually the wind would come around in the south, bring them back.

—Afton Farrin, Jr.

A foggy morning on the Thread of Life, just below Juniper Knoll. AUTHOR PHOTO, 1997

A LOT OF TIMES *you see these little puffy clouds coming from the nor'west and they don't mean anything. When you see little puffy clouds coming from the southard, you know that there's a wind. They also call them handbills. You know, they used to pass out papers and call 'em handbills. So these little puffy clouds, lot of times you can tell there's a gale coming by those.*

Then, of course, here on the Maine coast this time of year, in the winter or the fall, if you see a bank of clouds, a solid bank to the sou'west it always means a storm coming. Almost always—you can just about depend on it.

—Ralph Norwood

I'VE SEEN THIS *cottage [Bar Cottage] right here, the surf go so high that just the top of that chimney's sticking out of the spray—just the tippy top—the whole cottage was buried. When it finally come down it was just a shower of salt water coming off the roof of that cottage. That's where you get 'em, the big storms—usually start off east, then when they get southeast and really scream, boy, they can be hard.*

—Bill Kelsey

WHEN ED GAMAGE *had a Western Union office, the telephone line broke from high wind, and telegrams blew out into the Gut and covered the road. I'm one of the few who saw that.*

—Doug Thompson

WE HAD A SERIES *of storms in the '50s. I mean to tell you, we had a series of storms that was unreal. One right after the other like this; every month we'd get one. We had one that we had wind well over 100 miles an hour. We sat down here in the village and watched the trees over here behind the schoolhouse—huge, big pines and spruces—just toppling; just flattened them like rows of corn. And somebody lost a boat at the head of the bay, way up here in the bay, and the Coast Guard—one of them double-ended surf boats—came from Burnt Island across and up into John's Bay. And there'd be fifteen minutes at a time he'd be coming and you couldn't see him—disappeared in the troughs of those swells of the sea, the chop. Then he'd pop up, then disappear, then pop up again. It can get nasty.* —Bill Kelsey

THE SOUTHEAST *is the worst fog on this coast. Boy, she come right in heavy. Fog has always bothered me more than storms. After a while you kinda sense where you're going, I guess. Just a compass, just a compass: that was the only way to get around. I've got lost more than once. But you know the way the wind's blowing, you know where the chops are. You can get your direction if you know the wind's blowing south, if it's northeast, blowing offshore. Follow the wind and take all those into consideration. Usually when it's in the north, north or northwest, usually don't have too much fog. See, that blows it off pretty well. You know it's coming from the southeast. Northeast you're more likely to get rain, and some fog. You get some bad storms but not usually too much fog. South, southeast is the real foggy weather.*

—Afton Farrin, Jr.

*W*ELL, IN THE OLD DAYS *when they got fogged in, of course the first thing you do is slow your vessel way down, and then the next thing that you had to do was try to figure out where you were and what direction you had to go in to get where you wanted to go.*

Among the old-timers probably the smartest men were the skippers of the sardine carriers that picked up sardines all along the coast and took them to the sardine factory. They had to go in some very hard places, and as opposed to, say, an offshore fisherman, who's fishing way offshore, the danger isn't that you're off a long ways, the danger is that you're in close to the shore when it gets foggy—that's where the danger is. So these men who used to go, we'll say, from Portland east and west picking up sardines, they'd do it in the fog a lot. And in the beginning they didn't even have depth indicators of any kind, they had to use a lead. A lead weight on the end of a rope was the only way they could tell how deep the water was—a sounding lead.

So the way they'd do it then is still a way that you can do it now. We'll say you come out of Portland in a boat, you know how fast your boat's going. And when you come out on a good day, you write down the course that you've taken and how long it takes to get from lighthouse to lighthouse, from buoy to buoy, and then every time you make the same trip you write it all down. Then if you get it all written down, all the courses and times, and you've done it right and your compass is good, you can do it in the fog because you've written it down—the exact compass heading and the time it takes. And the only thing that fools you is you have to slow down in the fog, so that means that you've got to add more time on a foggy day than as if you were on a clear day. But that works out well.

When you left Monhegan headed for Portland, you left the whistler buoy at Monhegan and the next whistler buoy that you wanted to hear was off Damariscove, so you ran the time out, an hour and three quarters, then you stopped the boat, shut the engine off and listen. If you've done it right you'll hear that buoy right close to you, you'll be right there. Sometimes you're a little bit off so you have to go right to it, run right up to it 'til you can see it. Then take the next course that you know is proper from that, like the next one I think we used to run to was outside of Seguin to Halfway Rock Light, so that would be two hours and a half, whatever, and then you shut your engine off and listen and it would be within earshot, yup.

—Ralph Norwood

THE BOAT TRIP from Heron Island was a predictable twenty-two minutes. On this day, however, it would be reasonable to allow for a little extra time because the fog was as thick as pea soup.

A half hour passed with no land in sight. My father turned to Frank and said, "We should be there by now; I think we're lost."

"Nope, we're not lost, Floyd," replied Frank. "Don't worry about a thing."

Ten more minutes slid by as we ghosted through the dense passageway. "Now I know we're lost," lamented Floyd. "What are we going to do?"

"Now, Floyd," assured Frank, "I been goin' back n' forth for forty years and my father before me and never got lost before."

"Hold it, Frank," cautioned Floyd. "I hear another boat. Head over there and ask him where we are."

"Oh no," sighed Frank, "that's Pearly Spear, my lobsterman friend from Pemaquid. I'll never live it down."

"We're lost, Frank, and we've got to get to the mainland. Get over there," ordered Floyd.

Frank's boat edged up to Pearly's. We could just make out a faded yellow oilskin.

"Hi, Pearly. How's it goin'?" asked Frank feebly.

"Good."

"Ask him where we are," directed Floyd.

"Pearly, I got a question for you," Frank said haltingly.

"What is it, Frank?"

"I can't find Christmas Cove, Pearly. For the first time, I'm lost," confessed Frank.

"Frank Jordon … lost. My gawd, Frank, how many years you been doin' this trip and you're lost!"

"Enough, Pearly, just tell me where I am, for chrissake."

"Well," said Pearly, drawing hard on his corncob pipe, "tell you the truth, Frank, I don't know.… I just pulled the same goddamn trap three times in a row!"

—Romilly Humphries, *Summer's End*

Owned at one time by Mervin Rice, the old house on Clark's Cove Road attracted many lightning strikes. AUTHOR PHOTO, 1997

THAT OLD CAPE *was the top of a house. Moved up from down at the shore, house that was down at the brickyard. They cut that off and moved it up there. All the information I ever got on it was from Edna Kelsey. 'Course she was an old woman then, and her husband Everett Kelsey. She said that was the oldest house in Walpole. She said, "I can remember when they moved that house up there," and probably she could. Just down over that hill, there's a road goes down to the shore off to the right. Foundation is still there, right by the shore.*

When I was there, lightning hit that place twice. The first time it struck a little fir tree out at the end of the barn. Foom! It just disintegrated, that's all. But it come in and blowed the telephone right off the wall. Had the old crank telephone in them days, that was back before the war. Well, that thing went off and it was in a thousand pieces and it was just as black as—it just burned it right up. Blowed it right off the wall—it went off, BANG! That damn thing was on the floor. It come in on the wires of course, from striking so close, I suppose. And another time it hit right handy there and burned the water pump out.

When Whittaker lived there, Carl Monroe was there, and Whittaker's wife. They had a couch, you know how—iron springs in it, like that, coiled springs. Well, the lightning come in, it followed right along—they had an ell on it and then the main house. It come along that ell, it roughed the shingles right up along that roof, crossed over on that other roof. And there's a window up in that end there—way up in the peak of the house there's a window. It cut the nails right out of that window, right straight around the window—you could pick the frame right out. It took the nails right off. Well anyhow, Monroe and Whittaker's wife was setting on that couch and it throwed her off—it went into that damn couch, I suppose, I don't know—but anyhow it broke her leg. And him, Christ, it burnt the hair right off the back of his neck. Singed it right off. Whittaker was setting over in a chair, right handy there, and it burned his hair, too, right up the back of his neck, and numbed him, kinda. He come to all right, but her, it broke her leg. It throwed her right off—the shock of it, I suppose, just throwed her or something. But anyhow, it never set that house afire. I don't know what it was about that house, but it drawed the lightning. Wicked. —Mervin Rice

Undated photo of the old Pierce house on Thompson Inn Road. MARGARET FARRIN HOUSE

SARAH EMERY *didn't have electricity. They were too frightened that it might cause a fire. In the winter she would keep her food out in the shed, and in the summer she'd keep reheating it to keep it from spoiling. And funny, they didn't believe in electricity on account of fire, but the lightning struck her house. It came in—she had a telephone—on the telephone wire, went down cellar, burned the beams on the way, and come up through and under her kitchen table, and she had a kerosene lamp on it. And that lightning lifted that table right up, the lamp never tipped over or anything, set it back down. Sarah used to tell me that story.*

—Katherine Poole Norwood

PEOPLE REFER *back to the winter of 1934. I was a senior in high school at that time and I can recall that it got down to twenty-four below zero. The Guts were frozen over, especially the Eastern Gut was all frozen over; some of the current and tide kept the Western Gut from totally closing in. We didn't seem to mind these winters, even though the dampness on the seacoast makes the low temperatures feel worse. We still survived and had a lot of fun. I can remember walking a mile to visit a girlfriend down in Christmas Cove and walking a mile home later in the evening, and thought nothing of it.* —Doug Thompson

WE HAD ONE *Christmas Day, I think it was in the early '70s, and it was twenty-four, twenty-five below zero Christmas Day. There was so much vapor on the river you couldn't hardly see across.*

—Bill Kelsey

I'VE SEEN THE Gut froze over. And, I can't remember it, but they say they used to come in there with steamers and unload freight on the ice and haul it in on the Western Gut. That was before my time, but I remember when the Eastern Gut was froze over and we skated on it. But there was no boats, see, going in; now there's boats going all the time. 'Course there's a difference in the winters; a lot of difference in the winters. It's warmed up. It's warmer. —Mervin Rice

WE USED TO get ice skating by Thanksgiving, usually. Ponds would be frozen up by that time. It got colder earlier then, and lots of times we'd have snow. Sometimes we'd have snow by the first of November. We used to like that to go gunning on—tracking deer and so forth. The river would freeze up enough so there could be no transportation on it in the wintertime. Yes, winters were more rugged; seemed to me they were.

—Robert Woodward

The Western Gut, c. 1934, looking north from the West Side Road across to Harvey Gamage's and the Shipyard Road. MARGARET FARRIN HOUSE

This was the link of downriver towns with the outside world...

—Doug Thompson

...AND IT REMAINED so for many years under varying circumstances and changing boats. This was a major means of travel—a major means of freight transportation, not to mention mail.

—Doug Thompson

Ladies on a steamer, probably on the Damariscotta River. WILLIAM A. KELSEY

IN 1810 A liniment was put on the market which came to be a very popular remedy for common colds and enjoyed an immediate popularity. It soon gained a reputation for effectiveness and began to be used in large quantities, especially along the Maine coast. It was probably the most popular internal and external remedy of the Gay Nineties. It was called Johnson's Anodyne Liniment.

Some resourceful member of the company conceived the idea that it could be sold in larger quantities if some means were devised to bring it to people along the coast of Maine and on the remote islands. With this idea in mind the company contacted the boatbuilding establishment of A. & M. Gamage & Co. at South Bristol, Maine, in 1894. A design for a small steamer was submitted and approved, and the little steamer was built in 1885 and named the ANODYNE. Captain Elliot Gamage of South Bristol was engaged as master. For five years Captain Gamage went the length and breadth of the coast with this popular remedy and enjoyed a healthy business. Mr. Johnson himself accompanied Captain Gamage on the first trips.

The ANODYNE may have been Maine's first seagoing billboard. She was plastered with advertising signs which read, "Every Mother Should Have It in the House." She plied her liniment from town to town along the coast and often, to drum up more business and create goodwill, took ladies in sweeping crinolines and wide hats for an afternoon's cruise.

The liniment was advertised as a remedy for every ailment from colds to dandruff. It

The little steamer ANODYNE. Captain Elliot Gamage and his wife Annette stand on the bow.
NOBLEBORO HISTORICAL SOCIETY, IVAN FLYE COLLECTION

Advertisement from the *Boothbay Register*, 1893.

could be taken straight or camouflaged in sugar. Ingredients included 16 percent alcohol and 6 percent ether, turpentine, camphor, and ammonia.

In the pre-automobile days of the Gay Nineties small excursions and private parties on steamers were very popular. The little steamer ANODYNE was always in demand, and Captain Gamage conceived the idea of expansion and forming a regular steamboat company. He suggested the idea to various people in Damariscotta and Newcastle, and it received more than ordinary interest and approval. In 1900, the Corporation was formed and named "the Damariscotta Steamboat Company." Stock was offered at $25 a share and quickly subscribed. Plans were made to expand, and a new and much larger steamer contracted for at once. This new ship was to be named the BRISTOL. Completed in 1901 by A. & M. Gamage & Company, she immediately replaced the ANODYNE on the river.

It seemed certain that these two steamers could accommodate the demand but in the very first year of 1901, it was found that the demand was far greater, and a much larger steamer was planned, approved, and built by the same Gamage yard in 1902. This queen of the fleet was named the NEWCASTLE. Captain Gamage became master of this new steamer and "Uncle" Charlie Hatch, his engineer. Captain Plummer Leeman became the captain of the BRISTOL, with Uncle Charlie's son, Warren Hatch, as engineer. —Harold Castner, "The Castner Papers"

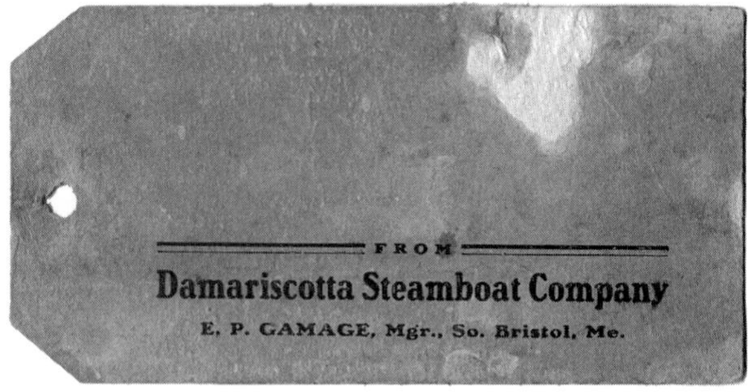

Luggage tag from the Damariscotta Steamboat Company. This tag was found in Elliot Gamage's Shipyard Road house by its present owners, David and Betsy Andrews. GEORGE KING III

The fleet of the Damariscotta Steamboat Company: steamers NEWCASTLE, BRISTOL, and ANODYNE.
PEMAQUID HISTORICAL ASSOCIATION

Damariscotta Steamboat Company

TIME TABLE

IN EFFECT JUNE 1, 1910

†Lv. Damariscotta and New'le	9.45 a.m.	3.15 p.m.	Lv. Christmas Cove	6.10 a.m.	12.10 p.m.
*Poole's Landing	10.25 "	3.50 "	Heron Island	6.15 "	11.45 "
*Clarke's Cove	10.30 "	4.00 "	South Bristol	6.40 "	12.30 "
*Willard Island	10.35 "	4.05 "	East Boothbay	6.50 "	12.40 "
East Boothbay	10.50 "	4.30 "	*Willard Island	7.10 "	1.00 "
South Bristol	11.00 "	4.45 "	*Clarke's Cove	7.15 "	1.10 "
Heron Island	11.20 "	5.05 "	*Poole's Landing	7.25 "	1.15 "
Ar. Christmas Cove	11.30 "	5.20 "	†Ar. Damariscotta and New'le	8.30 "	2.15 "

After June 28, the Steamer Tourist will connect with all boats for all Pemaquid Landings.

On and after July 4th boats will leave Christmas Cove at 5.20 P. M. (Saturday only). Return leave Damariscotta at 10.10 a. m., Sundays only.

*On signal. †Unavoidable delays excepted and subject to change without notice.

Through tickets can be procured and baggage checked through in New York, Philadelphia, Boston and all points on the M. C. R. R. to points on our line.

Write or Ask for Pamphlet

Timetable for the steamboat company. By 1910 travelers could buy tickets and check their baggage all the way through to their Damariscotta River destination before they even stepped onto the train in Boston, Philadelphia, or New York.
ELIZABETH ALLEY HOUSE

IN THOSE DAYS, Guy McFarland had a speed boat named the CIGARETTE, and they boasted that the NEWCASTLE once beat her, which indicates a top speed of perhaps twelve knots. NEWCASTLE and all the others cruised, however, at an economical eight to nine, and the trip down the river took about two hours, with stops at Poole's Landing, Clark's Cove, East Boothbay, South Bristol, Heron Island, and finally Christmas Cove. Often there would be a lot of freight to be unloaded at one place or another, and the trip took longer.

We had two boats a day from Bath. The NEWCASTLE made two round trips to Damariscotta; indeed, she blew her whistle at six every morning, which gave permission for the children to get up and play if they were quiet about it. The steamer ISLESFORD made the run to and from Boothbay three times daily, and the TOURIST spent the whole day going round and round John's Bay.

For whatever their faults, the little steamers were handy. They had immense propellers and large rudders. You could slide them alongside a dock at two or three knots, maintaining good steerage control. You then rang for full speed astern, and they stopped. The whole ship shuddered, and geysers of white water churned under the counter.

—John Sewall, *CCIA Notes*, Summer 1966

IT IS SAFE to say that Captain Elliot Gamage and Captain Plummer Leeman were two of the most popular men in this vicinity at that time. Those of us who were boys in those days will never forget them and also the dean of all engineers on the river, "Uncle" Charlie Hatch. We can still remember his immaculate engine room and those great pistons and shiny engine parts, and the kind and lovable countenance of Uncle Charlie looking up at us. He understood boys and his wisdom directed that it was not safe to let us loose among those moving parts, but Captain Gamage was very indulgent in the pilot house and some of us will never forget the thrill of turning that great wheel

The NEWCASTLE crew, left to right: Phil Woodwell, Walter Hayward, Charles Foster, Horace Kelsey, engineer Charlie Hatch, Randall Poole, Captain Elliot P. Gamage. MARGARET FARRIN HOUSE

and feeling the ship respond to our effort. It was a rather confusing process as all steering was called "steamboat style." This meant that if you wished to turn right, you turned the wheel left. It was from Captain Gamage that the writer first learned port from starboard.

From such men as Captain Gamage and Captain Leeman and Uncle Charlie Hatch, those of us who are grown men of today learned the object lesson of kindness and patience with children and may God rest their souls for the good influence they had on our lives. —Harold Castner, "The Castner Papers"

THE NEWCASTLE, THE TOURIST, and the ISLESFORD were owned locally and spent the night at Christmas Cove and South Bristol. Captains Gamage, Harrington, and Leeman were family friends, kindly and warmhearted. They knew us all by name. We liked them. We also admired them, for they moved and spoke with a firmness and dignity proper to their responsibilities.

—John Sewell, *CCIA Notes*, Summer 1966

ONE DAY Captain Gamage was warping the NEWCASTLE into Cottrell's Wharf at Damariscotta, and stepping along the rail, he caught his watch chain on a stanchion. This threw the watch out of his pocket and it dropped over the side into the water at the end of the pier. It was less than fifteen minutes before a group of boys were diving, and making every effort to recover it, but although some of them became almost exhausted, they were unable to find it and it is probably still lodged in the bottom where it has lain all these years.

—Harold Castner, "The Castner Papers"

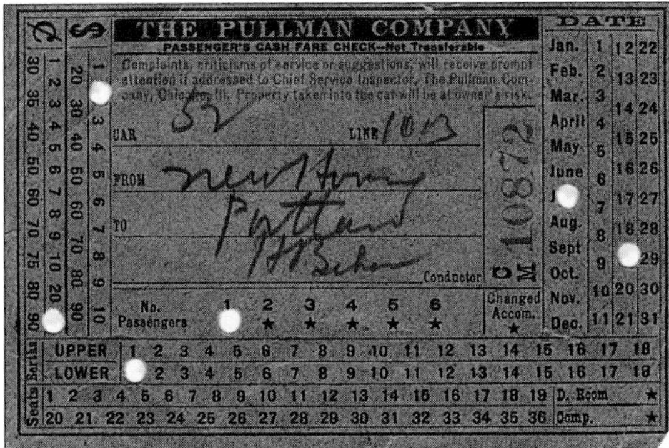

Train ticket, July 1915, to Portland, continuing on to Rockland. The fare, with a lower berth in the Pullman car, was $2.30. AUTHOR'S COLLECTION

AN ALTERNATE route was by train from Boston to Newcastle. That was quicker, but the trains were always hot and dirty. It was wonderful to get off the horrid train, put your handbags on a horse and wagon, and stroll through the quiet village to the dock where the old NEWCASTLE would be waiting. And she always had to wait because it took some time to put the mail and all the freight aboard. Everybody paced the decks alive with anticipation until, finally, the lines were cast off. And as soon as they got her turned and pointed south, they used to blow a good one on the whistle.

—John Sewall, CCIA *Notes*, Summer 1966

OCEANGOING STEAMBOATS—*New York and Boston boats—they would come in there, and sometimes they'd lay in there overnight with passengers. Smaller steamboats were coming down the Damariscotta River, making connections with the trains running into Newcastle, and this is how the people would arrive there to spend the summer.*

—Doug Thompson

Captain Elliot Gamage, holding his pocketwatch. Randall Poole stands to his right.
MARGARET FARRIN HOUSE

I HAVE VERY *fleeting memories of coming up on the train before they had built the Kennebec bridge—the Carlton Bridge—when they still had a ferry. These trains would come up to Bath, and then they'd break the train up into sections and push it onto this ferry. Then they'd take it across, and discharge the train on the other side. And then that train went to Rockland, and it made stops along the way at Wiscasset and Newcastle, and further up at Waldoboro; Rockland was the end of the line.* —Norman Hamlin

The TOURIST at the South Bristol steamer wharf, 1914. The arrival of another steamer is probably imminent: there appear to be more passengers on the wharf than could fit onto the little TOURIST.
ELIZABETH ALLEY HOUSE

ON AUGUST 26, 1918, the TOURIST was making dock at Cottrell's Wharf in Damariscotta. It was the "top of the tide" and Mr. Merrill threw the heaving line to Charles Etheridge and William Perkins on the dock. The steamer was making the usual headway as these men ran back to throw the loop in the hawser over a piling. They found that the steamer had so far advanced that they were unable to reach a piling and in sheer desperation, they tried to hold the steamer with their hands. Mr. Merrill stood there on the deck, ready to snub, but with nothing to snub. Capt. Etheridge, who was noted for his skill and care, gave an immediate bell to reverse the engine. There was no response and he shouted to Mr. Merrill to tell Mr. Spear to reverse. Mr. Merrill ran to the engine room hatch and looking down at Mr. Spear, shouted to reverse the engine. The sight which Mr. Merrill beheld was tragic. Mr. Spear stood there with blood streaming from his arm, but his hand was on the throttle. He had evidently met with a serious accident and due to the loss of blood, had lost the use of his arm. He looked at Mr. Merrill and tragically exclaimed: "I can't do it!"

Things happened quickly then. The steamer piled up against the rocks and the swift current carried it out sidewise, where the superstructure caught on the bridge. There was an awful moment when the hull began to curl under, but with a great crashing and scraping, the steamer turned almost over but passed under the bridge and drifted to the Newcastle shore.

It was a miracle that all on board reached shore except the engineer Spear, who perished by drowning. There were nineteen people aboard and several witnessed the accident from the bridge. During those awful moments under the bridge, Mr. Merrill overheard the mother of a small boy shout to him to hold on to the rail at all costs. As the steamer yawed in the current, this little boy held onto the rail tenaciously, reminding one of the familiar story of "the boy on the burning deck." As the steamer would roll, the rail would go under water with the little boy with it, but when it came up again, he was still holding on. This undoubtedly saved his life.

John Glidden came running from his home nearby, stood on the shore and quickly removed his trousers. He was wearing long, old-fashioned underwear. He plunged into the water and swam near the wreckage, doing whatever he could to assist the passengers, who were still aboard and intact. After he had been in the water for some time, he was obliged to return to the shore, where he discovered that the buttons on his underwear had been torn off, and he was considerably exposed to view, but remained unnoticed due to the general excitement. He soon recognized his difficulties and began looking for his trousers, but he could not find them and was obliged to retire from the scene where he might obtain sufficient raiment to cover his nakedness. Many rowboats and canoes soon appeared and began to gather the wreckage of all sorts and descriptions, including boxes, cushions, personal effects, and even a crate of hens.

—Harold Castner, "The Castner Papers"

The wrecked TOURIST, tethered to the shore in the Damariscotta River, August 1918.
CATHERINE JORDON WALKER

THEY SAID *the captain of the* TOURIST *was drunk when that happened. My mother-in-law was aboard.* —Annie Louise Alley Farrin

ACCORDING TO his grandson, Alfred L. Harrington—the original captain of the TOURIST—volunteered to accompany the new captain to aid him in the tricky docking maneuver at Damariscotta. The tides were known to be dangerous, and it was to be Captain Etheridge's first attempt at docking there. The offer was refused.

Repaired and put back into service, the TOURIST carried passengers in Maine until 1958, first on the Kennebec and then on Casco Bay. Renamed SABINO in 1922 she has been restored and now, the last wooden coal-fired steamboat still in operation, she carries visitors at the Mystic Seaport Museum.

Postcard home from Christmas Cove, 1908. The message reads, "Had a great trip. Not a bit sick."
WILLIAM A. KELSEY

Advertisement from the *Boothbay Register,* February 1889.

THE PORTLAND STEAMER, the ENTERPRISE, was a rolling old tub, and it was almost punishment to sail on her, even on a pleasant day.

For a time, ENTERPRISE carried passengers between Portland and Boothbay, but mostly she was used as a freighter, going where and when cargoes offered. Pretty flat on the bottom and having primitive machinery, she had the reputation of being a hog to handle.

The rolling ENTERPRISE—built in Baltimore—paid a weekly visit to Heron Island, Christmas Cove, East Boothbay and South Bristol after putting in first at Boothbay Harbor. Portland was her home port. She was primarily a freighter but had comfortable deck space for passengers willing to risk seasickness.
—John Sewall, CCIA *Notes*, Summer 1966

The NAHANADA and WIWURNA—later replaced by the less graceful EASTPORT and WESTPORT—made daily runs from Bath to Pemaquid Harbor. They stopped at Heron on signal, or if freight or passengers were on board to land. Coming downriver from Damariscotta, every day except Sunday, the NEWCASTLE, Captain Gamage, steamed out to Heron carrying passengers, freight and mail.
—John Sewall, CCIA *Notes*, Summer 1966

WHEN I WAS a kid we always went down around the wharf and waited for the boat to come bringing all this stuff, goodies and all. Where my wharf is, that's the old steamboat wharf. When the steamboat come in everybody'd be standing around waving, unloading barrels of molasses, boxes of dates, and all that kind of stuff. —Afton Farrin, Jr.

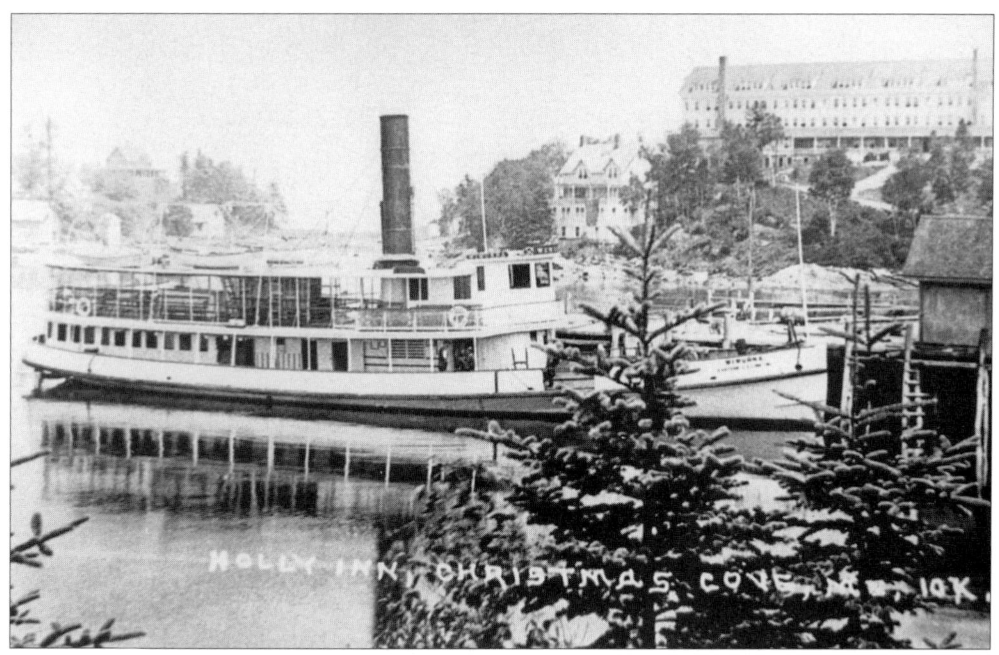

The steamer WIWURNA, docked in Christmas Cove. The Holly Inn can be seen in the background. PEMAQUID HISTORICAL ASSOCIATION

IN BACK OF Chester Clifford's market was the Eastern Steamship wharf. A great many of the supplies in those days, most of them, came down the river and were stored in the shed.

—Doug Thompson

ON ARRIVAL AT THE Cove by one way or another, trunks and suitcases were piled onto a wagon operated by Mr. Lewis Thorpe. He delivered them to your cottage almost as soon as you could make your way there on foot.

—John Sewall, CCIA *Notes*, Summer 1966

THE WHOLE WAY of life changed on the coast here when they stopped bringing goods by water. That's back when everything was brought by water, you know—by boat. Boats would come in from Portland and Boston until they put the railroad through in Damariscotta. There was a lot of activity that went by water. People would come here to stay in hotels and boardinghouses. They'd come with big trunks, and stay for a month or two. When I was a kid, it was mostly horses then. They'd just come out with the Model T. They'd put the trunks in the horse and buggy, and later when they started using the Model T Ford I can remember them putting the trunks on them to go to the hotels.

—Afton Farrin, Jr.

An expectant crowd awaits the steamer NEWCASTLE at the wharf in South Bristol. Although the photograph is undated, this image is from a card postmarked 1909. CATHERINE JORDON WALKER

A young woman waits patiently on the South Bristol steamer wharf, c. 1921. The large building directly behind her is the grocery store.
COURTESY MARIAN COUGHLIN

A horse and buggy go by the CCIA Casino and tennis courts in Christmas Cove. In the background, a large steamer can be seen docked at the wharf. WILLIAM A. KELSEY

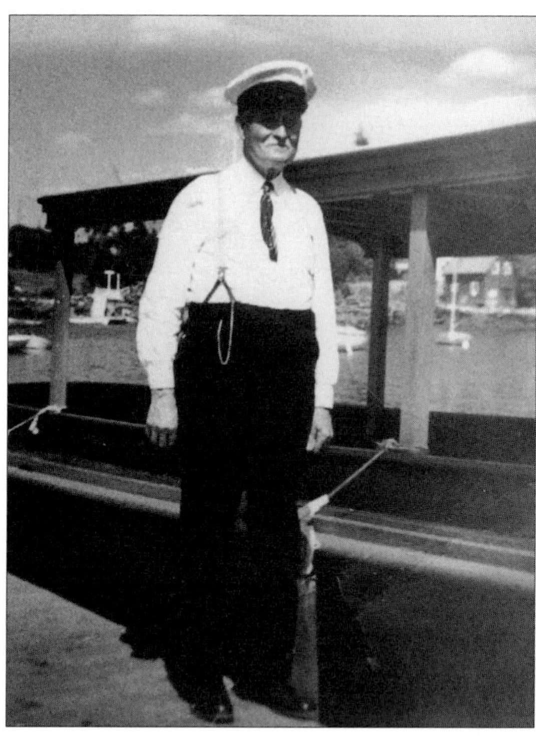

Captain Frank Y. McFarland, standing beside his launch in Christmas Cove.
FRANK Y. "PETE" MCFARLAND, JR.

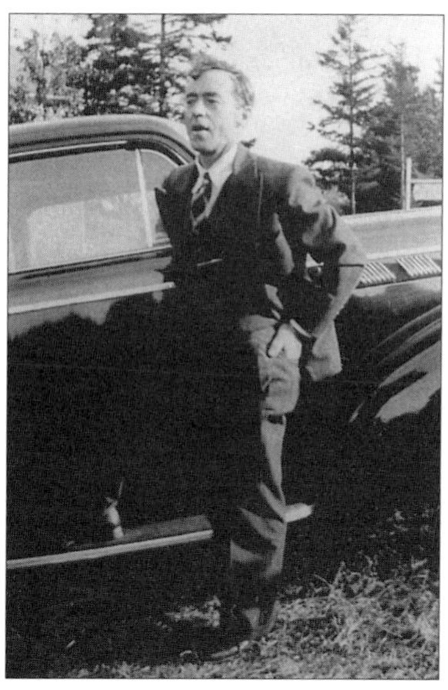

Captain George Kelsey. CHARLES KELSEY

GEORGE KELSEY later ran a sightseeing boat in and out of the area for a short time. George had a son Winslow who moved away at an early age.

—Doug Thompson

CAPTAIN FRANK MCFARLAND was a very accomplished boatbuilder, and he ran launch services from Christmas Cove to Boothbay Harbor. He would stop at Heron Island from time to time but they would go primarily to Boothbay Harbor. That was a regular route and it was taken quite commonly by people like my mother, who had to go shopping. It was easier to walk down, get on his boat, take it over to Boothbay Harbor, where it would land quite close to where the stores were. He'd give you an hour ashore and you'd do your shopping and have a nice trip back. Sundays he had a trip that was timed to coincide with church services that people that were here in the summer used to go to in Boothbay Harbor.

—Norman Hamlin

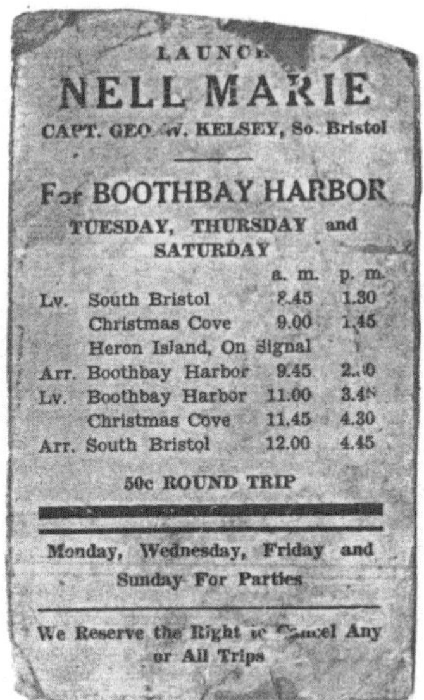

LAUNC[illegible]

NELL MARIE

CAPT. GEO. W. KELSEY, So. Bristol

For BOOTHBAY HARBOR

TUESDAY, THURSDAY and SATURDAY

		a. m.	p. m.
Lv.	South Bristol	8.45	1.30
	Christmas Cove	9.00	1.45
	Heron Island, On Signal		
Arr.	Boothbay Harbor	9.45	2.[illegible]0
Lv.	Boothbay Harbor	11.00	3.4[illegible]
	Christmas Cove	11.45	4.30
Arr.	South Bristol	12.00	4.45

50c ROUND TRIP

Monday, Wednesday, Friday and Sunday For Parties

We Reserve the Right [illegible] Cancel Any or All Trips

Schedule card for Captain Kelsey's launch, the NELL MARIE. CHARLES KELSEY

Captain Ambrose Alley. ELIZABETH ALLEY HOUSE

ACROSS THE STREET *next to Horace Kelsey's was Captain Ambrose Alley. Agnes was his wife. They had a daughter named Louise and they had sons named Stanley, and Ernest, and Richard. Ambrose ran a "party boat," a sightseeing boat. We always called them party boats—they were sightseeing boats. It was a long torpedo-stern boat, which was the style at that time. They were narrow, but they were supposed to be the thing. The name of that boat was the* ERNEST A*, and he ran to Pemaquid Beach, Pemaquid Harbor, Pemaquid Point.*

—Doug Thompson

THE TIDE IN THE *Damariscotta River was something that had to be reckoned with. Its force was something that had to be figured into the schedules. If the run up the river was against the ebb tide, or the run down was against the flood, extra time was allowed. By the same token, there was a great advantage if the run was being made with the tides. My father, Captain Thompson, was a master of taking advantage of the swirling eddies and currents that were running opposite of the main river's currents. He knew the river bottom and the shoreline so well that he could read the effects and safely leave the buoyed channel and have a fair tide rather than head tide most of the time.*

Captain Mark Thompson on one of his launches. Summer visitors who rode on his party boats would often take photographs and send copies back to Captain Thompson. J. DOUGLAS THOMPSON

Damariscotta River Line

THE Damariscotta River Line announces that it is now in a position to accommodate traffic on the Damariscotta River. Two 45 foot gasoline boats will ply on the river, ensuring connection with both forenoon and afternoon trains. These boats, the "Celia E." and the "Pilgrim" are staunch and comfortable, with ample accommodations for passengers and baggage. Experienced men will be in charge and the trip will be made in safety and comfort. Fare between Damariscotta and East Boothbay, South Bristol, Christmas Cove and Heron Island, 75c. From either end of the route to intermediate points, 50c. This includes war tax. Passengers will be picked up anywhere.

MARK THOMPSON, Manager.

Card for Mark Thompson's company, the Damariscotta River Line. J. DOUGLAS THOMPSON

The narrows at Fort Island and the ledges of both Merry's Island and Pitcher's Point, back of Carlisle Island or between it, was a place where whirling eddies caused a great deal of force upon the boats. His expertise was often called upon in later years to pilot down the river the draggers and minesweepers that were built at the Harry Marr shipyard in Damariscotta. —Doug Thompson

The J. Douglas.
Nobleboro Historical Society, Ivan Flye Collection

March, 1924

GOUDY & STEVENS
East Boothbay, Maine

A 50-footer, designed for fishing parties, is being built by this concern. Name, J. Douglas; started, January 10; finish, May 28; type, motor boat for fishing parties; building for Messrs. Thompson and Etheridge, South Bristol, Maine; designed by Goudy & Stevens; length, 50′; beam, 13′6″; draft, 4′3″; estimated speed, 10 m.p.h.; engine, 40 h.p. Sterling; propeller, Hyde, 34x34.

Excerpt from *Atlantic Fisherman* magazine, 1924. The Goudy & Stevens yard was just across the river in East Boothbay; many South Bristol ship carpenters were employed there over the years. Author's collection

This boat ran on the Damariscotta River quite a few years and it was named the J. Douglas, after me. I have memories of it with loads of people and lots of freight. It was large enough to carry freights; it was a double-decked boat to carry a lot of passengers and heavy cargoes. For years my father carried the mail and freight and they'd land there behind back of the store there at Farrin's Wharf—they called it the steamship wharf—and then go from there down to Christmas Cove. If there wasn't too much mail he'd throw it into his Model T and deliver it a mile down to the post office in Christmas Cove. Two trips a day. Good service then: we had two mails a day coming into Christmas Cove and South Bristol. He did that 'til the roads got so they were passable year-round, then the contract was issued to trucks.

He sold the J. Douglas down to Stonington, and they used it down there to carry workmen off to the islands where the quarries were, and then it went from there up to Saugus, Massachusetts, and I understand it's still in use—and that boat was launched by Goudy and Stevens in 1924.

—Doug Thompson

The Barbara J II, taking on passengers. She was named after Captain Thompson's daughter.
Catherine Jordon Walker

He made a contract with Harvey Gamage to build the boat in his yard. Then my father went into the yard and worked on that boat; helped with the construction of it. He didn't do it all alone, but he did a great deal of it. It was a fine boat—the Barbara J II. And all during my high-school days I worked with him on these boats, the trips that he made. We'd run to Damariscotta a couple of times a week and Boothbay Harbor three days a week, a morning trip and an afternoon trip, and a round-

The PILGRIM, with Captain Mark and Mrs. Sarah Thompson aboard. The photograph was likely taken from the South Bristol steamer wharf: the distinctive profile of Ed Gamage's store can be seen at the right side of the picture. J. DOUGLAS THOMPSON

trip to Boothbay. At that time it was fifty cents. Then on Saturdays and Sundays we made excursions, they were called. These were all-day trips for a dollar. Sundays we went to Monhegan, and then on Saturdays we made excursions to such places as Bath, Wiscassett, Five Islands, Friendship, and some of the other places of interest in the area. On the trips to Boothbay Harbor we had a lot of people from Heron Island who did their shopping in Boothbay; back in those days the refrigerators were ice refrigerators, and they'd take tubs or special canvas bags and pick up their ice in Boothbay Harbor, and then do their grocery shopping and put it ashore at Heron Island. I used to make pretty good tips waiting on those people.

—Doug Thompson

THAT'S THE BOAT *my father used to run. See the snow? Just as soon as the ice was out of the Damariscotta River, everybody wanted to get to Damariscotta, so he'd make trips. Sometimes he had to break ice up the river there to get up; he had a V-shaped piece of steel which he hung down over the bow of the boat so the ice wouldn't damage it. They had that house on there so they could keep warm. It was a big event when the rivers broke up. This was the link of downriver towns with the outside world.* —Doug Thompson

My father was a boatbuilder and my grandfather was a builder, and I guess you'd call me a builder, too.

—Pete McFarland

MY GRANDFATHER built, in his lifetime, over seven hundred. He had a record of every rowboat, every schooner, every sloop. The bigger boats, schooners, like that—they'd build them up in the field. Slide them down to the shore on timbers and launch 'em right there in the cove, yup. Wouldn't take too many men—they knew what they was doing.

—Addison McFarland

MY FATHER BUILT his first boat when he was twelve years old, a rowboat. We built fifty-three boats here, and rebuilt I don't know how many. My father, he'd buy boats and he'd do work on them and sell 'em. I think he had fifty boats—not all at one time. There were sailboats and powerboats and later on we built lots of yacht-club vessels. There were a lot of boats went over on Lake Michigan; they were kind of like a skiff. One of the sailboats we shipped out to Lake Michigan, and of course Portland, and Gloucester, and we sold a lot of 'em down in Cape Cod—all our own designs. Father would do the half model, and draft it out on the drafting board.

—Addison McFarland

William Addison McFarland, 1840–1929, grandfather of boatbuilders Winthrop, Addison, and Pete McFarland. His father, a mariner, died at sea when William Addison was only eight years old. The Walpole boatbuilder Samuel Kelsey was an uncle by marriage, and it's interesting to speculate whether Kelsey took the orphaned boy under his wing, giving him his start in the boatbuilding trade.
WILLIAM A. KELSEY

We are pleased to hear our veteran boat-builder, Addison McFarland, is rushed with business as usual. He has orders for ten boats to be ready for next season, and is expecting parties here, soon, S. T. & L. Nickerson from Provincetown, Mass., to close a contract for a steam launch. He has one of the best and most convenient boat shops in New England: the building is 27x66 feet, the carpenters room where the boats are built is 27x40, and adjoining this is a store room 26x27, where the boats are stored when completed. The second floor is used for storing lumber and building material. Mr. McFarland is a self-made boat builder, commencing about thirty years ago by building a 12 foot dory. He has worked straight ahead, and is now at work on his 332nd boat with nine orders on his books. He has built all kinds of crafts from the dory to schooners of twenty tons. He has orders all along the coast from Bar Harbor, Maine to Newport, R. I. He has orders for three boats from Mr. Brightman from R. I. Now he has all the modern improvements for boat building, and is a first-class workman in every respect, and has never failed to give his customers satisfaction. I doubt if there is another boat-builder can show as good a record. All persons desiring a first-class boat should give him a call.

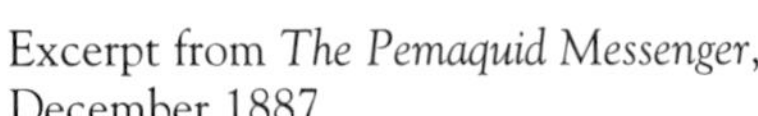

Excerpt from *The Pemaquid Messenger*, December 1887.

The McFarlands, father and sons, in their Christmas Cove shop: "Pete," Addison, Winthrop, Frank Sr.—and Lobo. FRANK Y. "PETE" MCFARLAND, JR.

McFarland's Cove, about 1910. W. A. McFarland's boatshop is on the shore at the lower left. CASSIE H. MANCHESTER TRUST

The launch DAUNTLESS II, outside the McFarland's boatshop. FRANK Y. "PETE" MCFARLAND, JR.

I STARTED IN at nine years old driving the plugs, you know, over the fastenings. And then as they'd rivet I would hold the rivet iron. They was all copper fastenings. We'd trade back and forth. We had an iron, 'bout so long, with a pin in the end that you held up in to hold the copper nails. And one fella inside with what we called a peen hammer. And you had to rivet those—with the round part of the peen hammer you'd start out flat, then you'd have to go round the edges. That would make a round rivet over a copper burr. One boat I know, there's five thousand rivets in—number six nails, almost the size of that pencil. That's a lot a pounding. But I was nine when I started drivin' plugs. They called it bungin'. —Pete McFarland

THAT'S THE DAUNTLESS II. She was beautiful. She was finished about as good as anybody could ever finish one. You could see your whiskers in the varnish! It was varnished mahogany bright. She was all bright—decks, seats, cockpit, floor, and all.
—Pete McFarland

Phil Page watches Sumner McFarland work on the JUNE B, c. 1961. At forty, the JUNE B still floats at her mooring on the Eastern Gut; at seventy-nine, Phil Page still fishes on her.
NOBLEBORO HISTORICAL SOCIETY, IVAN FLYE COLLECTION

Launching day, probably in the 1930s. Horace Kelsey and Will Alley flank the proud owner of the new vessel. MARGARET FARRIN HOUSE

HORACE KELSEY was a carpenter and boatbuilder. They owned the building in town that at one time was first a market and then a boat shop, and his partner was Will Alley. This shop of theirs was down at the head of the steamboat wharf in town.

—Doug Thompson

ARLETTA'S FATHER was a boatbuilder, too. He built boats, and her brother John, he built himself a Friendship sloop down there in the shop, the ELLIE T. I remember when he built that.

—Doug Thompson

HE JUST built pleasure boats, and a lobsterboat—stuff like that. He didn't have a lobster boat like they have now—he had a lapstrake open boat. He worked on boats when he was a young man. During the war he worked at Harvey's, and he worked at East Boothbay, but he built boats for his own pleasure, mostly. He sold one skiff—that was the first one I remember he built. It was a sailing skiff, and then he built a series of daysailers that got sold so he could buy lumber to build another one—that was the deal! One of them was a pretty big one, but most of them were daysailers after that.

There were two vessels that he admired very much; he must have either seen them or known of them as a kid. They were the MOUNTAIN LAUREL and the TWILIGHT. And he always wanted to build a boat that one of the old fishermen had had, but he had decided he could only name one the TWILIGHT—because he never would have a boat big enough to put the "Mountain Laurel" on the stern! —and he did indeed have a TWILIGHT—it was one of our daysailers like the half model over the fireplace downstairs. Just a little boat, but it was called the TWILIGHT—I don't know if he ever even put the name on her. —Arletta Thorpe Rice

Willard "Bill" Thorpe, with his wife Kathleen and little son John. Bill Thorpe was also a master carpenter who built several Christmas Cove cottages, helped transform the Miles Fresh Air Camp buildings into summer dwellings, and led the rebuilding of the Miles Tower. ARLETTA THORPE RICE

Clifton Poole in the shop, summer 1959, working on a boat for John Gay. Katherine Poole Norwood

Don Stanley, caulking the bilge stringers on the Hero. He and Pete McFarland had just finished caulking a 125-foot dragger, Hunter, sitting to the left of the Hero. Maine Maritime Museum

Clifton Poole retired from the Gamage yard after twenty-four years of boatbuilding, but soon found that "doin' nothin'" didn't suit him, so he began building small boats in the old family barn. He built lapstrake dories and skiffs out of "Maine pine and tough oak timbers." At Gamage's he had worked on hulls like the schooners Mary Day and Shenandoah, and big draggers like the Wawenock and the Pocahantas, but in retirement he drew upon his experiences from the days when he built dories for Admiral McMillan's famed vessel Bowdoin.

Large or small, all wooden vessels must be caulked, a task that requires considerable skill—and a strong constitution.

This is choking the cotton in. I did all the choking at Harvey's and I had helpers on driving. By that, you've got your caulking and your iron in this hand. The caulking goes over this finger, and as you choke that in, you take this here and drive it with a big heavy mallet. Put it in with your left hand and drive it with your right. That comes in a big package of cotton and we would pull it all apart, separate it and put it in the box here so it'd keep coming out of the box, right underneath where you're sitting on the box. The box we used was a paint box. I'd had four gallons of paint and I'd kept the top out and put cotton into the box.

Now the oakum was quite made up this shape, about so long, ten inches or a foot long. You had to pull that all out of the center, then you spun it over your knee, like that. Spin and stretch, spin and stretch. Then it goes in that box, and you start driving. The cotton goes in first, and the oakum over it. The oakum's sort of a hemp with pine tar—you're all greasy when you get through. Your pants or whatever you're spinning on is all covered with liquid. You come home smelling like it.

—Pete McFarland

Les Thompson, from Friendship, Maine, at work on the topsail schooner HARVEY L. GAMAGE. ROBERT K. WOODWARD

I'D SAY TO do a 100-footer I'd be a month, month and a half—decks and everything. That was steady pounding. I used to have pretty good muscles, boy. Quite a sound, just listening to a caulker. Every time you hit, it go "Ping!" When you was hitting your iron. "Click, click ..." or "Ping!"

Caulking is a hard thing to do. You end up with bad knees, bad arms, fingers all crippled up.

—Pete McFarland

WITH THE launching of the schooner JENNY LIND in 1854, the Gamage brothers, Albion and Menzies, began a half-century of building some of the finest vessels on the coast of Maine. Here we see a vessel being built at the A. & M. Gamage yard, probably in the 1880s.

A schooner, traditionally identified as the ARWILDA MORSE, under construction at the A. & M. Gamage yard, late nineteenth century. MARGARET FARRIN HOUSE

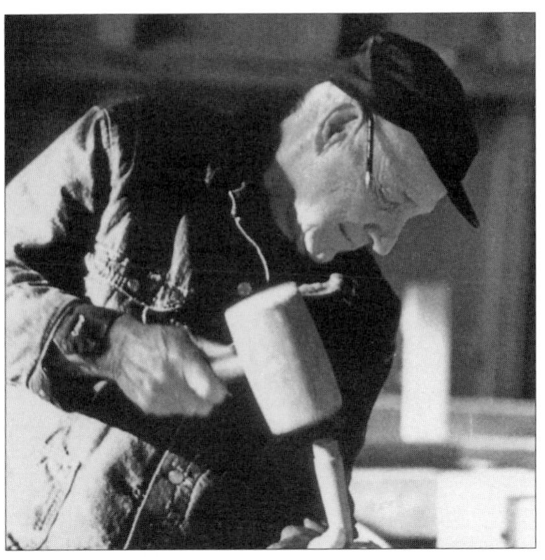

Harvey L. Gamage, 1898–1976, in a photograph taken in the early 1970s. Robert K. Woodward

Merton Stapels, front, and Clifton Poole wield adzes on a hull in the Gamage yard. Maine Maritime Museum

In 1925 Albion and Menzies' great-nephew Harvey Gamage built his first vessel, a John Alden design, on the site of their yard, and for the next fifty years continued to build vessels that helped reclaim South Bristol's reputation as a center of Maine boatbuilding.

Some think he was hard to work for, but I think he was a wonderful guy—always used me good. Once I had a bad back, used me up for twelve weeks. I went back up there and Harvey, I remember him telling me, "Come up to the house before you go. Don't get out, just drive up there," so I drove up and one of his sons-in-law come up and he put a bag of scallops in the car for me, about 60 pounds, wasn't it? I know it was an awful lot of scallops. And when his draggers come in for repairs he had gray sole, lemon sole, fish for us—take what you want, have a bushel if you wanted. Oh, he looked out for his crew, yes.

He was always a quiet person. Well, maybe not quiet, but he wasn't talkative. Especially if you came in to visit ... I guess he had the reputation of just plain walking off and not talking to you. One day we was working there and somebody come in. I guess Harvey didn't want to see him. He says, "Tell him the last time you seen me I was down on a boat at the dock,"—and there he was in the shop! When he got ready he went over and met him. —Pete McFarland

You can build a steel hull with only three men really knowing what they are doing, really expert at the job. The rest can be with helpers. With a wooden hull, every man has to be good.

—Harvey Gamage

When I went in there, from the start he put me out in that tin shed to put on a binnacle for a com-

pass. I says, "Harvey, I haven't never done anything like this." He said, "You worked for your father." I says, "Yup." "Well," he says, "If you're going to stay with me you got to do anything and everything." So I guess I did that.

Harvey didn't give up for a long time, and he went from wood vessels to "tin" vessels. Steel vessels. When I took this boat to build, it was a fiberglass one; I went up and he says, "I've gone to tin cans, Pete, and you've gone to Clorox jugs!"

—Pete McFarland

HARVEY's oldest employee was Merton Stapels, who in his eighties could still turn out a day's work to match any younger man's. He was renowned for his mastery of the old-fashioned hand adze—and for bringing vegetable soup for dinner every day of his working life.

MERT WAS *quite a worker. He lined all the plank, didn't want any help. He'd drag 'em out, get 'em on the bandsaw himself. And Clifton, he did all the planking.* —Pete McFarland

AS I WAS *growing up I recall many fun days at Gamage's shipyard. Saturdays and after school we would go there and play around in the boats and on the stagings. Harvey and his workers must have had a great deal of patience and love and understanding of kids to put up with us. It was great fun around the yard. There were many, many interesting things going on; the noise of the huge bandsaws and the planers as these huge pieces of oak and beautiful mahogany were being fashioned into something—it was something to be remembered.*

—Doug Thompson

ONCE IN A WHILE, *because my father was upstairs, I could go up there and just watch him work. I enjoyed it so much.* —Beatrice Plummer Rice

HARVEY'S BROTHER *Charles was a master in the mechanical and electrical, and other trades and skills of that type. He operated from a small building in the yard known as the blacksmith's shop. He was also a great prankster. A favorite of his was to catch some unsuspecting worker bending over to pick up some lumber. Then he would accurately aim a blowpipe made out of a piece of pipe and loaded with a wad of putty at the elevated butt of somebody, and—pow! A yelp from the victim and a good laugh for the shooter.*

Charles's skill in his trade was in the installation of the most scientific and technical equipment of the time, with which these minesweepers were equipped. Their work early in the war was almost beyond understanding. This man, it was no problem, no job, for him to install all of this sophisticated equipment. It was like child's play, and he was very fond of doing it.

The first electric lights in South Bristol village were from a generator and wiring which Charles put together. There's a story they tell about Charles, also: he invented a snow sled. He mounted a propeller and engine on some sleds and he got the thing cranked up. He was going through a town, and hit something, and the propeller exploded and took out a lot of the windows.

—Doug Thompson

Another master craftsman was Miles Plummer who had a joinery shop upstairs in the main building where he made cabinets and fancy trim which was later installed in the captain's quarters, or the staterooms, or a galley. Most of the wood that he used was mahogany. He worked in mahogany for many, many years—probably his lungs were red from the dust. He had great pride in his work.

—Doug Thompson

My father, he helped build an awful lot of the old boats, you see, at Harvey's—the wooden boats, yes. I guess he started when he was quite young doing that, and he really was good. He did all of that, really, all the carpenter work then, because there wasn't too many working, and he, well, he stayed there for a long time. I suppose that's all he did—that's where he worked. He was a good carpenter. Of course, he built houses, too. And he could build anything around the house, you know.

—Beatrice Plummer Rice

Wes McFarland's expertise was in planing. After the boats were planked he would plane them to a degree where they hardly needed any sanding, they were so smooth.

It was most fascinating to watch Fred Seavey and Drummond Farrin fashion a mast, or a gaff, or a boom, from a square stick. After being marked off on the corners, they worked on it with an adze and a broadaxe, mostly with an adze. Each corner would be taken off in turn until there were no corners—you had a round stick. The work was so precise and so smooth that it seemed to the layman that there was no need for any planing. Great skill, and a knack that these people had in doing that. —Doug Thompson

Miles Plummer—clearly not wearing his shipyard clothes—at a celebration for his stepmother, Mrs. Atwood Plummer. Elizabeth Alley House

Every launching was kind of a holiday. The local people all come in, kids come down from the school, and they'd put on food to eat, and liquor, and coffee, and whatever you wanted. Soda pops, everything like that. They'd set up plywood tables over there in the shipyard—it was a gala day.

—Robert Woodward

We had good launchings. I would say between five hundred to a thousand to a launching a good many times. They always had champagne. Every boat, every vessel, had one done up in ribbons, red and white ribbons. That was broke over the bow the second she starts to move. They're in the shop, and they're right on the ways, and they heave that bottle up there and crack it.

—Pete McFarland

Launching day for the FLORENCE, 1894. PEMAQUID HISTORICAL ASSOCIATION

THAT'S IRVING CLIFFORD'S place. You're looking northeast—there's the door with the stripes. They built several boats right there. It was built right there—that boat's brand new. She was built right there—and launched right there. In fact, that looks like launching day. See the rope hanging off the stern? They're getting ready. All new copper paint. Yessir, she's brand new. They put the logs and cradle under it—they're getting ready to put it in the water. The maul hammer—he's got his maul there to drive a wedge, pick her up off the blocks.

—Bill Kelsey

MRS. GAMAGE, she was always elected to provide the champagne bottle. It was covered so the glass wouldn't fly, hurt anybody, or get cut on it. She would use red, white, and blue ribbons, and she would wrap them 'round and 'round and 'round so it was well covered. When they first started in I think they'd just throw a couple silk stockings over the bottle, but that wasn't sufficient. She wrapped every launching bottle, always, that was her job that she always did. Usually afterwards they never threw out a bottle—all that ribbon wrapped around held it together, held the shape of the bottle, though it was pretty much crushed inside. And they'd usually make up a mahogany casket. Miles Plummer was one of the finish carpenters, and he

always made up these little caskets to hold this bottle in, and that was usually presented to the owners when they went away with the vessel.
—Robert Woodward

WHEN IT COME *time to launch, 'course we had cradles with timber, heavy timber. And between the piece that went on the ways and the one above, that was all wedged up by hand—topmauls. I think there was four of us in a bunch. I helped launch the most of 'em. We would go along and drive the wedges, about six hits each man, then the next man take over and drive again. That's the way it went up through 'til she was lifted off the blockings. And then we crawled up through on our hands and knees, and took the blockings out from under her. All the launching crew had to crawl up 'longside the keel and take the blockings out—that was not a good feeling! 'Specially when you get up to a hundred, hundred and ten foot. The way was here, and the block ahead, with oak cleats bolted to the two. Then you took a Skilsaw—either a Skilsaw or a crosscut saw—and those were sawed. They was graduated so you'd go down an inch, or two inches, or three. And when you'd go down so far they would crack, and let go—she would launch. Slide right in.* —Pete McFarland

HARVEY BUILT *a couple or three vessels for a man by the name of Mr. Carey from down in New Bedford. One of his launchings was scheduled at 2:00 and he hadn't arrived. But the vessel went down at 2:00—and was he some perturbed when he got there and saw his vessel out in the water, and he weren't there for the launching. Well, Harvey said, "'Time and tide waits for no man.' When it's high tide, the vessel's got to go overboard." We always launched at the top of high tide, to get plenty of water.* —Robert Woodward

WAWENOCK when she was new. WAWENOCK was one of three draggers that Harvey Gamage owned.
PEMAQUID HISTORICAL ASSOCIATION

WHEN THEY *launched the* WAWENOCK, *one of his bigger draggers, she got loose—she broke away on them. They had two big spring lines that went ashore. The first one caught on the well deck, up on the bow of the boat, you know—they got a big raised deck on the front end of these side trawlers, and the first one caught on the well deck and ripped off a chunk of it, and broke the line. Got too many tons on the bitt and snapped the hawsers just like that—and that went off like a gun. I guess they grabbed the second one, they had another one coiled on the other side of the deck—they'd coil them back on the deck of the boat in big long coils so they'd go out with no kinks in 'em, you know, so they could just wind them around the bitt a couple times and just ease 'em off. And the second one broke, and she just kept right on a-coming, she hit on the point over here, and stove the rudder, and done some damage, but not serious damage. She always leaked afterwards, but not bad.*
—Bill Kelsey

Launching of the Antarctic exploration vessel HERO, built for the National Science Foundation. In 1969 Governor Curtis presented Harvey Gamage with the third annual Award of the Maine State Commission on Arts and Humanities; in his presentation speech he cited HERO as "... probably the greatest keel laid down by a Maine shipyard in our time...." MAINE MARITIME MUSEUM

THE HERO. That was a big event when she was launched. She was one of the last ones as I worked on. She had big frames, I remember, must of been 12, 14 inches. Either 6- or 8-inch oak frames were built up two layers. It was built that way because it was going up to the Antarctic.

—Pete McFarland

I WAS OVER there several times when they was building the HERO and if you stepped up between these timbers, the HERO was built so tight and so reinforced that you could hardly wedge your body between them frames. And those frames were laid up double, and they were humongus.

They had granite blocks for the HERO. I think one was six ton, one was eight ton. Cables ran back up through the yard and onto the side of the ship here somewhere, side of the boat, and when she fetched up on those blocks she moved them so it eased the strain a little bit and eventually stopped her. But the HERO was heavy; she was wicked heavy.

They had quite a crowd when they launched that big boat that Harvey built for the National Science Foundation. Quite a gathering for that one—the HERO. Bill Alley and I, we used to go over there early to make sure we'd get on; quite often get in the boat and ride down on it. They'd let us up before they take the stagings, not a whole crowd, let two or three people up and give 'em a ride. It was quite a thrill. —Bill Kelsey

Pete Seeger and painter Richard Alley; Chester Gilbert and Thurlow Leeman are behind them.
©Dan Budnik 2003, courtesy Peter and Toshi Seeger

Launching day, and a jubilant Pete Seeger plays for an overflow crowd.
©Dan Budnik 2003, courtesy Peter and Toshi Seeger.

In 1969 the launching of the Hudson River sloop Clearwater was a huge event for the town. A resident at the time writes: "I was eleven years old when the Clearwater was launched. We woke up that morning and found "hippies" sleeping under the forsythia bush, braless women with flowing skirts and hair. Painting window weights copper orange for extra ballast, and under the old oak, smoking pot for the first time with the environmentally concerned young folks. The music—Pete Seeger in the town parking lot—wild and carefree dancing...."

That was a terrific crowd. Busloads from New York, you know. People parked up and down the road—everywhere, everywhere. It was a big crowd here that day. —Robert Woodward

They had a whole tribe—busload after busload of people, from New York I guess—they were just a hell of a crowd. There were buses clear up by the schoolhouse, lined right up. And all those people—you couldn't drive in the street. Harvey had a hell of a crowd over there for two or three of those launchings, but that Clearwater *was one good one. And Pete Seeger gave a concert down here in the village, down in the parking lot. Young kids were coming down the street. Oodles of 'em come up on these buses, just everywhere, all over the place they were. Man, they were just having a ball over there on the dock waiting for that boat to come out.*

And there's this Hudson River sloop—they're going to go down and clean up the Hudson—but you know, the next morning the whole shoreline had beer cans from one end to the other—beer cans and paper cups everywhere. —Bill Kelsey

The McFarland brothers—Wink, Pete, and Add—and Roy Rice, left, after a successful launching at the Bar in Christmas Cove. FRANK Y. "PETE" MCFARLAND, JR.

Another McFarland vessel heads down the "ways," also known as State Route 129. According to local residents, it was quite a sight to see these substantial vessels slide down the road past houses and yards. ARLETTA THORPE RICE

THAT WAS THE OSPREY that we'd launched down on the Bar. We used to take them down to the Bar, down here. Take down the wires, and roll 'em clear down from the shop. We'd take 'em down on greased boards. Oak boards, 30 inches long. Two rows. We'd take 'em down over those greased boards. From the shop clear down to the water.

—Pete McFarland

It just seemed like everybody was happier then. —Nellie McFarland Frey

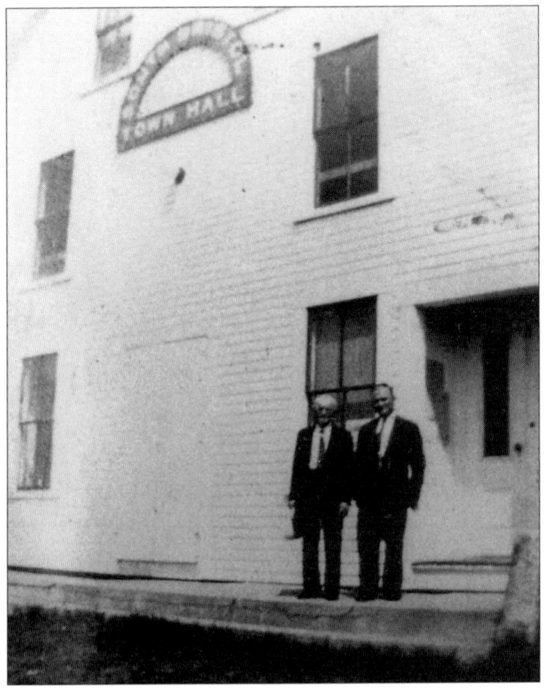

South Bristol Town Hall, 1936. Although no longer used as the town hall, the building still looks much the same today. Eugenie Woodward Cole

Didn't have to be running away off somewhere for their entertainment. They just made their own entertainment. It was a simpler life, but I think maybe better in lots of ways. We'd play cards, you know, and then they'd have dances, put on plays. The older folks used to put on plays, funny skits and stuff like that, you know. Have an evening of all kinds of entertainment and stuff. Used to be up in the old hall, lots of times.

—Nellie McFarland Frey

Usually every winter there'd be a little play in the neighborhood, over here in the town hall. They used to have a little play every year. Not only that, but up where the Koch apple orchard was, there was a store there and overhead there was a little dance hall; they used to have a play up in there in the wintertime. The local people'd get together, develop a little play. —Robert Woodward

At the town hall, on the second floor was a dance hall, too. They used to have dances there 'way back in the '30s, all summer long. There'd be a violin, and a piano, and maybe a saxophone. And they'd have dances: square dances, the old-fashioned dances, and modern dances.

—Robert Woodward

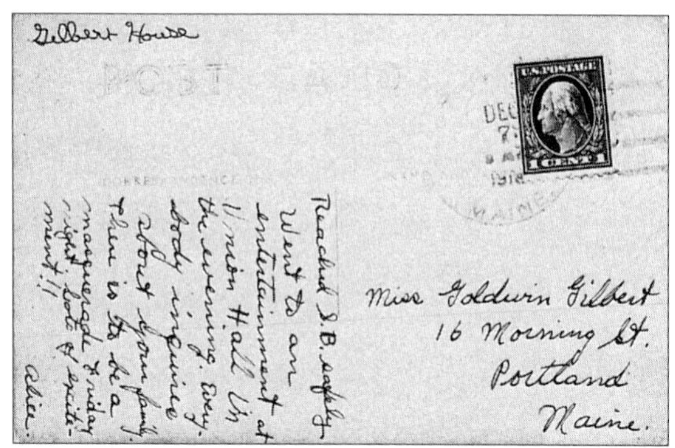

This postcard to Miss Goldwin Gilbert reads: *Reached S. B. safely. Went to an entertainment at Union Hall in the evening. Everybody enquires about your family. There is to be a masquerade Friday night. Lots of excitement!! —Alice.*
MARIAN COUGHLIN

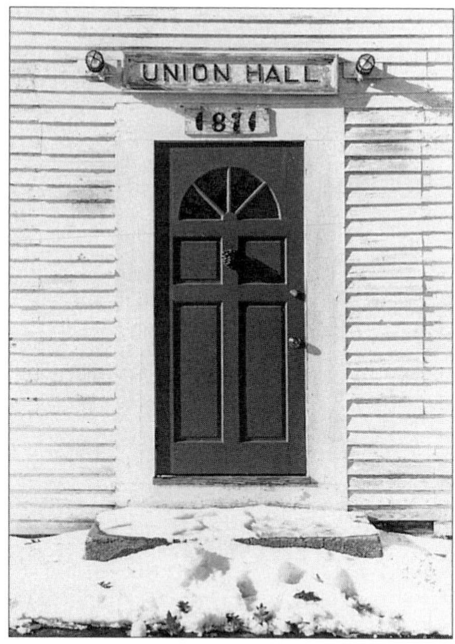

Entrance to Union Hall on Rutherford Island, erected by the Masonic Lodge Association in 1871.
AUTHOR PHOTO, 1997

THAT'S WHERE we did everything, in the Union Hall. Oh, heavens, in the old hall—we played basketball in there; kids came from other towns and we went out to other towns and played basketball. We had dances, and used to have plays there, just high school plays. Used to have what they called the "Chizzle Chizzle Fair," which was like a bazaar thing, had booths and stuff like that. 'Bout every spring we did that. And we used to sing up there now and then. We used to have all kinds of entertainments up there. The Masons used to have their meetings upstairs and so did the Stars. At one time I was Worthy Matron of the Eastern Star and we used to have what we called Guest Officers Night. We'd invite officers from other chapters in the area to come and fill our chairs, we'd call it, take our offices for the evening. And one night we had a hundred up there—and that old floor was going just like ... but it never gave way! —Nellie McFarland Frey

THIS HALL was used both by the Masonic Order and the Redmen. The Masonic Order used the upstairs and the Redmen down. Over the years the Redmen used it pretty much as they wanted to and after a while, it even became a question as to who owned the hall, in the minds of some people. Well, the Masons decided that perhaps it was time to take over full use of the hall, so they asked the Redmen to move out. This immediately caused a great rift in town. It was a real hot issue and it was so bad that even families split up, or neighbors didn't speak to each other, and this went on for a long time. Eventually it was resolved partially by the fact that my grandfather up on Kid Hill had a piece of land next to his house, and he gave that to the Redmen and they built their own hall. So that more or less helped to resolve that situation, but the differences of opinion and the feeling between families went on for years. —Doug Thompson

MANY YEARS AGO, *when I was real little, they used to have dances up at the old hall. And Mama and Dad took me; I guess the parents all took their little ones—we didn't have babysitters in those days. We'd walk up to the old hall. Dad would carry me on his shoulders with my feet hanging down, and I used to set up there and watch them dance. They were such good dancers.*

Raymond McFarland played piano, Lauriston Little played the violin, and I can remember somebody played the bones, too. And then they used to have a piano player and Will Alley's wife would sing "My Wild Irish Rose," and things like that, and Will played the harmonica.

—Nellie McFarland Frey

Class play in the Union Hall, 1950s.
MARGARET FARRIN HOUSE

OF COURSE THIS PLACE *wasn't very large. The circles overlapped. The baskets weren't too far apart but we had some hot old games in there. Back in those days most of the places where basketball was played were of the same type: they were the existing halls in all of the communities, and that's where they'd play basketball and the local high schools would use them. We had netting around the sides to keep the ball from going out and breaking the windows or we might have bars across the windows.*

The hall was heated by stove. It had two woodstoves and we would go onto somebody's lot where there was mostly standing dry wood, or dead dry wood, and we would cut the wood, cut it up, haul it out, and take it up to the hall. We would go up after school or perhaps at noontime, get permission to go up and build a fire, get the place warmed up for practice in the afternoon or for a game at night.

—Doug Thompson

PEARLY FOSSETT *used to run movies in South Bristol once or twice a week. Silent movies, up to Union Hall. Sadie Gilbert used to play the piano in tempo with whatever was on the screen, and he had movies there a couple times a week. Pathé News, and there'd be a serial every week so that the people would come back.* —Doug Thompson

WE HAD SILENT MOVIES, *and somebody would play the music, the piano, you know. Raymond McFarland used to play, and Alice Page used to play. Every week somebody would put on a movie up at the old hall, and we had them later down at the church. But they'd be continued—a serial—next week, when somebody would be in a burning building or things like that. We couldn't wait to see the next chapter of the serial.*

—Nellie McFarland Frey

Postcard with the Fraternal Order of Redmen emblems and poem, copyrighted 1908. At one time the South Bristol chapter was quite active; a 1936 newspaper article describes an installation ceremony at the hall with fifty members in attendance.
William A. Kelsey

A good crowd has turned out at the two dances which are a regular feature of the neighborhood, the "Hacienda" and Centennial hall, in spite of the hot weather.

A large crowd attended the all night dance, Monday, at Centennial hall. Dances will continue as usual, every Thursday night throughout the fall months.

Excerpts from the *Lincoln County News*, 1930s.

We had radios, but they weren't too efficient, and of course no televisions. We did have parties and we went to dances. There were dances that were held in the Redmen's Hall and also at the Union Hall. The women of the town were kind enough to teach some of us younger folks how to dance. And it paid off later—we could have some good times after we learned to dance by going to dances all over the place. I can recall during my high-school days, during the summertime, every Thursday night we went to a dance at Centennial Hall, the town hall up in Walpole. That was a weekly event that we all went to. These were held in the summertime, and in the summer we all waited for the hotels to open and for the summer visitors to come because the summer visitors brought some girls with them who did the cooking and worked for them, and then there were the waitresses who came to the inns and hotels, and of course that was of great interest to us. We also used to go to dances over to Pemaquid Beach. The Lewis Pavilion was operating. They had some real good orchestras there. We had a lot of fun doing that. —Doug Thompson

We used to have an awful lot of fun at the Redmen's Hall. There'd be a piano player, and a saxophone, and trumpet, I guess, and violin, and stuff like that. And that was a big orchestra, you know, that was great when you had an orchestra. We did have waltzes, and lots of square dances, too. 'Tisn't very big but we had an awful lot of fun—had lots of good times in there.

—Nellie McFarland Frey

Lena and Will Alley played in a harmonica band. She played the piano, and Will the harmonica. They had a group, five or six more harmonicas. They played at dances all around the area.

—Doug Thompson

Somebody'd have a fiddle, somebody'd play piano. Somebody from here, or maybe somebody from Pemaquid or from Bristol. Waltzes and foxtrots and square dancing. Oh, I used to love square dancing. My husband and I, we used to dance like everything. One night they had prizes for the best dancers and he and I won the prize—I don't know that we were the best dancers, just for some reason or other we won. Maybe we got $2 or something like that. —Nellie McFarland Frey

Hacienda Hall, part of today's Brannon Bunker Inn on State Route 129. AUTHOR PHOTO, 1997

Former dance hall building on Cavis Cove, newly reshingled. It was originally built as a residence by Thomas Cavis shortly after he purchased the property in 1796. AUTHOR PHOTO, 1997

THAT WAS THE *Hacienda Hall. Probably it was an old barn at one time, hooked to the house. And then I remember when Mama and Daddy were young, once in a while they'd go up there and dance—they'd have dances up there.*

—Katherine Poole Norwood

OVER ON THE S ROAD *there's a little small building, in Cavis Cove. That little building was where they used to come across from Boothbay, and they'd come across from Back Narrows, come across by boat, and go to those dances over there. And that building's still standing. That would have been before my parents, I think.*

—Katherine Poole Norwood

Lincoln County Fair in Damariscotta, c. 1920s. NOBLEBORO HISTORICAL SOCIETY, IVAN FLYE COLLECTION

WHEN I WAS little it was a thing for all these surrounding towns to go to Damariscotta on Saturday night, and I can remember my grandfather sitting in the back seat all dressed up with a suit on, and a soft hat. Mama would be dressed right up—silk stockings—and Daddy had a suit on.

That was the big thing of the week, everybody going to Damariscotta. People would visit in the stores and then we'd usually end up going to a movie. We went in a car, but when my Daddy was little they used to go by horse and buggy and my aunt told me once they were kinda worried they didn't get home, so they'd go and put their ear to the ground—they thought they could hear the horses coming.

Of course before we'd go up to Damariscotta on Saturday night we'd be all afternoon getting cleaned up for it. We didn't have electricity in the house up there, so we'd drag in this great big galvanized tub from the barn. We'd all have to have a bath in that before we could go shopping. My mother was a great sewer and usually I'd have some pretty dress on that she'd sewed. My sister and brother would dress up, too.

—Katherine Poole Norwood

PEOPLE USED TO visit a lot in the afternoon. I remember going with mother to call on a friend of hers just to sit and talk and visit for a little while. I can't remember ever calling ahead—not everybody had telephones then. It was just neighborly; it felt comfortable dropping in.

—Catherine Jordon Walker

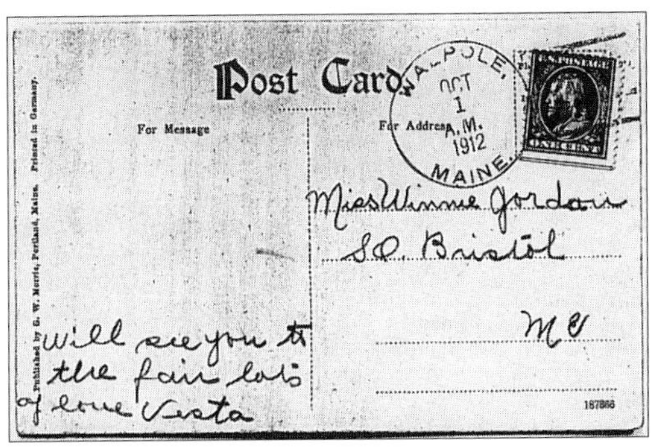

1912 postcard to Winnie Jordon in South Bristol, from her friend Vesta in Walpole. "Will see you to the fair...." CATHERINE JORDON WALKER

PEOPLE WOULD VISIT. *First they'd go to your house, then you'd go to their house. So these two guys worked at the boatshop; they'd visited the other fella's house last week so this week they went to his house. The host happened to be on his way in from the outhouse just as the neighbor drove up, and the neighbor stepped out of his automobile and said to his wife, "I hope they don't have those damn' peanut-butter sandwiches again this week." So when it came time to serve the refreshments the man said, "Well, I'm sorry, but we've got those damn' peanut-butter sandwiches again this week!"*

We used to visit and play games before television came, and even after television came we used to visit back and forth. We'd play checkers, Chinese checkers, all kinds of checkers!

—Ralph Norwood

WE ALWAYS *used to go to the Lincoln County Fair in Damariscotta. Oh, that was something to look forward to all summer. It was a country fair: merry-go-round, and Ferris wheel, and all the sideshows and all the attractions. It was a big thing to do, a big thing to look forward to.*

—Nellie McFarland Frey

WE'D ALL GO *to the fair. They let us have one day off school. We always went the middle day for some reason—there was more stuff, more going on the middle day. First, second, third day of October. First three days that used to come on a Sunday in October, for years and years.*

That fair, that closed in 1947. They had a race track there; raced horses. Three days of it—a three-day fair. They pulled horses there; wrestling matches, and boxing matches, and all that stuff. If you wanted to go in and wrestle somebody you could go in if you wanted to. They always had a man come with the fair, see—"The Terrible Greek," or something like that. I seen Walter Gilbert go in and wrestle and pound hell out of that old Greek. Walter was, God, he was strong. Jeez, he was strong. He'd go in there with that old Greek. The old Greek would go like this, and he'd have a big beefsteak and he would say, "I'm going to pound him!" Oh, he'd go on and on. Time Walter got ahold of him and threw him around a little bit, half killed him, he didn't feel so smart.

They had sideshows. Girlie shows, they had them, of course. They'd charge you so much to get in, then a girl would come out, she'd take off part of her clothes. Then you give another 50 cents and go in another part, and she'd take off some more. I guess if you paid enough she wouldn't have any on! They done big business—you know how that works. So, they had one of them, but they barred 'em out after a while.

They had Beano, stuff like that. And a big expo building there where they had chickens, and pigs, and all 4H stuff. Ladies' Aid, where they'd knit, and made pillows or made blankets or something, they had all that. Vegetables and all that stuff was in that building. It was worth seeing, really. Good in them days as it is now—better.

—Mervin Rice

It was just plain good Christmas.
—Nellie McFarland Frey

MY LAND, *the Christmas presents were nothing like now. Mama used to send out to Sears & Roebuck catalog, or Montgomery Ward catalog, and get me a new doll. Gerry Tibbetts and I used to see which one of us got the most handkerchiefs for Christmas. And then we used to get packages of writing paper. And just simple things—it wasn't simple to us then. It's what we looked forward to. Mother would always make doll clothes. She used to buy a doll and dress it for me for Christmas, make several outfits for it. And my father made a doll's bed for my dolls; I had that for years—made the head and the foot of the bed, and the sides, and then he put string across to hold the mattress, like a spring. And Mama, every year she'd make new bedding for it: a little mattress and sheets and pillowcase for it, and a little quilt, and new clothes for the doll.* —Nellie McFarland Frey

Trying out the new rocking duck on Christmas morning. MARGARET FARRIN HOUSE

CHRISTMASES WERE *nice family days. We always went in the woods and cut our own tree. We always got the Christmas tree, and it was the family job to decorate it. We had various decorations—some that were commercial, some things that had been handed down for a long time. When I was a little child, popcorn was a popular decoration. There was always some exchange of gifts. You'd get a pair of stockings, a new muffler. And mittens, mother used to knit mittens.*

—Robert Woodward

Home Made Gifts.

As the holidays draw near a general query rises of what to make for presents A gift which is the work of our own hand usually has a greater value than an arti [illegible] something particularly desired by the recipient. Wisdom in selection may make a little money go a long way, and there is already but little time left to make things

In several families of our acquaintance the custom of putting up a Christmas list, two or three weeks previous to the day. Each member hangs up a card on which he writes what he would like, and the watching of these lists as they appear an the whispered consultations over them furnish a great deal of amusement. No limit is given to the imagination, and perhaps father wishes for a pair of horses, and mother writes a request for a satin dress, but with wise forethought they also put down something which the little folks can get or make, like a pair of mittens or a book-mark. The younger ones enjoy the indulgence of wishing which always has its charms, and they are perfectly satisfied if two or three of the more humble requests are met. Already, by the writer's desk hangs nine-year-old Ethel's list, which has been the result of hours of careful meditation, and includes a black kitten, a box of paints a thimble, a little doll's tea set, and some yarn Obliging grandmother, who somehow has a suspicion of what has [illegible] hurredly put away every time she [illegible] in, has headed her list with a [illegible]. These trifling matters are mere [illegible] to show how much pleasure may be taken from what to many is a burdensome and exravagant custom, and something to be yearly dreaded.

"Home Made Gifts," *Pemaquid Messenger*, December 8, 1886.

We never had turkey in those days; they'd always go out and kill the chickens that were right there on the farm … and we had the Christmas tree in the dining room because the whole house wasn't heated then, and the woodstove was in the dining room. Go anywhere and cut a tree—Grampa used to even give them away. If anyone wanted a Christmas tree he always used to let them go out and get one. —Katherine Poole Norwood

The schoolhouse was crowded. And it was before electricity, you know—long before electricity, the tarred roads, anything. I didn't want a great big tree, because it would have been hard to take care of. The children—I didn't bother with it—I told them it had to be pretty and even; they would bring the tree and we would put it right on the table that was for the little folks. Then, they didn't have as many ornaments, no electric light ornaments. Well, I wouldn't want them anyway because I would be afraid of them. So sometimes someone would string a load of cranberries. Well, we had that, and when my mother used to keep the store, used to get a lot of stuff there. Candles; they had that tin foil, you know, the kind on the string, and this was red and green, and the wooden balls, and of course a star for the top, and an angel or two.

Money was scarce; these children didn't have extra money. So some of them would string popcorn. You know there is quite a trick to stringing popcorn: you have to pop it and let it set so it would get soft. Some would bring some of that, some would bring some cranberries, and I would have all this other stuff. I would let them fix the tree. And of course, I supervised after school, and they draped it all. I said, "Now you stand here and see if that is all right." They would see something out of kilter and they would fix it. Oh, it was a lot of work! The schoolhouse was all deco-

rated; it was really beautiful. As I look at it now, I think what a lot of work, and was it worth it? But then I was young.

—Sarah Emery, 1975 interview

AT CHRISTMASTIME *the stores were well stocked, way beyond the imagination of what might be taking place in South Bristol at that time, between probably 1927 or '28 and 1934.*

Ed Gamage always had stocks of extra things for Christmas; all of the stores did. Nat House had the store where many years later J. R. Little operated, and then there were two dry goods stores there in town, and they were heavily stocked with items for Christmas—all kinds of items that would make good gifts. There were toys, and there were books, cloth goods, perfume, gift sets, things that people could use. There was a great deal of shopping right there—back and forth all the time between these stores. People were traveling back and forth through the snow from store to store, and visiting the library which was upstairs over Clifford's store.

The whole town was busy, busy, busy as it could be, people in the stores, making their way around way into the evening. Stretching their money as far as they could make it go.

—Doug Thompson

FOURTH OF JULY *at our house, we always had a big family dinner. It was always fresh salmon with egg sauce, and fresh peas from the garden, and lemon meringue pie. We had that every year. Relatives would come and spend the day. There was a good fish market in South Bristol that was under that building next to Farrin's store. Irving Clifford was the fish man, and lived upstairs. You could always find almost anything there, and that's where we'd get our salmon.*

—Catherine Jordon Walker

When the Fourth of July came around, many South Bristol families relied on Irving Clifford for their fresh salmon dinner. CATHERINE JORDON WALKER

THE FOURTH OF JULY *was always a picnic day. The family would get together and have a picnic; that was a real family day.* —Robert Woodward

EVERY HISTORICAL HOLIDAY *was celebrated in school. On Memorial Day, or the nearest school day to Memorial Day, we always were taken to the cemetery by the teachers and put flags and flowers on the veteran's graves, and had sad poems read, you know, things like that; it meant something. I can't remember ever having a parade, but I know we always took flowers. We took apple blossoms and lilacs and my mother had a lot of white narcissus that grew, just sprung up there all over the front of the house. So fragrant. I always went with her and took jars of those flowers to put on my grandparents' graves.*

—Catherine Jordon Walker

We had a great childhood.
—Nellie McFarland Frey

WE MADE A LOT OF our own fun, our own entertainment. —Nellie McFarland Frey

WE USED TO slide half the night—we used to call it sliding, not sledding—practically no cars, and we could start a sled going up at the top of Kid Hill, go down, and we'd go across both bridges, we get speed enough so it'd carry us across both bridges and almost up the hill on the island. And then we'd get off and walk up and go all the way up by the school, by the church; sometimes we'd go all the way up to Union Hall and start there and slide back down. Then you'd go up on Kid Hill and come down the other way and go halfway up this hill. That's the way we did—back and forth, back and forth. Slide down, walk up; on the way home, slide down, walk up to the house. Remember, there were no automobiles then, or sand on the road to pack down. They were gravel, and the snow and ice formed on them. In the wintertime—when sliding was good, you could slide halfway to school. —Doug Thompson

Tobogganing on the Thompson Inn Road. MARGARET FARRIN HOUSE

Snowy view down through the village, looking north towards the mainland. "Kid Hill" would be just to the left of the double-gabled house in the center background. The bridge structure indicates that this was taken some time between 1903 and 1925.
PEMAQUID HISTORICAL ASSOCIATION

DURING THE EVENINGS *when it was good sliding, there were many, many people out on these hills. Some of the older boys had what we used to call double-runners. They were sleds with a plank from one sled to another—could be steered by the front sled. Some of these were very large and there were a couple there that could hold up to twenty people. They'd go roaring down the hill and sometimes they'd upset and you'd have quite a jumble of people, but I don't recall anybody ever getting hurt badly. Oh, the sleds were fast.*

—Doug Thompson

SLIDING AND SKIING *and skating and everything. Just cross-country skiing mostly, and snowshoeing—just what anybody could do in a small place like this. Used to be some of the older fellas that had these big double-runners. Sometimes there'd be twelve or fourteen of us on one of those double-runners. It was wide, and had runners on the front and on the back, and wood in between. The boys would steer it—I don't know as the girls ever tried to do that—but we'd all pile on, a gang of us, and the boys would steer it. Somebody would stay on the back and push—get a start and then jump on. We'd start all the way up by the old hall here this side of the church and go all the way down to Farrin's store. And then we'd go up on the hill up by where Harborside is, and come all the way back down to Farrin's store.*

—Nellie McFarland Frey

Margaret Farrin about to set off on her snowshoes, c. 1930s. MARGARET FARRIN HOUSE

Skaters on Nellie's Pond, c. 1930s. The pond still remains in existence on the West Side Road, though much overgrown and smaller in appearance.
MARGARET FARRIN HOUSE

View across Wawenock Golf Course towards the site of the old Morris Sproul farm. AUTHOR PHOTO, 1997

ACROSS FROM *the McFarland's was a pond that was created by excavating and taking out gravel. We always call this Nellie's Pond. It made a great skating pond in the winter and we used to walk down there on winter evenings from uptown and skate.* —Doug Thompson

BETWEEN THE *golf course and the Morris Sproul farm was a big meadow. In the winter, they'd wait for the fields to freeze over, and every Sunday they had horse racing on the ice there. They'd put steel calks on the shoes and they raced with sulkies. Straightaway. That was a favorite pastime in the winter out there.* —Doug Thompson

Two teenagers in bathing costumes, poised to take the plunge in Long Cove, c. 1914.
MARGARET FARRIN HOUSE

Farrin boys take to the Gut in a sailing skiff.
MARGARET FARRIN HOUSE

WHEN I WAS A KID *in the summertime, boy, first hot day we'd head for the cove and go swimming lickety split—get down and get in the water. That shallow water, that sun would warm up the flats mud.* —Bill Kelsey

SUMMERS, *we spent most of the time swimming and fishing and stuff like that down around the cove here. It was cold, but it was all we knew—it didn't bother us that much. Hardly missed a day from usually first of June right straight through 'til time for school to start.* —Nellie McFarland Frey

AS KIDS WE *used to play around the water all the time. We didn't do much swimming—the water was so cold that swimming wasn't much of a pastime. But we did play in boats. I guess I was twelve or thirteen before I learned to swim, and that was out of necessity. I was threatened by my father: "Either learn to swim or stay out of those skiffs."*
—Doug Thompson

Alice Gamage rowing, June 1914. This was not normal attire for a teenage girl back then. In her album she captioned the photo, "When Betty and I were boys...." MARGARET FARRIN HOUSE

I SAILED *since I was a kid, you know, born right into it. Growing up on an island we either rowed or sailed—so we sailed all we could.*
—Ralph Norwood

Wallace "Foggy" Bridges, 1931. Mervin Rice

We always called him "Foggy." Story was, he was born on Damariscove, one of the outer islands where they were living, on a very foggy night and he got the nickname of Foggy. There was a very unfortunate thing happened to these boys. They'd been working on the farm on a hot day and went down to the river down back of the house, to Seal Cove, to swim, and both of them drowned. It was a real tragedy for the town. —Doug Thompson

Wallace Bridges, and George, those boys were both drowned, just about graduation time. They lived up what we call the S Road, up on Seal Cove, the big cove that makes in up in there. Well, they lived near the water there and they went in swimming and apparently they couldn't swim that well and went too deep, and one of them got too far out and the other one tried to save him and they both drowned. Not far from home, and they were high-school age. George was in my class and when we graduated we had an empty chair for him.

—Margaret Farrin House

Brooks McFarland and a friend, getting in a little target practice out by the woodpile.
Margaret Farrin House

Hunting was a great pastime. Throughout the fall, during the partridge season, in the winter during the duck and rabbit season; also we went deer hunting during the deer season—but that was after we got a little bit older. I started hunting when I was quite young. My grandfather had a single-shot .22 rifle; I guess I was around twelve years old when he used to let me borrow that. I'd go tracking through the woods with it. Then I must have been no more than thirteen when I got my own .22 for Christmas—that was a great gift. My father also had a shotgun and I was allowed to use it. So all of us kids were brought up with guns, and most of us retained that interest throughout our whole life, when we were interested in hunting.

Up on High Island was a great place to hunt rabbits and then we used to walk all around the shore on stormy days and there would be ducks trying to get out of the wind on the shore.

You could get a hunting license without any problem. I probably was around twelve or thirteen years old and my hunting license cost 25 cents and it was supposed to be good forever—for a lifetime.

—Doug Thompson

George Herman Ruth—the Babe. LIBRARY OF CONGRESS

Carroll, left, and Mervin Rice with hunting dog Trailer. MERVIN RICE

I RECALL *Mrs. Miles bringing a man to the schoolhouse one time, and he was known by everybody. It was Babe Ruth. I will always remember him. I can see him now—he was dressed in a big raccoon coat. He looked so big to us there, and this was in the height of his career. Dressed in his coonskin coat he was quite a sight, and he signed autographs for us. He signed my hunting license; I was very young then.* —Doug Thompson

*I*N 1933 OR '34 *he come to the school; he went and signed his name for all the kids, saw all the kids. He was connected somehow with the Miles Estate over there. And so he showed up here and he wanted to go rabbit hunting. And Stanley Alley was working there, and he said that I would take him out, I had the dogs. He says that he'd be glad to take you. So, we went in November, and it was cold, but it was raining—snow and rain mixed. One or the other—it was just raw. Oh, it was cold, that's all there was to it—and wet. And I told him, I said, "It's not a fit day to go. I don't think we can even find a rabbit today, they're hid out somewhere. I don't think they'll be much of a hunt." But he wanted to go. 'Course he had a big fancy gun, and he had a bottle of booze shoved down each pocket, and big hunting coat on, you know. He was all head and shoulders, he got no hips, no legs, he was just all from here up. Great big fella from here up, but he could run, I guess, playing baseball.*

Anyhow, we went just this side of Wendell Holmes's on the bay side, on the east side of the road. There was a wood road went to the shore. There wasn't no house there then. So we went down in there; we'd caught a lot of rabbits down in there. "Oh", he says, "if you get cold," he says, "you can have a little nip anytime you want it." I says, "I don't use that stuff when I'm hunting, anyhow."

"Oh," he says, "you wanta call them dogs, we'll get out of here. It's too cold, too wet." And he put that old gun in the air and he let her go five times. "That'll call the dogs," he says, "That'll call 'em, they'll come." And they did come. We only went 'til about noontime, and it was so wet and cold he said, "I guess we've had enough." But the next day he went over to Pemaquid Point. They was thicker than the devil over there, and he shot some rabbits. So he had a lot of fun before he left, anyhow.

—Mervin Rice

South Bristol High School girls' basketball team, 1934. Left to right: Miss Lord, coach; Victoria McFarland, Nellie McFarland, Verona McFarland, Cleo Gamage, Margaret Farrin, Grace Seiders, Hazel Farrin. MARGARET FARRIN HOUSE

Lincoln High School's championship basketball team, 1931. The name of the island school had yet to be changed to South Bristol High School. Seated, from left: Frank Farrin, Mel Thompson, John Thorpe, Daniel Seiders, Lewis Kelsey, Maxwell House. Standing, from left: Laurence Page, principal, J. Douglas Thompson, Wallace Bridges, Mervin Rice, John Frey. MERVIN RICE

WE HAVE A picture of the team, and Gerry isn't in it. Once there was a dance at Redmen's Hall; Miss Lord told us nobody could go because we had a game the next morning—if anyone went to it she wasn't going to let us play anymore. And Gerry went to the dance, so Miss Lord wouldn't let her play basketball. That was kinda mean. She'd played with us all year. Oh, she was a good player.

Miss Schmidt was nice, but she was so awkward. We had only one basketball—the boys and the girls had to share the one ball. We raised enough money to buy another one, and she went out and bought a medicine ball—big heavy thing you pass back and forth for exercise. We were so mad!

—Margaret Farrin House

WE WON THE championship—that's why this picture's here. We played Lincoln Academy to get that. 'Course, not that first team, their second team 'cause we were just a small high school. That just took about all the boys there was in high school to make a team. Oh, we played Waldoboro, and Lincoln, and we went over to Boothbay and played, and played Barter's Island. We played everything around. —Mervin Rice

THE BOYS AND GIRLS both had basketball teams. This, we always thought, was one of the advantages of having a small school—everybody got to take part. All the kids. Any of the entertainments or the plays or anything, any kid in high school could make their move to be in it. And they all had a chance to play basketball, baseball, stuff like that. —Nellie McFarland Frey

Everett Gamage's store. The first floor was a general store, the town post office, and even an ice cream parlor. The hall, used for entertainments, dances, and basketball games, took up the entire second floor.
WILLIAM A. KELSEY

ACROSS THE STREET *was a building that was owned by Everett Gamage. At one time he was postmaster and the post office was in there, and that, too, was an ice cream parlor. Up over that building was a hall with a hardwood floor where dances used to be held, and also we used to play basketball up there. It was lacking in height and it was pretty difficult to shoot baskets other then to bounce them off the ceiling. The ceiling was in bounds, and there was barely room for the ball to get down between the ceiling and the basket. There were some hot old games up there. They had wooden bars across the windows so nobody would go through them. The referee would blow the whistle and say "Play!" and they'd all go at it until somebody scored a basket. And they would get pretty rough sometimes!* —Doug Thompson

WE'D PRACTICE *up in the Mason Hall there. At first we practiced at that building on the right as you go across the bridge had a post office downstairs. Upstairs we'd have dances and all that stuff, and we'd play basketball—and the ceiling weren't much higher than this here living room. Ball would just fit in over the basket. 'Course, we'd practiced there, so those other teams come from out of town, why, they was licked. Christ, they couldn't do nothin' with it. But we'd just stuff it right in there, you know. But it was the only place we had to play.*

Finally they let us go up to the Mason Hall. They put net around the wall so it wouldn't stave up the plaster, you know; they put a fish net all the way round. And we played in there—that's where we played. That had plenty of height. We had to learn to play all over again. After playing in that thing, we'd go somewheres else, we lost. Jeez, we couldn't shoot a basket no more than—well, we soon changed over. —Mervin Rice

WE PLAYED BALL *right next to the high school there. It wasn't much of a field, but we made do.*
—Doug Thompson

WE WERE DOWN *in front of Everett Gamage's store. The trailer is hitched to the minister's car.*

Mrs. Page was so much fun. We'd go to these 4H field days, and she would—"Rah! Rah! Rah!"—she would cheer us on.
—Margaret Farrin House

AT ONE TIME *there were three different 4H groups. We were the Merry Maids, and then they had the Helpful Handy Home Hustlers—those were the younger girls—and we had the Tick Tock Toilers. Our 4H group used to go places, down to the Union Fair, different places with Jennie Gamage and Mrs. Little—they had our 4H group.*
—Nellie McFarland Frey

Boys' baseball game, probably out behind the island school.
Margaret Farrin House

The 4H group Tick Tock Toilers in front of Everett Gamage's store, on their way to a field day. Left to right: Grace Seiders, Hazel Thompson, Verona McFarland, Hazel Farrin, Margaret Farrin, Lizzie Rice, Ferne Seiders, and Mrs. Clifford, the minister's wife. Margaret Farrin House

The Handy Home Helpers, 1940s. The 4H clubs were grouped by age, each with their own distinct name. Margaret Farrin House

Project Pushers' 4-H News

The Project Pushers held their meeting January 25 at their assistant leader's home, Mrs. Mildred Little.

The Sewing girls discussed the proper way to care for the clothes, while Gwendolyn Haley and Phyllis Hatch made a chocolate pudding. Later they served it with whipped cream and cake.

Later all went out tobogganing. After many a spill and good laughs the party separated anywhere from four to half past.

The club will hold their next meeting Feb. 7 at their local leader's home, Meadow Brook Farm.

Martha E. Little, Club Reporter.

Excerpt from the *Lincoln County News*, mid 1930s. The Project Pushers was a Walpole group, up on the main.

May basket, made with an oatmeal box and wallpaper samples. AUTHOR PHOTO

WE'D MAKE May baskets. We'd get together in someone's home and make these pretty baskets for the first day of May. We'd fill them with candy, and we'd "hang 'em" to somebody, a boyfriend or a friend that we liked, and they'd have to chase us and catch us and kiss us. We usually set it on the doorstep. Full of candy—sometimes penny candy, peanut butter kisses, whatever; but quite often we made fudge, too, and then once in a while someone would do flowers.

They were pretty. We'd fix them with tissue paper; we'd cut out pieces of wallpaper books, too. We made cones and crinkled tissue paper on them. We'd make them like umbrellas, parasols: just pretty baskets. Quite often we'd take an oatmeal box and cut it in two—then we'd have two—and then we'd cover it and put a nice pretty handle on it. —Margaret Farrin House

WE USED TO GO DOWN to Florence and Ethel and Helen's house, and make big May baskets. 'Course, Florence, Ethel, and I were just young enough to be kind of nosey—eight, nine, ten, something like that. Johnny Thorpe, he used to be quite sweet on Helen, and we heard one night that Johnny was going to hang a May basket for Helen. So we hid over in the bushes across the road there because we wanted to see her kiss him, or him kiss her. And we stayed there and we giggled and giggled and giggled, and watched for Johnny to come up the road and hang that May basket. And finally he did, and he hung it on her door, and hollered at her, and she came running out, and he ran just as fast as he could go, way down the corner to Coveside and around, and of course she was after him. And they got way out of our sight and we never did see them kissing! Oh, wasn't we disappointed—we didn't get to see Helen kiss Johnny for that May basket.

—Nellie McFarland Frey

We'd holler, "May basket for Johnny!" "May basket for Mary!"—and when they'd start out the door whoever'd hung the May basket would run and then the one that the basket was for would chase them and kiss them.

—Margaret Farrin House

Sarah Emery used to tell a cute story. Sarah was an old maid and it was May basket day. Mark Russell, he wasn't married—they was just young—and he came up with a May basket for Sarah, and she didn't want him kissing her so she ran around and around that tree—still stands out by Ronnie's house—ran around so Mark couldn't catch her and kiss her. —Katherine Poole Norwood

Mark Russell was tall, and like a beanpole. His mother was a little funny ... she used to like to go around the neighbors—her husbands were all dead—and take this boy along with her. But once she heard them say I like olives, and he decided to make me a May basket. I heard a knock on the door. I went to the door, and there was a bottle of olives. Well, I saw Mark, and of course, you have to chase them and was supposed to kiss them.

There was this big ash tree out here, you know. Well, I chased around, and I didn't try too very hard to catch him. And Mark would get his hands on his hips and knees bent kind of awkward, it was cute. My father said that it was the funniest sight he ever saw. Mark would keep just a little way ahead of me, you know. I had no intentions of kissing him. Well, I said, "Mark, if you're not going to let me kiss you, I might as well go into the house." So I went into the house and I can remember my brothers saying, "A bottle of olives!" He didn't know, he would go where angels feared to tread. I guess it was funny.

—Sarah Emery, 1975 interview

Viola Gamage with her doll, 1909.
Margaret Farrin House

Annie May and Ruth Naomi Farrin, with their cousin Virginia Gamage, wheel their doll carriages through the village about 1929 or 1930.
Margaret Farrin House

I had a china doll with eyes that opened and closed and her name was Gladys, I remember. That was my favorite doll for years. Mama used to make new clothes for her 'most every year. I think the arms and legs were china, and her body was stuffed, if I remember right. And then I remember one Christmas I came down—always came downstairs and looked at the tree, see what was there—I found quite a big doll she had sent away for, had real hair and everything. And a carriage to wheel her in—and I'd wheel her all up and down the road. —Nellie McFarland Frey

Tricycle gang on Thompson Inn Road, with the Thompson Inn wellhouse in the center background: Evelyn McFarland, Neil McFarland, Gloria House, Ronnie House, Bobby Eugley, Paul Farrin.
MARGARET FARRIN HOUSE

THE LITTLE HOUSE in the back there covered the well for the Thompson Inn. As kids, we'd climb up one side and slide down the other—if Father had known he'd have killed us.

—Margaret Farrin House

WE USED TO make up our own games. I played with my brothers a lot in the evenings. We had one of the big bedrooms, and we'd go in there and there was a big shelf across there. It was about the time, I guess, that Lindbergh flew across the ocean. We'd make these paper airplanes and throw them, and try to make them stay on that shelf. If they went on the floor we lost it. We made up our own rules and we played for hours to see who could get the most of 'em. We'd tear up, make those airplanes; I think we used old Sears-Roebuck catalogs—whatever we had. —Margaret Farrin House

WHEN I WAS home we always used to play games. We had Parcheesi, and Flinch, and we'd play checkers, and Chinese checkers. We liked canasta, and "63" was a game we loved to play.

—Nellie McFarland Frey

WE JUMPED ROPE, and we played marbles. We made the clay marbles. Down by the old well, down back of Denny's house, there was blue clay and we'd go down and dig that out and roll these little marbles, and then we'd set them in the sun for a while, for a couple days, and they'd bake, and we'd play with them.

—Margaret Farrin House

I CAN REMEMBER taking marbles to school and we'd play, and sometimes we'd gain a lot of marbles from somebody else, and sometimes we'd lose them. If you hit one you could keep it. Some of the kids, if they lost their marbles, they would cry, and feel so bad about losing all their marbles. We'd have to knock the marbles out of a circle, we did that, and then we used to dig a hole, too, and try to roll it in the hole. —Nellie McFarland Frey

IN THE SUMMERTIME, when I was a kid growing up—this was when I was quite small—every summer, a man would come around, walking around the island here. He'd have a real live monkey, and he had an organ grinder ... and the monkey would dance. His monkey used to have a cup for pennies, and I'd save up my pennies when I knew it was 'bout time for him to come around, to put pennies in his cup. The monkey wore a suit, and a cute little hat. Couple times every summer, usually, there was a man and his monkey.

—Nellie McFarland Frey

Organ grinder and monkey, c. 1892.
HAMILTON OVERSPECK PHOTO, LIBRARY OF CONGRESS

Paper dolls, c. 1915–20.

WE HAD QUITE A *gang going down this way … we had a great time together. If two of us were playing and a third one showed up there'd be a fight, and somebody would go home mad, and then inside of half an hour everybody would be back together again. We played dolls, something the girls don't seem to do that much anymore. Dolls, and paper dolls. Gerry Kelsey and me, we'd sit for hours and make paper dolls, cut out paper dolls, and their clothes and stuff. After we got a little bit bigger, you could buy books with the paper dolls you could cut out, and the clothes and everything. We used to use a lot of imagination when we played with them, too. Dress them up for skating … play that way.* —Nellie McFarland Frey

The roller coaster at Old Orchard Beach amusement park, 1917. MARIAN COUGHLIN

MISS SCHMIDT was such a good old soul. She had a car and she'd call it "Hepzibah," and when we graduated—in my class there were four girls—she took us to Old Orchard, to the amusement park. She lived in Saco, and in her family, they had a shed with a chamber over it and we camped out up there. We had some way to cook things and we stayed one or two nights. And she took us to Old Orchard. We'd ride around in that old Hepzibah ... and I can remember I went up in the roller-coaster. I'd never been on a rollercoaster—I was a senior in high school and this was our senior trip! And we went up in this rollercoaster and I just loved that and I said, "I'm goin' again—anybody goin'?" and Gerry said, "Not me!" But I did. I went around again. I think Doris maybe went with me, but Grace and Gerry didn't—they were scared. But we had a good time.

—Margaret Farrin House

AND THE BIG THING to me, we used to get a package—I guess it was when Crayola crayons first came out—I think there'd be eight in a box, and there was always a paper folded up, with these pictures on it to color with the crayons. And I can remember when I would be sick, maybe have a bad cold or measles or chickenpox or something ... my favorite aunt, I always wanted her to come down when I was sick. She'd bring me a package of those crayons with the strip of paper with the different pictures on it to color. Oh, to have a new package of crayons and pictures to color—my, that was somethin' to look forward to—worth being sick for! —Nellie McFarland Frey

Imagine the schools that was in town—up at the fork in the road, the little one up by the golf course, the one down by Four Corners, and then this little Roosevelt School. —Katherine Poole Norwood

AND OF COURSE *when we went to the Roosevelt School the school downtown was always monstrous to us; we'd always think that that was a great big school.* —Katherine Poole Norwood

BEFORE THE big schoolhouse was built, island children went to school in the building that is now known as Clugston's Barn. When it was built, in 1848, townsfolk thought it much too grand for a mere schoolhouse.

Clugston's barn, across from the Union Church on property adjacent to the big school house. By most accounts this was not the original location of the structure. AUTHOR PHOTO, 1997

THERE WAS ONE BIG ROOM *for the primary school. At that time there were thirty-four or thirty-five kids in school with one teacher, for four grades. And then in the same building was what we called the grammar school, and there were four grades in there, too, with one teacher. Far as I know, it was wonderful.*

When we went to class, they always had one class—like first grade—come down front and sit in the seats, and then the second grade would come down and sit in the front seats. Two to a seat when we'd go down front, but I think we had separate seats the rest of the time—desks, the little old-fashioned ones. The teacher would say, "First class excused," and we'd get up and go back into our seats in the back of the room and work on our next lesson. Then the second class would come forward, right straight through to the fourth, just the same. —Nellie McFarland Frey

THE OLDER CHILDREN *helped the teacher, especially in the grammar school. I remember I used to be asked to write questions on the blackboard. One advantage, I think, of the one-room schoolhouse is that the younger children absorb a lot that they're not being taught, just by listening; and also the older children, we took care of the younger ones. It was just assumed that you were going to. Almost everyone had younger brothers or sisters, so you looked after them.*

—Catherine Jordon Walker

Arletta Thorp, who earned these certificates of merit, was born in 1836. Miss Lydia Crooker taught at the earliest known school on Rutherford Island. AUTHOR'S COLLECTION

The Lincoln School, built in 1898, was originally a single-story structure. The school was on a lot next to the Summit House hotel and for a period of time teachers boarded with its proprietors, the Gamage family. MARGARET FARRIN HOUSE

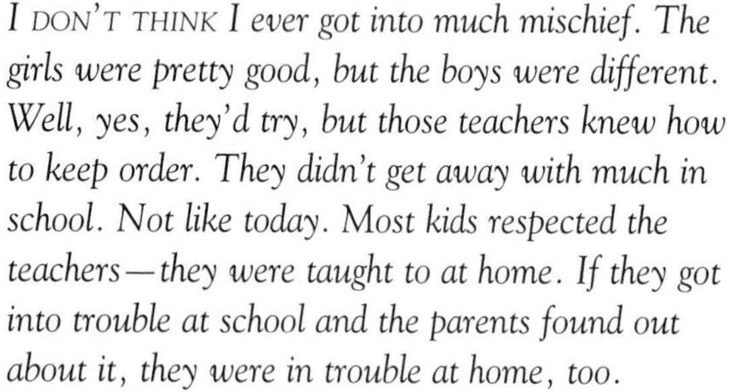

I DON'T THINK I ever got into much mischief. The girls were pretty good, but the boys were different. Well, yes, they'd try, but those teachers knew how to keep order. They didn't get away with much in school. Not like today. Most kids respected the teachers—they were taught to at home. If they got into trouble at school and the parents found out about it, they were in trouble at home, too.

—Catherine Jordon Walker

I LOVED TO READ, and I'd get up in that library and I'd get a book and I'd put it like this—if we had a book we wanted to read, we'd put it inside of the lesson book and hold our lesson book up with the book we were reading inside it so the teacher couldn't see it. Well, they probably knew what was going on. —Margaret Farrin House

THEY COULDN'T CHANGE ME anyhow, but I never done anything harmful. I raised hell when I was a kid, but I never messed with anybody or stole anything.

In my class there was five boys and a woman teacher. It wasn't a good combination. Oh, we raised the devil sometimes. She was a good teacher, she was a good person. She was a great, tall, burly person. She was smart, and she was a good teacher, but we gave her the devil sometimes. We'd try about anything—raise hell. The principal, though—there was no fooling around when you went in that room. Boy. Sent us back into that room—you didn't learn nothing *that day.*

—Mervin Rice

The scholars of the Lincoln school, about 1922. Front row, left to right: Afton Farrin, Jr., Lewis Hatch, J. Douglas Thompson, Maxwell House, John Thorpe, Addison McFarland, John Frey, Frank Eliphalet Farrin, Lewis T. Kelsey, Phillip Hatch, Daniel C. Seiders. Second row: Marion Wall, Charlotte Farrin, Margaret Farrin, Louise Alley, Hazel Farrin, Ferne Seiders. Third row: Robert Farrin, George Farrin, Elbridge House, Weston Poole, Carl Foster, Kenneth Farrin, Raymond McFarland, Frank Frey, Hazel McFarland. Back row: Herbert Tibbetts, Winthrop McFarland, James Plummer, Carlton Farrar, Lula Ada Gamage, Thelma Plummer, Vera Foster, Catherine Jordon, Mabel McFarland, Annie Otis (peeking), Kathleen Wilcox. MARGARET FARRIN HOUSE

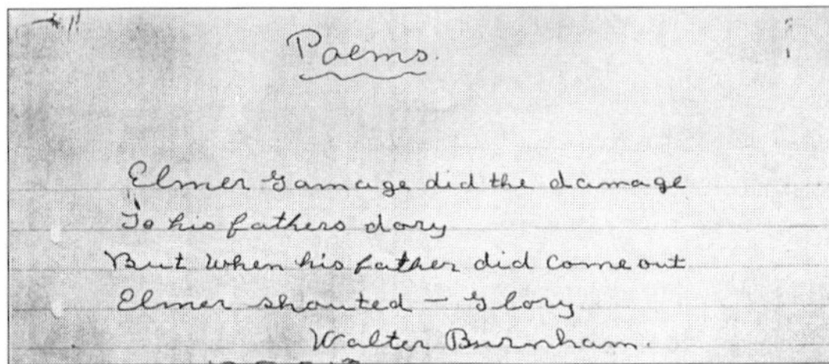

Poems.

Elmer Gamage did the damage
To his fathers dory
But when his father did come out
Elmer shouted — Glory
Walter Burnham.

Poem from the Lincoln School's handwritten newspaper, "The Schoolboy's Magazine," 1915.
MARGARET FARRIN HOUSE

The naughty Elmer Gamage, 1911, with a string of flounder. Whether that's his father's dory in the background is a matter for conjecture.
MARGARET FARRIN HOUSE

THEY SAT *two to a seat, and they didn't behave themselves any better than they do now, if you ask me. Somebody was always sticking a pen into someone, making 'em squeak, or pulling hair or something. The boys were bad. They'd pull the girls' braids, so you didn't like to be that near anyone, especially someone you didn't like, or someone that just wanted to tease you.*

—Kathleen Thorpe

OF COURSE, *we went all twelve years right up here in the school, you know. The downstairs was just the eight grades for a long time and then for a while they just had a two-year high school here, and then they enlarged it to a four-year high school. Built the top on to the high school. It was probably just two or three years before we went into high school that they put the top story on.*

—Nellie McFarland Frey

An undated photo of the Lincoln School, with the completed second-story addition. William A. Kelsey

A rare glimpse of the interior of the Lincoln School, showing Rita Turner's class in the early 1950s: Connie Seiders, Patty Kelsey, Beverly Haley, Alden McFarland, Adrian Chapman, Stanley Wall, Vaughn Seiders, Jimmy Frey, Janice Farrin, and Kelly Farrin. Nellie McFarland Frey

All the rooms in this building had several pipes, probably three inches in diameter, on three sides of the room—where there weren't any doors. They ran along under the windows. Those were heat pipes—they carried the heat—steam. And down in the basement was a huge boiler. And that boiler was covered with asbestos as were all of the pipes down there. That furnace heated all of the building. It burned soft coal so there was a lot of dust and smoke. There was a janitor who spent a great deal of time down there stoking the furnace when he wasn't cleaning the rooms upstairs.

We had an outdoor toilet in the early days and then came the improvement, which was a chemical toilet. There was a big tank, and the upstairs toilet room was divided—one side the boys, and one side was the girls. The chemical tanks were in the whole area and sometimes there was a splash—an occasional splash—and it caused a burn. Well, that was quite an event when that happened because probably everybody knew about it.

—Doug Thompson

As you sat there you listened to the other classes doing their recitations. You were supposed to be doing your work, but I think you probably learned a lot just through listening to the other classes, and you sort of got advanced when you came to the things that they were studying about. We learned a lot from that.

When the classes were in session they sat down in the front of the room—that group did. In the front of the room was a stage on which the teacher's desk sat, and his or her chair, and sometimes some mischievous acts took place. A couple of boys, during recess, would go up and set the front legs of the desk right over on the edge of the stage and then somebody would ask for help and be asked up to the teacher's desk—and as they would work he would lean on that desk and over it would go. The legs would go over the edge and the desk would go upside down. Books, clock—there was always a clock on the desk—whole thing would go down in a jumble on the floor. And there was a bell, of course, the bell would go with it. Every teacher had a bell for signaling the end of class or calling the students back after recess. —Doug Thompson

The front yard of the Randall Rice house in South Bristol village, where the 1935 graduation was held.
AUTHOR PHOTO, 1997

ALPHABET WAS *across the blackboard, and then there was a multiplication table, the "times tables," as we called them, as well as the division tables, addition and subtraction examples. The "goesinta tables," we called the division tables: because 2 goesinta 4, 4 goesinta 8, and so forth. It was sort of a joke among the kids. And these examples, they got firmly embedded in one's mind. In fact, I can see them to this day.* —Doug Thompson

MY FOLKS WERE *thinking of sending me to Damariscotta to board with somebody so that I could go to Lincoln Academy. In other words, the transportation was not as frivolous then—they would not have thought of driving me fifteen miles in the morning and then fifteen miles back.*

At one point the South Bristol people were required to take students up there. They bought or rented a wagon. There used to be a bakery wagon that wasn't a big box truck, but just like a cheap kind of stationwagon is now, but with no windows. So that's what they rented as a school bus for the kids. And because it looked to somebody in South Bristol like a Nissen's Bakery truck, they called them "the South Bristol Biscuits."

—Arletta Thorpe Rice

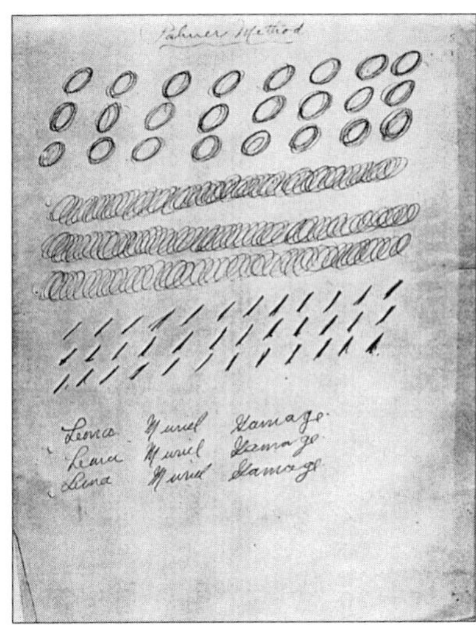

Page from "The Schoolboy's Magazine," 1914. This is a practice page—the Palmer Method was traditionally used to teach cursive handwriting.
MARGARET FARRIN HOUSE

ALWAYS HAD *the graduations in the church ever since I could remember, except the year Charles graduated there was the scarlet fever scare, and then one other year, when one of my cousins was graduating. It was outdoors, in the front yard.*

That was '35. The graduation was just on the lawn. I can remember there were a lot of people and they lined up on the road, up and down the hill. They had it outdoors because of the scarlet fever; somebody had scarlet fever. And of course the first graduating class at the high school the same thing happened: they didn't even have the graduation. And that was too bad because that would have been the first class to graduate from the high school. —Nellie McFarland Frey

I JUST DIDN'T LIKE *school very well. I was some glad when the last day come. But school wasn't the worse place you could be—sixty years later, you can make your living a lot easier with your head than you can with your hands.*

—Mervin Rice

THE ISLAND NEWS

No. I SOUTH BRISTOL HIGH SCHOOL, DECEMBER 14, 1951 Vol. V

FISHING CLASS PHOTOGRAPHED BY COLLIER'S WEEKLY

On Friday, November 30, the publishers of Collier's Magazine sent a photographer to our school to take pictures of the members of the Fishing Class and their activities. As this class is unique in its purpose and curriculum, the publishers want to portray to their readers the possibilities of such a program. They became interested in a picture of the class and of Mr. Boothby, our principal, taken by the Sea and Shore Fisheries Department and sent to many newspapers throughout the United States. Mr. George Woodruff, Collier's photographer, took pictures of Farrin's Lobster Pound, showing the students selling lobsters, of students in the boats hauling traps, "Danny" Seiders rowing in his boat, standing up, of Mr. Cook making traps, of Oscar Otis assisting with the knitting of pot heads; of Coastal Warden Daniel Davis, etc. In the afternoon, Mr. Donald Harrington and two other gentlemen from the Boothbay Harbor Experimental Station came over and Mr. Harrington gave a lecture and a demonstration pertaining to the clam structure. He also explained about the borer which has destroyed so many traps.

It is not yet known when this article will appear in the magazine. Our school is a small one, but it can still make the headlines!

(With assistance by Roger House)

*****

BASKETBALL SEASON OPENS

This year's undersized girls' basketball squad is composed of seven members, three of which are in junior high school. The team members are: "Betty" Alley, Gloria Chipman, Beryl McFarland, Evelyn McFarland, Diana Foster, Rosalie Rice, Ruth Gamage.

Our forwards are the same as last year's except they do not keep their eyes on the basket as yet. The loss of three of last year's four guards has left the burden on our one experienced guard plus the younge[r]

On the boys' team one member of last ye[ar]
line up available unti[l]
Christmas vacation.
improvement has been
and if all boys woul[d]
the game as interesti[ng]
hunting, we could have
ter team than we were
on the floor at any ti[me]
son. The boys' squad
the loss of "Donnie" F
to illness.

The other squad m[embers]
Roger House, Harry Pet[erson]
Hassan; "Ronnie" House
Eugley, "Billy" Kelsey
rin, Lewis Kelsey, Nei[l]
Arthur Wylie and Den
The junior high boys w
few games this season
other junior high tea[m]
vicinity.

We hope to give a
of ourselves even i[f]
winners. We hope o[ur]
porters will enjoy
much as we do enjoy
tunity to play them.

*****

The Island News, the South Bristol High School student newspaper, December 1951. It was big news when a national magazine came to the school; the concept of a commercial fishing class was quite innovative. MARGARET FARRIN HOUSE

Inset: one of the *Collier's Magazine* photographs of the high-school fishing class, 1951. Oscar Otis demonstrates knitting to the class, as principal E. Harry Boothby looks on. Roger House holds the needle while Billy Kelsey, Harry Peterson, Dan Seiders, Bruce Hassan (Otis's grandson), and Paul and David Farrin watch. ELIZABETH ALLEY HOUSE

The S Road School, where Sarah Emery taught for so many years. Its official name was the Roosevelt School, after Teddy Roosevelt. AUTHOR PHOTO, 1993

THE 1861 *Report of the Supervisor of Schools of the Town of Bristol* describes what came to be commonly known as the S Road School as "... a new and commodious house, built during the summer at an expense of six hundred dollars ... the scholars here, after waiting so long, now have the best schoolhouse in town."

I SET HERE *many hours. The seats were double, and when I first started school they made me sit with my sister. I'd do my work, and anything I'd do, she'd erase it. That used to bother me awful!*

We used to come out at recess and we had those little dinner buckets, and we thought so much of such stuff then; it had a little thermos in it. We'd sit on that doorstep and eat our dinner. And the teacher even used to let us—there's a big ledge up in here—let us go up there and eat our dinner.

One door went in to what they called the woodshed. The left one was the woodshed, and the other was the one we used to go through to school. And at Christmas we'd have a play; all the parents would come. I can remember going into the woodroom to change our clothes and put costumes on. They kept wood in it until later when they built a woodshed on.

There used to be a nice picture of George Washington in there. You'd stop and take your coats off. And they had a water jug out there; we had to fill it from the old—Thompsons lived up there then—from the Thompson well, and the woodstove sat right here. We'd go out and skate at noontime, and fall through sometimes, and the teacher dragged us in and set us around the woodstove to dry off. —Katherine Poole Norwood

THERE WAS *an anniversary for George Washington and by sending to Washington, D.C., we could get a picture free and then have it framed. And then the picture came, and of course, a frame was very expensive. I remember a Mrs. Andrews over on the Neck, and years ago her husband or father-in-law had made these picture frames. And I got one of the picture frames and put the picture in it.* —Sarah Emery, 1975 interview

MARGARET'S *mother Annie could remember when the S Road Schoolhouse there was on the other side of the road. Then they moved it over here. My father went to school in that schoolhouse, way back there in 18-somethin', and I never heard him say 'twas on the other side of the road. He went to school with Sarah Emery for a while—Sarah Emery's first job. When I went to school there, it was where it is now but generations before me went there when it was on the other side of the road. Oh, yes, it must have been well before 1900 that it was on the McFarland Cove Road.*

—Katherine Poole Norwood

The Gladstone School, at the intersection of Route 129 and the northerly end of Clark's Cove Road. AUTHOR PHOTO, 1997

Gladstone School scholars, c. 1915. EUGENIE WOODWARD COLE

A STORY IS TOLD that when the Civil War came, the teacher at the Gladstone School went off to fight, and seventeen of his students volunteered at President Lincoln's "first call" in 1861, joining the colors in defense of the Union. The school shut down until the war was over.

I WENT EIGHT GRADES THERE. One room, eight grades. That was good education back in those days. It really was—better than we got today. It was just wonderful. You had just that one teacher, and she always had somebody that kind of tended the fire for her, and brought in the wood, kept that big firewood box filled up for the wintertime. And she did the whole thing.

If you lived a mile and a half away from school you could get transportation. We used to have an old retired sea captain that used to haul the kids down from the north end of town to the Gladstone School. He had an old open wagon—doubled-seated wagon—and that was the way he brought them to school. —Robert Woodward

The former Four Corners School, now moved to a location north of Ridge Road; a contemporary addition has been put on the front. AUTHOR PHOTO, 1997

THERE WAS ANOTHER one-room schoolhouse just below what we call the Four Corners; just a little below that, on the knoll, there was a one-room schoolhouse. Kids from Clark's Cove and over the top of the hill coming north went to school there, and the kids up around the golf course and north of the golf course, going towards Damariscotta, went to the Gladstone School. Then eventually they closed up that one down there and they all came up either here to Gladstone or to the Sarah Emery School. —Robert Woodward

THERE'S A LITTLE HOUSE that was moved up from Four Corners that used to be a schoolhouse. Now that's what I've been told, and I guess it was, because Austin Sproul, when he was alive, he could remember it. —Katherine Poole Norwood

ONE OF THE TEACHERS at the Four Corners school was Wilbur Bearce. Bearce, one of the first selectmen in South Bristol, was never known for his warm personality. His lack of popularity with his students is legendary, if a bit far-fetched. One tale describes the day that some of the older boys stuffed him into a barrel and floated him in the river. Another tells how the boys picked him up and threw him out the window. He didn't go back.

The Upper School, on State Route 129. The ell on the left has been added to the school structure, and it has been moved from its original location near the fork where Routes 129 and 130 split.
AUTHOR PHOTO, 1997

THE HOUSE that I was born in, it used to be a schoolhouse. There's an ell been added on to it, but the rest is pretty much how it was. Dr. Farnsworth owned it, and he moved it down from just below the Forks. —Robert Woodward

THE UPPER SCHOOL appears on the town map of 1857, and is believed to have been built sometime around 1815. Though unsubstantiated, one story tells that it was moved downriver from Damariscotta on a scow.

SARAH EMERY, born in 1883, taught school for forty-nine years, all but two of them in South Bristol, first at the "S Road School," that is, the Roosevelt School, and later in Walpole. She retired from teaching in 1953 at age seventy-one, and even then continued for many years tutoring local children in her home. In some families she taught two successive generations. She was fondly thought of and much admired in the community.

WE HAD A teacher by the name of Sarah Emery. She had eight grades and they all got their lessons. She put on a little Halloween play, a Christmas play, all those things all by herself. She had to go through the whole routine: teach 'em little songs, and music, all the things like that. I don't know how the woman ever did it. And she put out well-educated kids for the time. Reading, writing, and 'rithmetic—they knew! —Robert Woodward

WELL, WE HAD our entertainments upstairs in the hall. Everybody had some part, even the little folks. The parents—my parents anyway—they would bring a gallon of ice cream and a cake to sell. And the boys would buy the cake and ice cream for the girls, and so on and so forth. Some would have just a piece to speak, some would be in a dialogue, and there were tableaux, maybe one skit. We really had a lot of fun.

—Sarah Emery, 1975 interview

Miss Sarah Emery and her scholars at the S Road School, about 1914. KATHERINE POOLE NORWOOD

SARAH EMERY taught eight grades for years and years—all the time she taught, I guess. In that schoolhouse it was all double desks—two kids sitting on one bench. They usually sat one younger one and one older one so you wouldn't get up to nothing. They filled that school up—every seat. Them days we all walked to school, you know, on the S Road. We never had no snow days—we went every day—snow, rain, whatever, we went. Sarah Emery lived right up the road; she walked to school. She never had a sick day—she mighta had an ugly one, but she never had a sick day. Them days you couldn't do nothing *right—whatever you done was wrong. She'd have one of them days once in a while.* —Mervin Rice

THERE WERE NO LIGHTS. When it was a thunderstorm and we couldn't see to study, I used to have gymnastics on some of those days because some of the children were frightened to death and cried all the time.

We had to go through all kinds of weather, snow and everything else. I've waded down to the corner 'way up to my waist in snow. We never had a holiday because there was a storm. We went through everything. If there were five children there, we kept school. If there were less, I sent them all home and I traveled home myself. But you had to plow through all that snow, because the men on the road hadn't got there yet. Why, I don't know I bothered much after I got accustomed to it. As I look back, the hardships don't seem to come to me the same as the humorous things do.

—Sarah Emery, 1975 interview

SHE WAS AN awful nice person. When we went to high school we were way ahead of them guys when it came to figuring. I could use figures good. She'd pound that in to me, boy. And you didn't move on until you knew what she was teaching you that day.

—Mervin Rice

*S*ARAH USED TO *come over and spend Christmas with us. She was quite a musical old lady. We had a tambourine, and boy, could she play that. She'd hit it on her elbow.*

I used to take her shopping. She never got anywhere hardly when her mother was alive. Once in a while, she'd go with me, and after her mother died she went with me quite often, with my mother and me. We took her to Brunswick—she hadn't been to Brunswick for years and years and we went in Grant's, and she looked around, and when we come out she said, "My, there's so much we don't need." And she was right.

She didn't have electricity in that house. She'd lug all her water. And to keep stuff from spoiling she'd reheat it, and reheat it, and reheat it. And in the winter—what we used to do—she'd put it in the shed so it wouldn't spoil. Sarah said she didn't want electricity because, she said, "Lightning does come in on the wires, you know." But she did have a telephone put in, and darned if we didn't have a thunderstorm and lightning come in and smashed everything all up. She didn't have any electricity, but it came in on the telephone wires, and burned everything right by the telephone, went right down in the basement.

—Katherine Poole Norwood

I WENT TO *school with him one year. He taught school one year at the S Road when Sarah Emery was gone; Afton taught at the S Road School one year when Sarah Emery went on vacation to California for a year. Gee, he was a hard teacher, too, boy. He had law and order, I'll tell ya. Jeez, he'd start off in the morning, he'd take this big geography book, he'd slam that down on the desk. It went off like a cannon and boy, you took notice! When he spoke you went into your shoes. God!*

That man taught on Barters Island; that's over in Boothbay, north of Boothbay Harbor. He'd row across the river in a dory all winter—cold, you know, zero, ten below zero, whatever it was—a snowstorm and everything. He'd go across the river in a dory, land in East Boothbay, walk from there to Boothbay Center—which is three, four miles—teach school, walk back, row back 'cross the river, and then—he kept a bunch of cows—do chores. They said half the time he'd come home, he'd lay right down behind the stove—that's where he slept. He was an awful hard-working man. 'Course, you know, the way he worked I don't suppose some nights he had much rest. He worked twenty hours, twenty-four, seemed like—so tired some days he probably didn't feel like teaching school. But he was tough. —Mervin Rice

Photograph from a school newspaper tribute to Afton Farrin after his death in 1948. MARGARET FARRIN HOUSE

Afton Farrin with scholars at the S Road School.
Margaret Farrin House

Afton Farrin, with students at the Lincoln School, possibly around 1915. Katherine Poole Norwood

Most of the kids were great readers.
—Doug Thompson

Christmastime, one of the biggest things we asked for were books. We received a number of books, and then after we had read ours we'd exchange them with our friends and we'd almost have contests to see who read the most books in a week.
—Doug Thompson

For many years the village library was on the second floor of the building that housed Merritt Thompson's—later, Chester Clifford's—grocery store. The Maine Register lists a "Rutherford" library as early as 1891, with Mrs. Flora French as librarian, and 1,500 volumes by the end of her tenure in 1914. Other librarians in subsequent years were Sarah Thompson (Doug's mother) and Cora Thompson, the storekeeper's wife.

I vividly remember her as a great patron, carrying a bag of books to and from her home in Christmas Cove along with her daughter-in-law Ora—Flora and Ora. —Doug Thompson

The parsonage of South Bristol Union Church, on the Middle Road, was built for the church association by Warren Gamage in 1908. Author photo, 1997

At the time our minister was George Woodwell, and up in the third floor of that house he had a library full of books for children and that was probably before our other library, maybe before it was established, or anyway they didn't have that many children's books. So we all went to Sunday school and he would encourage us to come and borrow books to take home. And if you took care of the books and you were careful and brought them back when you were finished, he gave you one. So I accumulated books like that.
—Catherine Jordon Walker

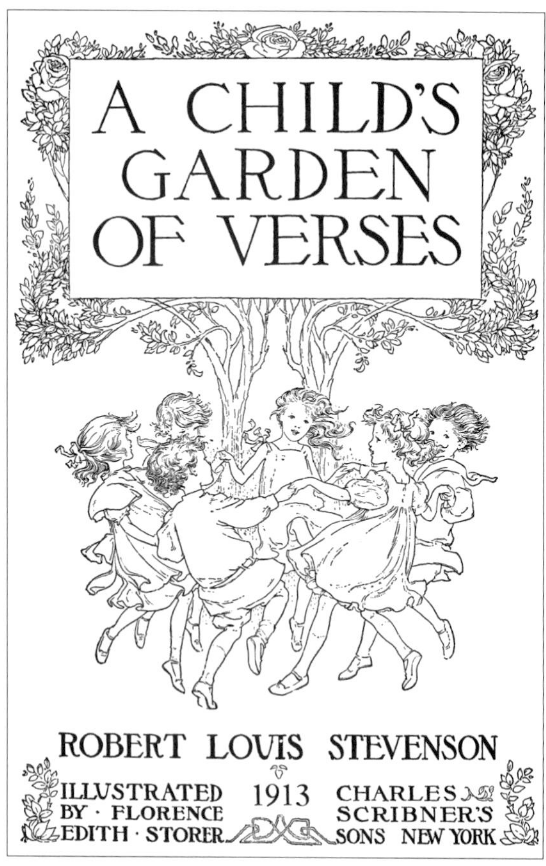

Title page from an illustrated edition of *A Child's Garden of Verses* by Robert Louis Stevenson.
AUTHOR'S COLLECTION

THAT'S MY FAVORITE—*poems that I used to love when I was young—*A Child's Garden of Verses. *My sisters and I used to play school and we used to learn these little verses. I used to love that book.*

I remember how I loved the Thornton Burgess books about the animals—Reddy Fox, and all those other animals. They were stories about different animals, and he had a name for each one. Squirrels, and fox, and little animals that live in the woods that everybody's familiar with. They were just fun stories to read; there was always sort of a moral to it, too, like Aesop's Fables. *I remember having those. Someone gave me one for Christmas; I had that for years. I read it so much and I used to read it to my sisters. Sometimes I wonder what ever happened to a lot of those things, but I guess we just wore them out.*

—Catherine Jordon Walker

THE "RANCHMAN POET," *Larry Chittenden, was from Texas, and he had all sorts of steer horns and odd things in his house. He was the one who wrote the Christmas Cove poem that has a line starting from each letter of the words Christmas Cove.* —Arletta Thorpe Rice

PEOPLE WOULD *donate books to the library. He'd make a big ceremony of it when you brought your* Bobbsey Twins *book. He'd take a bookplate and glue it in with old-fashioned mucilage and brush, and you would autograph it.*

—Arletta Thorpe Rice

MY UNDERSTANDING *is that Larry Chittenden came here from Texas. I don't know what brought him to a little town like South Bristol. And it may be that we didn't have much of a library at the time, but he got the idea of making this a memorial library—that's what he called it—and asked for donations of books and it was just free for everybody. It was called the Autograph Library because everyone who gave a book could sign their name on this label that they had given it.*

—Catherine Jordon Walker

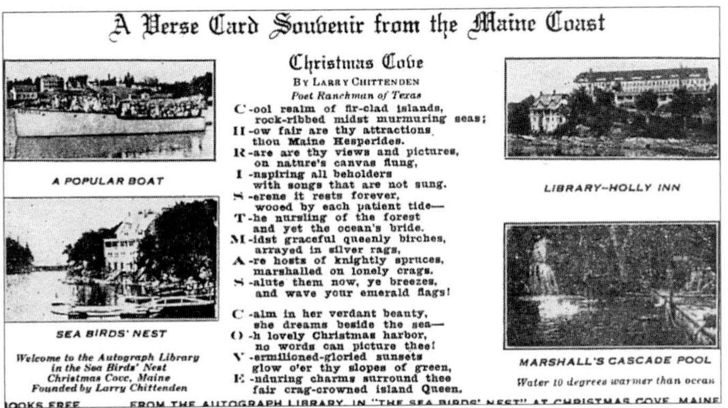

A Verse Card Souvenir from the Maine Coast

Christmas Cove

By Larry Chittenden

Poet Ranchman of Texas

C-ool realm of fir-clad islands,
 rock-ribbed midst murmuring seas;
H-ow fair are thy attractions
 thou Maine Hesperides.
R-are are thy views and pictures,
 on nature's canvas flung,
I-nspiring all beholders
 with songs that are not sung.
S-erene it rests forever,
 wooed by each patient tide—
T-he nursling of the forest
 and yet the ocean's bride.
M-idst graceful queenly birches,
 arrayed in silver rags,
A-re hosts of knightly spruces,
 marshalled on lonely crags.
S-alute them now, ye breezes,
 and wave your emerald flags!

C-alm in her verdant beauty,
 she dreams beside the sea—
O-h lovely Christmas harbor,
 no words can picture thee!
V-ermilioned-gloried sunsets
 glow o'er thy slopes of green,
E-nduring charms surround thee
 fair crag-crowned island Queen.

A POPULAR BOAT

SEA BIRDS' NEST

Welcome to the Autograph Library in the Sea Birds' Nest Christmas Cove, Maine Founded by Larry Chittenden

LIBRARY–HOLLY INN

MARSHALL'S CASCADE POOL

Water 10 degrees warmer than ocean

"A Verse Card Souvenir from the Maine Coast," with Larry Chittenden's famous—or infamous—Christmas Cove poem. David W. Andrews

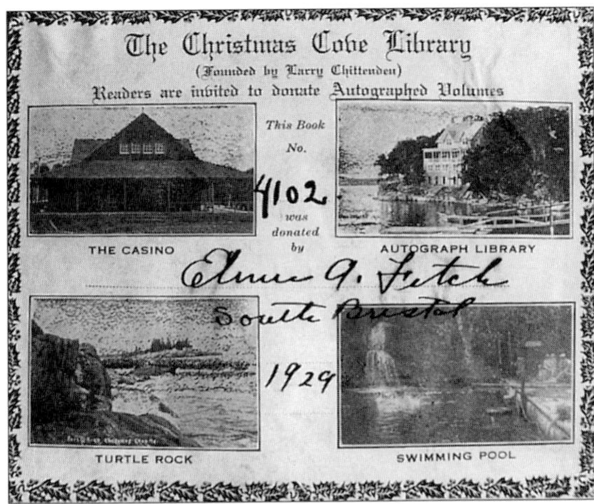

Bookplate from the Autograph Library. The four photographs are all scenes from Christmas Cove: the library, of course; the CCIA Casino and tidal swimming pool; and Turtle Rock, on the shore of the Thread of Life. William A. Kelsey

A partial view of the interior of the Autograph Library, "Texas Corner." To judge from this and other photographs of the place, practically every square inch was crammed with books, artwork, signs, and objects. William A. Kelsey

He wasn't a big man at all, but boy, I'll tell you—when he spoke, you trembled. —Bill Kelsey

THERE WAS SOMETHING *about him—look at his face. I don't think I ever saw anybody defy him—not in my lifetime.*

He had a puttputt boat—little, small 20-foot boat Sumner McFarland built him, with a little make-and-break engine in it; hauled his traps by hand. Had a rope on each side of the boat and he'd steer with his rope, pull his rudder back and forth. If he needed runners for his traps he was apt to take the door right off the house, saw it into runners. He'd go out and cut his own boughs, you know, spruce boughs, spruce limbs—cut the big spruce limbs, then you bend 'em 'round into a stick of wood—make your frames for your old wooden lobster traps, he'd make his own. He taught me how to knit. He spent hours over there showing me how to knit pot heads. Used to knit 'em for me when I first started.

Dad used to buy him a bottle once in a while. He never was a heavy drinker. He never did drink too much, but boy when he did.... there was a little tiny room there in the back of the house. Dad would buy him a bottle of hooch, and every once in a while he'd go out in the back room there and have a little drink, you know. "Whew!" You'd hear him blow like this: "Whew!" You could always tell—"Whew!" Then he'd just come back out. He was quite a cat.

Herman W. Kelsey, 1873–1961. WILLIAM A. KELSEY

He didn't very often wear a belt—he used an old rope to hold his pants up. He worked in the quarry over at Round Pond, and he was supposed to be dead when he was forty-something, from rock dust. He claimed he took creosote and milk—built himself up from one drop to several drops. He says that's what cured him, but God only knows. But he lived to be eighty-seven or something.

—Bill Kelsey

George William McFarland, 1854–1938, known to all as George Will. MARGARET FARRIN HOUSE

UNCLE GEORGE WILL MCFARLAND was well known; he was known as the Butterfly Man. His talent was magnificent carvings and paintings of butterflies, which he sold by the hundreds to summer visitors. It was George Will McFarland's shop that we kids visited—much time was spent by the neighborhood youngsters watching him, and we'd stop off at the house with Aunt Nora for cookies. We were always welcome in Uncle Will and Aunt Nora's house.

Sylvanus McFarland lived down the road on the same side, at the top of the hill overlooking the village. He carved and painted birds.

—Doug Thompson

South Bristol, Maine Nov. 20, 1919.

Dear Sister Christine:-

Father received an order for some butterflies Tonight and has got to have them ready to send by Next Thursday and hh has no small wire for the smellers. Will you please get him some as soon as possible? We owe Arthur for some screw eyes and some wire. Will you please pay him for them and let us know how much we owe you? We think Ava is having a good time by the way she writes. Father is making butterflies This Evening and Mother has been shelling some beans to bake. Harlan was up to Damariscotta Today and saw Uda. Gee I am glad I am free. Doris and her baby are getting along fine. Aunt Dea is as well as usual. Well this is all I can think of to write so will close now with love from us all.

Your Brother Harold.

Letter from George Will's son Harold to his sister Christine. Born in 1884, Harold was thirty-five when he wrote this from his parents' home. MARGARET FARRIN HOUSE

Hilda Hamlin among her lupines at Juniper Knoll, June 17, 1963.
Norman Hamlin

A summer resident of Christmas Cove since her first visit there in 1916, Hilda Hamlin was the real-life inspiration for the heroine of Barbara Cooney's award-winning children's book, *Mrs. Rumphius*. She died in 1989, just two weeks short of her 101st birthday.

The true legend of Hilda Hamlin as "the lupine lady" first became widely known when *Yankee Magazine*, in 1971, published an article by W. Storrs Lee:

For almost three-quarters of a century, Juniper Knoll has been Hilda Hamlin's summer hideout. Here she first began "flinging" lupine seed, imported from her native England, over the thin soil of the headland. They took hold. The biennials grew and blossomed in glorious wild profusion, until her hillsides became the garden show of Lincoln County. Every August she harvested bundles of dried stalks, shook out the seeds, and strewed them over a wider area. Handfuls were doled out to her neighbors, who started lupine patches in their own backyards, and they in turn made community contributions of more "boughten" seed. From the first there was contagion about the dissemination.

Then Hilda adopted the habit of filling a pocket with seeds, and on her tramps to the post office, would fling a few into roadside thickets, work them into the soil at a curve in the road where there was a pleasant backdrop of boulders or balsam, or cast them generously down an embankment, wherever a green thumb dictated they would do best. She discovered, for instance, that they germinated readily and grew most profusely on the site of old woods fires.

From Christmas Cove she went farther afield. Though she never drove a car herself, her friends did, and when they took her for a spin, she was prone to toss handfuls of seed from the car windows into spots she felt needed floral decoration. Any number of unknown disciples have appreciated the fact that lupine tends to run out after a few seasons, and have supplied the seed and emulated the original strewer.

Like her disciples, Hilda has always kept her plantings strictly anonymous. Only her closest friends were wise to her avocation. Even exclamations expressed in her presence about the beauty of the approach to Christmas Cove were commonly received in poker-faced agreement, with nary an admission of her complicity. It was her practical jest on the public and nature—her private secret. Only on one occasion did she break down and confess all to a complete stranger.

"I was enroute to the P.O. on a mid-June morning when the roadside lupines were especially fine and numerous," she recounts. "Suddenly I heard a queer squeaking sound, and around a bend in the road came a Model T Ford, complete with running board and all of the other accouterments of a Tin Lizzie. Behind the wheel sat a regular old-time New England schoolmarm, her gray hair done up in a bun and her prim figure rigged out in a high-necked, long-sleeved cotton dress. She stopped the car, begged pardon for the intrusion and inquired: 'Madam, can you explain the source of these beautiful cultivated lupines growing along the roadside like wildflowers?'

"'Yes,' said I, 'at the end of the road lives a queer old bird who has so many hundreds of lupines on her land that she has acquired the habit of scattering the seed when it ripens. Her friends call her Hilda Lupina.'

"'Wonderful!' said the old gal. 'How I'd like to meet her and shake her by the hand and thank her.'

"'Would you?' said I, extending a paw. 'Shake. I am Hilda Lupina.'"

"Woodchuck Corner," at the intersection of State Route 129 and the West Side Road on Rutherford Island. AUTHOR PHOTO, 1997

Milton D. Thompson, with his invention the feathering propeller. Although first patented in 1909, the use of feathering props is still widespread today. KATHERINE POOLE NORWOOD

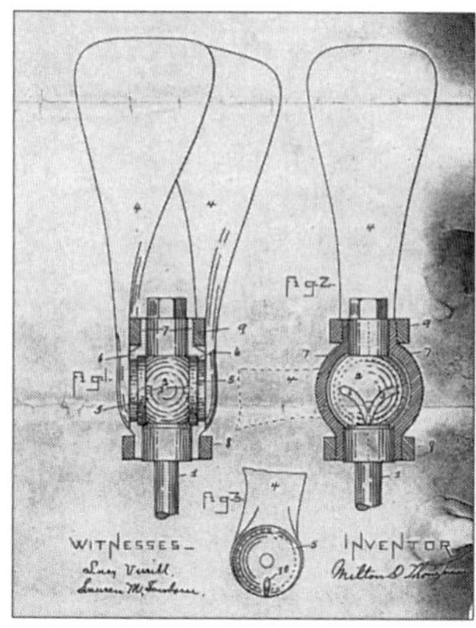

The original engineering drawing for the propeller patent. DONALD M. THOMPSON

AT THE CORNER of the West Side Road was a house known as "Woodchuck Corner," where Dan Chittenden lived. It's said that this name came from the fact that people would bring "Uncle Dan" the woodchucks that they'd shot, and he would cook and eat them with great relish. You can see his gravestone in the island cemetery: "Uncle Dan, Everyone's Friend."

UNCLE DAN owned that house when you go down the West Side Road, the house on the right. I can remember when we used to walk to school; I was in grade school then. Uncle Dan had that house just full of all sorts of curiosities, all sorts of things he'd collected over the years, and he let the kids come in and look at them. He had just everything you could think of, I guess, that he had collected in his travels. He liked children and he knew everybody. —Catherine Jordon Walker

A GENTLEMAN lived there, and his name was Dan Chittenden. He had lots and lots of books in his place, and he had a monkey there, and souvenir-type things that kids used to like. He had a brother named Larry who had a library down in Christmas Cove.

And I remember the time we "borrowed" a cannonball that was on Dan's lawn as a decoration—for a shot, since we didn't have one for the high school track team. —Doug Thompson

MY UNCLE Milton Thompson invented the feathering propeller for sailboats, which is still in use today. He had a unique demonstration device, which was a glass tank on the running board of his car. Cars had running boards in those days. He would go into the village and haul people out of the stores to see it. —Doug Thompson

Elliot Brewer had a compulsion of growing and wearing giant dahlias in his buttonhole. And he gave me my first formal gown!

—Arletta Thorpe Rice

He'd get up on the porch there with a great big pine candle under each arm, wave it over his head, and let out a hoot—scare the people right off the tennis court. —Bill Kelsey

Elliot Brewer in his flower garden.
ARLETTA THORPE RICE

Bain Young's sister Lottie, they called her—her real name was Charlotte—Sarah Emery was her daughter. She used to love flowers, and at the south end of her house, for years after she died, it came up nothing but flowers.

—Katherine Poole Norwood

Charlotte Young Emery in 1957 at the age of 92 years, 11 months. KATHERINE POOLE NORWOOD

Samuel A. Miles, 1862–1932.
NOBLEBORO HISTORICAL SOCIETY, IVAN FLYE COLLECTION

The "Fresh Air Camp" that Samuel Miles built on the shore of John's Bay. Leonard Tibbetts and Willard Thorpe built the camps, which have now been converted into summer homes. WILLIAM A. KELSEY

WHAT A NICE MAN. *Once a week he'd have silent movies there, and the townspeople were invited. And he threw parties every fall for all the little kids, you know. He got a great kick out of that. Every kid headed up there near the tower where he had his house. Back then it was considered somewhat of a mansion. He had all the kids up there and they all got not just little trinkets for presents—every one of them had a good present. Big dolls and things—REAL presents, real nice things, and games, nice games. I can remember he had a great big umbrella hanging up from sort of a cathedral-type ceiling, and then they'd lower that down full of presents. And he played the piano, and to this day I can hear him singing "In My Heart There Rings a Melody." That was one of his favorites. A great man.* —Doug Thompson

DURING THE DEPRESSION, *Mr. Miles was a real philanthropist. He did a great deal for the town. He had a lot of men working for him, and he did this just to provide employment. The Miles Estate started right next to the high school land and it went all the way down on the east side of the island, down beyond House's Cove, all the way to the lobster pound that was down there. S. A. Miles had that fence put in there during the depression: they set posts the whole length of the road on the west side of his land, strung aluminum cable, capped those posts with aluminum, and they're still there today, many of them. They've lasted over the period of seventy or more years. He was a great philanthropist and everybody around here thinks, to this day, the same thing: he simply put that fence in to give some people work—that was his objective.* —Doug Thompson

MR. MILES *gave great Halloween parties—he'd give us a half pound of Fannie Farmer candy when we left!* —Annie Louise Alley Farrin

HE ALSO FINANCED *and built several barracks-type camps down on the shore, down on John's Bay. During the summer for many years he paid for the operation of a Salvation Army summer camp for needy boys and girls throughout the state. The Salvation Army did the work, and he paid the bills.* —Doug Thompson

WE'D SAY, *"here comes the Miles kids." I remember them coming in buses, singing the camp song.*
—Margaret Farrin House

Lumber scow on the Damariscotta River.
NOBLEBORO HISTORICAL SOCIETY, IVAN FLYE COLLECTION

I REMEMBER *Eben Otis because when we went to school the older boys used to tease him—you know how boys can be. They'd go over there and do all kinds of things to annoy him, and he'd always get annoyed, of course, and come out and yell at them. He was an old man then, when I went to school. Ellen Shew's house was where he lived.*

—Catherine Jordon Walker

EBEN R. OTIS was one of those old googers who always seemed to be mixed up in some escapade or calamity of a humorous nature. There were some who owned and operated large barges with sail power and who made occasional trips to the towns with assortments of cargo and returned with a variety of material for downriver delivery. One such was owned by "Uncle" Eben. He was a venerable old sailor and familiar with the river and the area down by the ocean. One day he sailed his scow up the Damariscotta with a load of flour for Flint & Stetson grocery, which had been transferred from the steamer ENTERPRISE at South Bristol.

While he was unloading the flour he was approached by Mr. Austin Hall, who was a lumber dealer. Mr. Hall had an order for a load of lumber to be delivered to South Bristol. Uncle Eben sailed across and tied up at Cottrell's Wharf and loaded on the lumber. It was quite a load, but it was well stacked and he made ready to sail. It was a flood tide and he hastened to "shove off" before the current would set up through the bridge.

Just at the head of the dock was the marble and granite works of Marias Page. They had finished a gravestone for a customer downriver and, seeing Uncle Eben going that way, he went to the dock and inquired if the stone could not be carried along on the same trip. This was agreeable to Uncle Eben, but he began to have concern for the current which was increasing up through the bridge, which would make it difficult, if not hazardous in getting underway, but the stone was soon on board, lying on top of the lumber, and willing hands cast off the line and as the bow swung around, Uncle Eben, close-hauled, quartering with the wind, set a tack for the other side. He soon realized that he was confronted with a problem. He gained on the tack, but the swift current converging between the two wharves caused him to lose what he had gained. After a series of luffs, jibes, and tacks, his predicament attracted several people crossing across the bridge. Others gathered and it began to appear that Uncle Eben might not be able to extricate himself from the trap he was in, and it meant certain disaster if he was carried up to the bridge, where the mast would catch and the whole thing capsize. Making one last effort to tack, he saw it was hopeless, let go the main sheet and, standing there on deck, with his white hair waving in the breeze, he looked up at the people on the bridge and shouted, "Tell Marias I've gone to Hell, gravestone and all!"

—Harold Castner, "The Castner Papers"

The ferry from East Boothbay, which was known then as Hodgdon's Mills, they found, was a small open sailboat, manned by "Eben" clad in pants that didn't meet his boots, vest that didn't meet the top of his pants, no coat, and an old straw hat that we were to know for years, which allowed strands of hair to appear through the top.

It was foggy. In time the crowded boat drifted and beat across the river to South Bristol, whereupon Eben suggested sailing these new city people "around the 'Pint' into the Cove." No one knew what they were in for, but as there was wind against the tide, most of those city summer people were sick and disgusted when they arrived hours later at the Cove.

At Boothbay, that year 1883, Eben Otis met us in his little boat, mainsail and jib, and we found that he had sailed over the day before and had curled up in his boat cuddy all night. In went the trunks, lowered by tackle from the dock of the Wiwurna, and stood on end in the cockpit. Did the wind hold good? Often it didn't, and a long tiresome sail it was around Ocean Point and Linekins Neck to the Cove. If we arrived at noon we were lucky.

—Henry M. Seaver in a letter to his nephew, 1937

At one time Uncle Eben acquired a contract to row the mail across from East Boothbay to South Bristol. He traveled this water route in all kinds of weather and with his apparent knowledge of "dead reckoning," the mail went through in darkness and fog. On an August day, however, he left East Boothbay in a thick fog, and by some strange reason became confused. After rowing around for some time he decided it was time to send out a distress call. Shipping the oars, he stood up, spat out a generous wad of tobacco, and filling his lungs, began shouting at the top of his voice: "Who am I! Who am I! I'm Eben R. Otis, lost in the fog!" Actually, Uncle Eben was not far from a line of cottages. Everyone knew him and after several repeats of this unusual SOS, some of the people shouted through the fog, informing him about where he was. The only reply they received was a disgruntled groan and some words that sounded like profanity, and they heard the unmistakable shipping of the oars and the rhythm of noises in the tholepins, that assured them Uncle Eben had got his bearings and was on his way.

—Harold Castner, "The Castner Papers"

Willard Metcalf's studio, just south of the ice pond, probably in the mid-1930s. The house in the left background was once one of the boardinghouses for Bristol Ice Company crews. Eugenie Woodward Cole

Spring on the River, by Willard Metcalf, 1904. Oil on canvas, 8¾ x 11 inches. The back of his parents' home is in the center, flanked by a barn on the left and Metcalf's studio on the right. This is the southerly end of the meandering pond used by the Bristol, later American, Ice Companies. Private collection, photo courtesy Spanierman Gallery, LLC

In 1903 American Impressionist Willard Metcalf moved to his parents' home in Clark's Cove seeking, and claiming to find, a spiritual and aesthetic renaissance. He arrived penniless, and during his time there the family lived off meager savings and his father Greenleaf's Civil War pension of twelve dollars a month. Fish and lobsters were plentiful then, and Metcalf and his mother would often fish for their supper off a flatboat on the Damariscotta River. The miller's cottage served as his studio; although modest in size it afforded a spectacular view overlooking the ice pond and the old stone bridge that spanned a Damariscotta River inlet. In the 1950s, without knowing why, the local children playing at Clark's Cove still called the old building "the studio."

According to his own records, it was on a snowy Christmas Day, 1906, that Metcalf spent all day painting *The White Mantle*, depicting the stone bridge; the iceworks superintendent's house and an ice crew rooming house appear behind it. A local postcard from the same period looks back across the bridge from the opposite shore, showing Metcalf's studio and just beyond it his parents' house and outbuildings.

Willard Metcalf painted between twenty and twenty-four landscapes during his Clark's Cove period. *Spring on the River* is a view looking south from the bank of the old ice pond, with his studio and the Metcalf homestead in the background. Thurlow Kelsey used to tell how, as a small boy, he would sit in the small warming shed to put on his ice skates.

The White Mantle, by Willard Metcalf, 1906. Oil on canvas, 26 by 29 inches. From this point of view, the ice pond would be on the right and the inlet from the Damariscotta River on the left.
PRIVATE COLLECTION. PHOTOGRAPH COURTESY OF HIRSCHL & ADLER GALLERIES, NEW YORK

Postcard of the stone bridge at Clark's Cove. The photograph is undated, but the postmark, verso, is 1907. DAVID W. ANDREWS

'Course, he was my doctor when I was born. —Mervin Rice

Dr. Henry Fernald, 1866–1943. Dr. Fernald came to East Boothbay in 1893 and practiced in the Boothbay region for nearly fifty years. BOOTHBAY REGION HISTORICAL SOCIETY

I CAN REMEMBER *him coming for the younger kids. I was old enough to remember when he come—every time there was one born it was the middle of the night, it seems though. They'd go over on a boat and bring him back. He'd come with his old, long, black fur coat on. Gosh, he was an awful guy to stick a needle in you. No matter what, he'd stick a needle in you—pink pills and a needle. That'd cure you. Old black fur coat, dragging on the ground—I bet that thing weighed twenty pounds. Well, he had to, you know—open boat, and damn' cold weather, and he had to come across the river. No matter what the weather was, call and he'd come. He'd come. There was only one place to land with a boat, and they'd meet him there with a horse and take him wherever he was supposed to go.* —Mervin Rice

DR. FERNALD *came from East Boothbay. I can remember when I was much younger and had flu or something. My memory of that is that he came over by boat to Christmas Cove landing over down here. I knew he was coming and was very anxious. He always took off his rubbers when he came in the cellar way; maybe it was snowing. I was in bed upstairs. I could hear him, and would think, "Uh oh, here he comes," and then wait for him to take off his rubbers and he'd mumble around here and then come up. One particular time that he came it seems to me it was at night, and he said that I needed clam broth to "break the phlegm." My father went out in the dark and dug clams, and my mother cooked the clams—and how I hated clam broth. It seemed to me it all happened at the edge of the night.*

I remember being fascinated by the racks of colored pills that he had in the valise. A black valise, and it opened up on a hinge so that you could look in and see red pills and pink pills and white pills. Coated pills, some of them, and others were just sort of chalky. —Arletta Thorpe Rice

I REMEMBER *when I was a kid they had the flu 'round here and nobody could do anything. Perhaps you've heard this: Dr. Fernald took the Luden's cough drops. I guess he melted them and mixed them somehow and made a syrup of them that worked on the flu, got rid of it. I don't remember just how it was, I don't know who would tell you about it, but I remember them telling at the time about it. Nobody here ever died from the flu.*

—Pete McFarland

*W*HEN *I* WAS *five years old in 1918, influenza hit the area. I was the only one in my family who wasn't infected. So I dispensed the pills that Dr. Fernald made to my family. Every time the doctor came, he would tell us that a neighbor had died.*

—Annie Louise Alley Farrin

*V*ERY OFTEN *the* PILGRIM *or the* CELIA E *was called upon just to make trips from South Bristol to East Boothbay, and also at that time the* ERNEST A, *owned by Captain Ambrose Alley, was called upon as a river ferry, and there was a man in East Boothbay by the name of Fred Hodgdon who performed the same duties. All were often called upon to bring Dr. Fernald, who resided in East Boothbay, over to South Bristol to take care of somebody that was sick, or to deliver a baby. This happened all the time and he depended upon these people to transport him, especially Fred Hodgdon when he was on the home side of his river. I was delivered by Dr. Fernald at our house in South Bristol and my father went across the river in the boat to pick him up.* —Doug Thompson

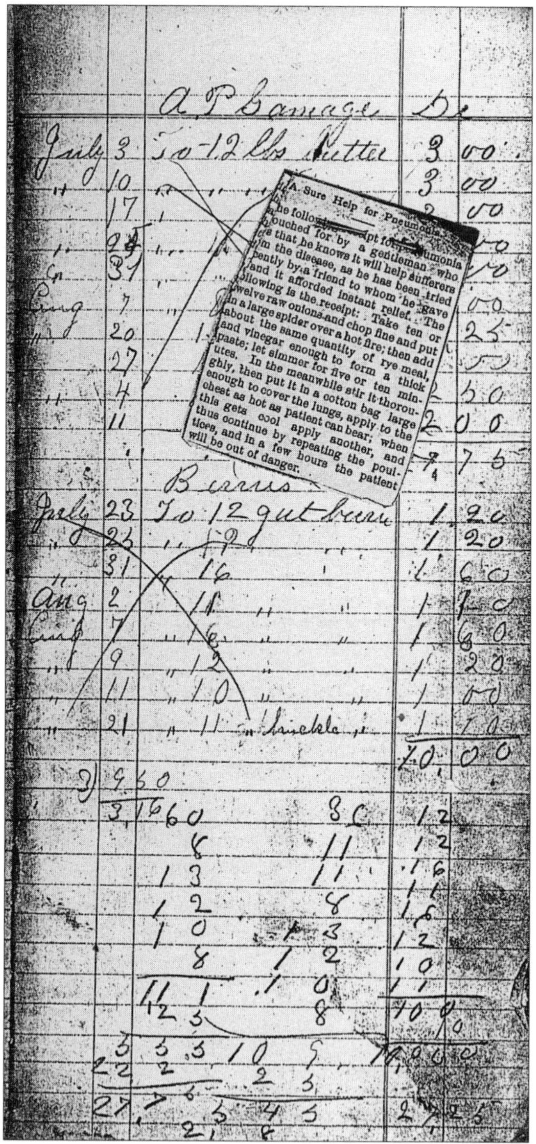

A Sure Help for Pneumonia.

[illegible]he follo[illegible]pt for [illegible]umonia [illegible]ouched for by a gentleman who [illegible]s that he knows it will help sufferers [illegible]m the disease, as he has been tried [illegible]ently by a friend to whom he gave [illegible]and it afforded instant relief. The [illegible]llowing is the receipt: Take ten or [illegible]welve raw onions and chop fine and put [illegible]n a large spider over a hot fire; then add about the same quantity of rye meal, and vinegar enough to form a thick paste; let simmer for five or ten minutes. In the meanwhile stir it thoroughly, then put it in a cotton bag large enough to cover the lungs, apply to the chest as hot as patient can bear; when this gets cool apply another, and thus continue by repeating the poultices, and in a few hours the patient will be out of danger.

Home remedy recipe found pinned to old ledger pages. LALEAH CONDON KENNEDY, EUGENE B. SPROUL FARM

*W*E NEVER CALLED *the doctor unless someone was really sick. Someone would always go across the river and bring him to South Bristol, and then he came down in a sleigh in the winter. It seems to me he always came in the winter. I can't remem-*

ber him coming in the summer. He always wore a big bearskin coat. And he had a fascinating case of pills—all different colors—that he brought with him. They say he made his own pills—I wonder if they did any good. But you thought they did, because you'd called the doctor, and you'd paid him, and so—I think people got well whether his medicine helped or not. —Catherine Jordon Walker

WITH THE CLOSEST DOCTOR a mile and a half across the river, people couldn't fetch the doctor for every illness and complaint. Common sense and folk wisdom were the order of the day; women dispensed the cures and home remedies they'd learned from their mothers and grandmothers.

THAT'S WHAT all the old folks did—mixed up all these potions for healing and for different purposes. Sulfur and molasses—that was a spring tonic. I used to love that—oh, it tasted good. Sulfur and molasses. Every spring my mother would mix up a whole lot of that. We took that every day, springtime. Got the winter out of our bones.

—Nellie McFarland Frey

IN THE SPRING Momma always gave us sulfur and molasses for a spring tonic. That was supposed to clear the blood. She mixed it up and kept it on the back of the stove. It was sort of spongy—sort of a sponge on the top. I hated it. The molasses was just to cover up the sulfur taste, but it didn't. I don't know that it ever made any difference at all, but people thought it did.

If we had a sore throat my mother would always put some kind of grease on your chest with a flannel over it, and you'd go to bed until you got over it. And there was Musterol; it came in a little jar like Vaseline, only it was very strong. They used that for muscular problems.

—Catherine Jordon Walker

I CAN REMEMBER some kind of liniment that we got for throats. They'd drop a few drops of this liniment, which I think was a rubbing liniment—horse liniment, probably!—into a spoon of sugar and we'd chuck it down to help a sore throat or cough or something. —Arletta Thorpe Rice

WHEN MY GRANDMOTHER, Mertie Curtis, *had her first child—my father—he was very tiny and at risk. She had to go to Damariscove Island with my grandfather and was very worried about her baby. Someone told her to take a goat with her to the island and to use the milk for her baby—which she said she did, and the baby grew and thrived. She attributed his survival to the goat's milk.*

—Claire Curtis McNamara

When I was a child there were quite a few families in Christmas Cove, families with a lot of children.

—Catherine Jordon Walker

William and Loletta Jordon, probably on their wedding day in 1875. A master carpenter and housewright, Will Jordon built many of the cottages on Heron Island and on the western side of Christmas Cove. He came from Georgetown; Loletta was a South Bristol native, daughter of Lois and Webster Gamage. Catherine Jordon Walker

Will Jordon, 1849–1914. Not only did Will Jordon build many of the cottages on Heron Island and the west side of Christmas Cove, but as a fine carpenter he made furniture as well. She was only four when he died, but his granddaughter Catherine Jordon Walker still has the tiny rocking chair that he made for her. Catherine Jordon Walker

Above right: Helen Russell Jordon. Her family was from Bristol Mills. She married Will's son, Frank Jordon, and they raised their four daughters in the house that Will Jordon had built on the west side of Christmas Cove. Catherine Jordon Walker

SEEMS AS THOUGH everybody came to our house. We had an extra room off the living room that they called the playroom because it was too small to use for anything else. My father had put up a blackboard on one wall from the bowling alley on Heron Island when they closed it, and we played school in there—it was just a nice place to play.

At our house, my father's sister played the piano and my father liked to sing—and that was part of the entertainment—something we did just 'cause it was fun. Everybody who felt like it could sing. And we would often make candy. Father enjoyed cooking; he liked doing things like that, and he was the one who usually got us started. We made pull candy—taffy—and fudge, and peppermint drops. They didn't last long—everybody ate it.

Catherine Jordon Walker

WILL JORDON was a man to match wits with anyone, in humor and homespun philosophy.

—Floyd Humphries, "Boyhood Memories"

HELEN JORDON was a devoted wife and mother, a lovely lady, cultivated in every way.

—Floyd Humphries, "Boyhood Memories"

SHE ALWAYS had crisp molasses cookies on hand, and thin sugar cookies. Whenever any children came to the house they always had some of her cookies. Children used to come over to our house a lot. We always had cookies on hand.

—Catherine Jordon Walker

FRANK JORDON became the first island caretaker and store keeper, the first and only Heron Island U.S. Postmaster. On the kitchen stove he dried a mixture of Prince Albert and Bull Durham tobaccos—for his constant companion, a pipe.

—Floyd Humphries, "Boyhood Memories"

Frank Jordon on the porch of the Heron Island store where he was caretaker, storekeeper, and postmaster for many years. CATHERINE JORDON WALKER

HE USED TO MAKE dandelion wine—he'd pay us kids a nickel for a bucket of dandelion blossoms. And elderberries. I think we used to go off in the boat on a Sunday. He had one of those one-cylinder—make-or-break they call it—engines, and he would take my mother and the children out to some of the off islands for all day to pick berries—elderberries and sometimes raspberries. She'd make jelly out of the raspberries and he must have made wine out of the elderberries. In the spring we'd all go out in the woods and he'd tap maple trees and boil the sap and make maple syrup.

Another thing I always remember ... my father was always making things for the children, like stilts and kites. He made the first pair of skis I ever had. He made whistles out of alder branches for boys—good things like that. And he not only made them for our family—he made them for all the children around—he liked doing things like that.

—Catherine Jordon Walker

"Wellie" and "Winnie"—Wellington and Winnifred Jordon, born 1891, twin son and daughter of Will and Loletta. Catherine Jordon Walker

Wellie Jordon on Heron Island. Wellie assisted his brother Frank in looking after Heron Island and its summer residents; the visitors would sometimes send the Jordons copies of the photographs they had taken. Catherine Jordon Walker

We loved Frank Jordon.
—Romilly Humphries, "Summer's End"

Wellie, Frank's younger brother, was a handsome young man with the physique and strength of a gorilla. He could carry alone, if necessary, a heavy trunk up two flights of stairs—for which feat he usually received as tip a good five cent cigar.

—Floyd Humphries, "Boyhood Memories"

This was my Uncle Wellington Jordon who died in World War I, and this is an old contraption that they built. Some kind of a little truck that they had down there on the island. That's quite a vehicle, isn't it? They must've made it out of old parts.

—Catherine Jordon Walker

My father's sister was quite a bit younger and was not married; she used to work in the hotels around here in the summer as a waitress; in the winter she worked somewhere else out of town.

—Catherine Jordon Walker

When my father was a little boy, my grandfather took him along to visit the old sea captain who lived in what's now the LaMond's house. When it came time to leave, the old man said, "Would you like to stay to dinner? We're having fried bellybuttons!" My father remembered it all of his life.

—Catherine Jordon Walker

The home of Mary Norwood Gamage, 1717–1821, on the "Neck," off the upper end of the S Road. The house was built sometime between 1795 and 1815.
Author photo, 1997

Mary Norwood Gamage's story is quite well known in South Bristol, possibly because it was told in Nelson W. Gamage's *Short History of South Bristol*. He described her as "a small but very active woman, intelligent and quick-witted; she had bright, black eyes and hair that never turned gray. Her mind yielded to the touch of time a few years before her death, but her bodily usefulness remained to the last."

There was a Norwood woman buried in South Bristol, over on the Neck. She came to South Bristol and married Nathaniel Gamage. Some ancestors in England died and left quite an estate; Nathaniel Gamage headed to England to sort out what he had coming, when he was quite a young man, and he disappeared and they never saw him again. And they believe—at that time the British were impressing people in press gangs for labor on the sail vessels—they thought that he might of got kidnapped.

Mary Gamage was over a hundred years old when she died, and her hair was just as black—her hair never turned white. They say her mind went at the last of it, and she'd sit and mend on Nathaniel's clothes. Of course he'd been gone fifty years. She used to say she had to get his clothes ready 'cause Nathaniel was coming back.

—Ralph Norwood

The children of Skipper Tom and his wife "Waty" Thompson.
MARGARET FARRIN HOUSE

"SKIPPER TOM" GAMAGE, a great-grandson of Mary Norwood Gamage, was born in South Bristol in 1794. He, and the schooner he built there, were well known in both the fisheries and the coasting trade.

The children of Skipper Tom and his wife Waitstill Thompson: Standing, left to right: Thomas W., also a sea captain, and sometime owner of Gem Island; Asa, a seafarer; Albion and Menzies, owners of the famous shipyard; Lebbeus, grandfather of Harvey Gamage; and Nelson, Civil War veteran and later the proprietor of the Summit House and a village general store, and author of South Bristol's only published history. Seated are Margaret Gamage Norwood, left; and Ellen, right. The empty chair is for their sister Hannah, who had died in 1876. Waty was seventeen years old when their first child, Thomas, was born; when their youngest, Nelson, was born, she was forty-one.

"Skipper Tom" Gamage, 1794–1877.
MARGARET FARRIN HOUSE

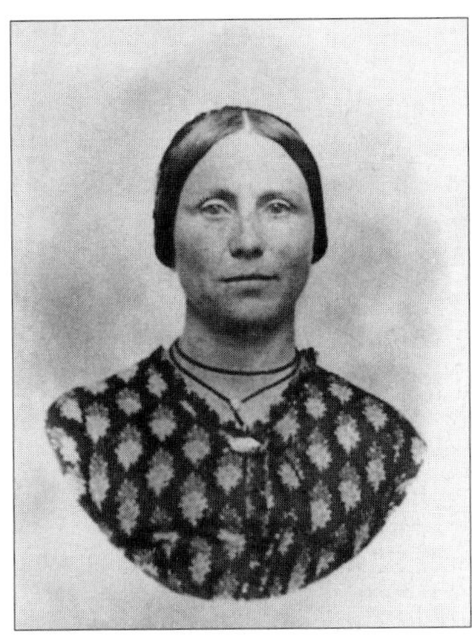

Margaret Gamage Norwood, 1821–1910, one of Skipper Tom's children. When her first husband Davis Gamage died, she returned to Jones Cove and supported her children and herself as a seamstress. She maintained this independence even after her marriage to Jonathan Norwood. MARGARET FARRIN HOUSE

Jonathan Norwood, born 1813; an independent spirit. MARGARET FARRIN HOUSE

WHEN HER first husband died, after he come home from the sea, her brothers took dories and went over to Pemaquid and loaded the lumber that he had gotten to build them a house. They took it back to Jones Cove and used it to build an addition on to Skipper Tom's house, and then she lived there.

She was a seamstress—that's how she made her living while Jonathan was off roaming. After her father died she continued to live in his house, but she was so far out of the way she thought it was too far for people to come out from town, so she swapped the house for one on the West Side Road. And that house was moved on a scow to where it is now at the head of Long Cove. In those days the land was open, and they say she could see people coming all the way up on Kid Hill, all the way from her house there on the West Side Road. She'd go out and butcher a chicken, dress it, put it in to cook, and when the people got there it would be ready to eat. They'd stay there all day while she worked on their dresses.

He was a wanderer. He peddled wares from a boat; he'd go off, then come back. Margaret would mend his clothes for him, and he'd go off again. He played the fiddle and the jew's harp. He'd swim, and he'd make Margaret go out and do exercises—people thought that kind of stuff was odd back then, but Nannie Pierce used to say he was just way ahead of his time. —Margaret Farrin House

THE NORWOOD family of four brothers originally lived on the east bank of the Damariscotta River. They were all quite eccentric and each had some peculiar trait that predominated his life. Three of them made "hawkin'," or peddling, their leading vocation, though any of them could build a boat, stock a gun, or mend a clock or watch. Jonathan, later called "the Hermit Boatman of House Island" in Portland harbor, was a picturesque dancer. In his early days he operated a little boat around the harbors of Lincoln County, selling various wares and dancing at all the entertainments.

—Harold Castner, "The Castner Papers"

Eben[ezer] C. Poole, 1806–96, was the one who put the "e" onto the Poole name. Sitting on his lap is his grandson, Sam Poole's son James. When Eben married Martha Plummer, he gained land from the Plummer family; the Poole farm then stretched all the way from the Damariscotta River on the west to the shore of Wurlin's, or Wurling's, Bay on the east.
KATHERINE POOLE NORWOOD

THIS DEED OF 1881, passing the family homestead from Eben Poole to his son Everett, is typical of many of the era, whereby children gained possession of the family property and at the same time assured their parents of care and living quarters for the balance of their lives. Such deeds were often specific in their terms.

DEED

Know all men by these present that I, Everett Poole of Bristol, in the county of Lincoln, State of Maine and held and firmly bound to Eben Poole and Martha Poole of said Bristol in the sum of $3,000 to be paid to said Eben Poole and Martha Poole or their attorney for which payment to be made, I bind myself, my heirs, executors and administrators firmly to these present. Sealed with my seal, dated the tenth day of October 1881.

The condition of this obligation is such that if the said Everett A. Poole shall during the natural life of Eben Poole and Martha Poole suitably support and maintain the said Eben and Martha and provide them with suitable clothes, food, drink, medicine and nursing, and all other things necessary in the house of the said Everett Poole or in such suitable house which said Everett A. Poole may provide and live in himself, and allow them the northwest rooms, northeast entry, and bedrooms adjoining the same, the use in common of the front entry and the firewood and fire by themselves if requested by either said Eben or Martha Poole. Then this obligation shall be void, otherwise shall remain in full force.

Signed and sealed, delivered in the presence of Thomas Thompson, Justice of the Peace and signed by Everett Poole.

EBEN AND MARTHA Poole lived there, in the two back rooms of the house, until they died.

When Sam Poole was a boy, he was carrying hot coals from the family house to be used in starting a fire at the smokehouse. He dropped some live embers onto the floor of the house and it burned to the ground.

Samuel Poole, born in 1841, one of Eben and Martha's sons. The house, which may have been built by Bedfield Plummer as early as 1763, burned in 1850.
KATHERINE POOLE NORWOOD

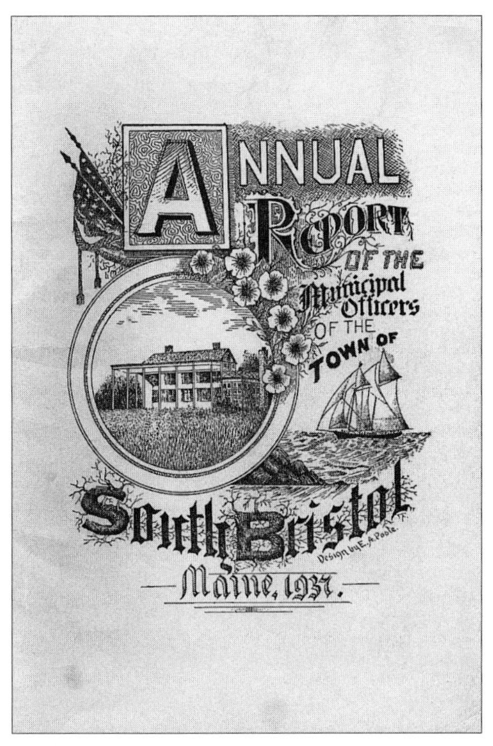

Cover of the *South Bristol Town Report, 1937*. Many in South Bristol fondly remember this design, which for years graced the covers of the town report. By 1937 Everett Poole had been South Bristol's town clerk for twenty-two years, the only clerk since the town's incorporation in 1915. South Bristol Historical Society

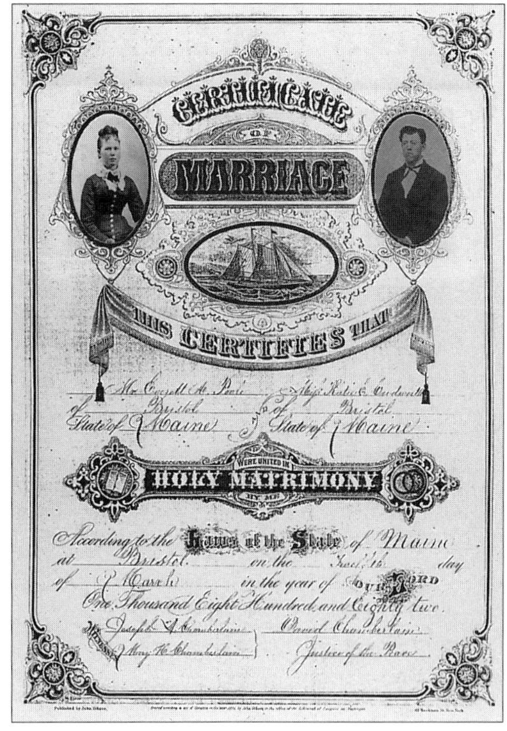

Marriage certificate of Everett Poole and Katie (Katherine) Cudworth. The ornate script that records the names and dates is in Everett's own hand. Katherine Poole Norwood

Everett Poole was South Bristol's first town clerk, and a skilled calligrapher of wide repute. In work ranging from calling cards to his own marriage certificate, his designs were a combination of script and decorative elements.

I remember him doing his work in the living room when we were little. We had to be really careful not to run through the dining room where he was working, 'cause you know, it was real fine work. He did it on the dining room table, and then he had an easel. He used wooden pens, that you'd put a pen point in. You had to shove the point up in, then he dipped it into an inkwell. And he did have a nice desk when he was town clerk, all these pigeonholes and a rolltop.

—Katherine Poole Norwood

Orris McFarland, 1858–1943, in the doorway of his fishing camp on Long Cove Point.
NELLIE MCFARLAND FREY

Henry, 1887–1975, and his sister Elsie McFarland.
NELLIE MCFARLAND FREY

MY FATHER'S FATHER *used to live with us in the wintertime. He had a camp right up on the river—a beautiful place down on the point just this side of Long Cove. He was a fisherman, you know, lobsterman, and just caught all kinds of fish. He had a camp down there and I used to love to go up there and visit him. My favorite aunt lived right across the cove there from him. And my mother and my aunt used to take turns on Saturday nights baking beans and making biscuit and brown bread and stuff like that, for my grandfather, and I would take it up to him when it was my mother's turn. I would take the baked beans and stuff up to him. And then, he couldn't live there in his camp in the wintertime, 'cause it was too cold, so part of the winter he would live with my aunt, other times he lived down with us. Orris McFarland. He was a good old fella.* —Nellie McFarland Frey

THAT'S MY FATHER *and that's his sister Aunt Elsie. That would have been about 1890. And see, the boys wore dresses then. When my oldest kids were born they were still putting dresses on little boys, until they got a little older. When my second boy was born—well, my first one, too—his baby picture, Jim's baby picture has a dress on. And they would wear long stockings and high shoes. See, both of those got high boots, high shoes on. And they used to wear, what did they call them—I know the girls wore them and I imagine the boys wore the same thing—they had these "waists," they called them, and they had buttons and they'd button on to here and they were long, almost like bloomers, kind of, with lace on the bottom.*

—Nellie McFarland Frey

Alice Dodge McFarland, 1889–1971. A masterful hand at needlework, cooking, and gardening, Alice McFarland was a mainstay of the Ladies' Aid and Pogonia Chapter, Eastern Star. NELLIE MCFARLAND FREY

Henry McFarland, in his later years.
NELLIE MCFARLAND FREY

THEY USED TO have a nice vegetable garden out back of the house, and Mama used to have beautiful flower gardens. She always planted from seeds. She used to save nasturtium seeds over from one year to the next. They used to come up just as nice second or third or fourth year. She always planted sweetpeas. Oh, she had beautiful sweetpeas, and nasturtiums, and asters, just everything. Beautiful rose bushes. She had beautiful gardens.

—Nellie McFarland Frey

FATHER WAS A carpenter—built our house and a lot of cottages down on the east side of the Cove. They always called him first-class carpenter. He'd be astonished at some of the wages people get now. I can remember when he would get eighteen dollars a week, and that was good pay.

—Nellie McFarland Frey

FRANKFORT OCT. 15TH 1846
Dear Wife—
I take this opportunity of addressing you and by the way let you know my health is good hopeing yours is the same.

We arrived here on 12th and are now discharged—tomorrow we should commens loading with lumber for Boston. I have had rather a hard cruise since I left home—if the wind is unfavorable we shall com in hom when bound to Boston if we do not I shall quit in Boston as I do not feel perfectly reconciled to my situation.

Last evening I was at capt. Sprowls. they are all well.

Mrs. C is on board she come on board at east Tomastown and I suppose will remain untill we com in hom or go to Boston probably we may leave here next sunday. If we do not call in write me at Boston. Today I feel rather low in spirits a little homesick with all—but close as I cannot think of much to write. So I remaine your husband
Wm. McFarland Jr

WILLIAM MCFARLAND, JR., who was born in 1807 and died at sea in 1848, established another branch of the McFarland family on McFarland's Cove Road. He was the father of Abbie Jane, Leander, Bainbridge, and of William Addison McFarland, patriarch of the boatbuilding dynasty, whose sons later moved to Christmas Cove.

Frankfort — Oct 15th 1846
Dear Wife
I take this opportunity of addressing you
and by the way let you know my health
is good hoping yours is the same.
We arrived here on 12th and are now
discharged - tomorrow we shall commens
loading with lumber for Boston
I have had rather a harde cruise since I
left home — if the wind is unfavourable
we shall com in hom when bound to Boston
if we do not I shall quit in Boston as I
do not feel perfectly reconciled to my situation
last evening I was at capt [illegible] they
are all well
Mrs Cox is on Board she come on boards
at east Tomastown and I suppose will
remain untill we com in hom or go to Boston
probably we may leave here next sunday
if we do not call in write me at Boston
to day I feel rather low in spirits & a little homesick
with all — but close as I cannot think of much
with. So I remaine your Husband
Wm Mc Farland Jr

Letter from William McFarland, Jr., to his wife Caroline Foster. The text is on the previous page. Margaret Farrin House

William Addison and Annie Young McFarland, 1844–1946, in front of their McFarland's Cove farmhouse. Annie, born on Matinicus Island, lived to be 102 years old. Cassie H. Manchester Trust

When I was a kid, after school we'd go over and talk to her. Gee, she could tell you some awful stories. She could go back, her mind was just as good, you know. Set in a wheelchair there the last of it, but she could tell you stories—boy, I'm telling you. —Mervin Rice

The houses of the feuding brothers, William and Frank Y. McFarland, shown as summer boardinghouses about 1905. "Rock Ridge," left, was owned by William and his wife Flora French; Frank Y.'s house, "Salana," on the right, is still occupied by the McFarland family. DOUGLAS THOMPSON

THERE WERE *two brothers who lived right across the road from each other and they say they didn't speak to each other for years and years. In those days there were a lot of feuds. I always heard it was the wife—she had kind of a temper. She was kind of a spitfire, I guess, and she didn't get along with the other side of the road. She never had a good word for anybody. They used to say that the other ones taught their cats to go on the other side of the road.* —Adele McFarland

THEY ALWAYS *fought one another; they could never get along. One wouldn't speak to that one, that one wouldn't speak to the next one, that's the way they lived. And their mother lived in on the McFarland Cove Road there, and she lived to be a hundred and two or three years old. And they couldn't go visit her—one to a time had to go 'cause they didn't speak to one another and they'd fight, so only one could go. Then when he'd gone, the other one could go. That went on for years.*

—Mervin Rice

WHEN MEDORA *became ill, my father had been living with Willard and Medora, and she gave the baby to Arletta to raise for Willard when she died. And then Willard married Abbie Jane, and I don't think my father ever lived with his father except maybe in one of the two Clifford houses.*

—Arletta Thorpe Rice

Medora Clifford Thorp, 1847–1891, daughter of another old Rutherford Island family, the Cliffords. ARLETTA THORPE RICE

Willard Thorpe and his Aunt Arletta at the old Thorp homestead in Christmas Cove, probably about 1895. The little boy seated in front is Arthur Wells, son of Captain Frank Wells.
Arletta Thorpe Rice

Willard N. Thorpe, Medora's son, and his bride-to-be, Kathleen Geyer, about the time of their marriage in 1909. Arletta Thorpe Rice

ARLETTA WAS *a spinster. I don't really know what she did, except take care of Willard, but as soon as the first summer people came she became one of the boardinghouses, also. Obviously she was a spinster and didn't have much of a life as we look at life now, but she must have done her duty.*

He was pretty young when he left Arletta. I don't think he had much care taken of him. She was John's daughter, a real old maid—I don't think they called him "Bill" when he lived with Aunt Arletta. —Arletta Thorpe Rice

I BELIEVE *that he first met her at the hotel over here, the Holly Inn; that's how they met, with all the young people who were working at the inns here. He rowed a boat of some kind to Pemaquid to court her, and when he would go back and forth to Pemaquid Harbor to see her he took her chocolate-covered almonds. And when they were out spooning one night they sat down by a tree. She leaned back and she got pitch in her hair, and it was awful because in those days they wore the big pompadours and the rats, as they called them, to hold the pompadours up and she had a terrible time shampooing her hair after that.*

—Arletta Thorpe Rice

Albert C. Thorp, 1853–1928, known fondly as "Dud" to his family, and his wife Emily Hatch, 1858–1929, known as "Empy." ARLETTA THORPE RICE

SHE ALWAYS *wore long skirts. And when she met someone on the road she swung her hand up in greeting but she didn't say hello or good morning. She said, "That that!" That's what she said, "That that." Meaning—nothing. Nobody knew what she meant.*

As I remember him, he was sort of a gentle man. He did his work outside, but not vigorously. But of course he was old then, as you can see from the picture. —Arletta Thorpe Rice

Jonathan P. Thorp, 1844–1872. Arletta Thorpe Rice

The brothers John and Eliphalet Thorp came to Christmas Cove in 1829. They bought all the land from the Bar south and gradually established an entire fleet of fishing schooners, kept a general store, and sold salt-preserved fish to the Boston market. Their sheep and cows were pastured all the way down to the point. Bristol valuation books show that as late as 1885, they still owned 172 acres on Rutherford Island.

A WPA abstract in the Maine Maritime Museum shows that Eliphalet Thorp was part owner of the 64-ton schooner Solon in 1835; by 1842 he and his brother John were sole owners, with Eliphalet listed as master. In the decades following they had a fleet of schooners, employing scores of men, but by 1870 were reduced to eight men on two vessels.

For many years, John and his brother Eliphalet Thorp had sent out their fleet of schooners to the Grand Banks for cod fishing and had an enterprise that employed about all the men in the nearby community, but then, on account of Gloucester's foreign-manned boats, these Maine fishermen were crowded out of the business. They were hard hit, and all the sons and neighbors of the Thorps sailed on their boats. All the schooners were sold, except one, the Twilight, which floated several years at the wharf, 'til one day, her sails were brought out from storage, and were hoisted by strange men, perhaps from Gloucester, and she too sailed away.

—Henry M. Seaver
in a letter to his nephew, 1937

They always told me it was the Portuguese fishermen that drove them out of business—from lower down—you know, Massachusetts.

—Arletta Thorpe Rice

Eliphalet and Elizabeth's son Jonathan may have been one of many of the Thorps and their neighbors to venture out to the banks fishing. Born on Washington's birthday in 1844, he died at the age of twenty-eight. The inscription on his tombstone is typical of the time:

Dear as thou wert,
and justly dear
We would not weep for thee
One thought shall check
the starting tear
It is thou that art free.

I hope we shall not have no more bull runs & Fredericksburg fights….

—Albert Hatch

Nathan C. Hodgdon, 1824–92, Co. I, 21st Regiment Maine Volunteers. In this image, probably taken about 1885, Hodgdon sits with his granddaughter Lena Kelsey. EUGENIE WOODWARD COLE

Oliver B. Spear, c. 1909. 1842–1925, 2nd Maine Battery. MARIAN COUGHLIN

NATHAN HODGDON was already in his late thirties when the Civil War broke out, but volunteered nevertheless. When Lincoln's "first call" for volunteers came, many Walpole men quickly enlisted, regardless of age or physical condition.

THE QUOTE ABOVE is from a letter written by Albert Hatch to his parents in Walpole, January 1863. One-quarter of all the federal troops in the first Battle of Bull Run were from the state of Maine, and many were casualties in that terrible conflict.

Albert Hatch, 1834–1914, 20th Maine Volunteers.
PHILLIP HATCH

ALBERT HATCH returned from the war with a Purple Heart, and became a pillar of the Walpole community, serving as postmaster for a time and operating a successful brickyard on the banks of the Damariscotta River. His letters home to his wife Helen, excerpted here, begin at Camp King outside of Portland and continue through the months following the Battle of Antietam on September 17, 1862.

Portland
August 13/62

DEAR HELEN as I have time I shall write to you I am in the tent in camp King on the old race coars it is a butiful place and we enjoy it much. The 17th regiment is hear and they had a good meeting last night and we shall have some soon i hope we tent 5 in a squad and I have prayers Jok Ford & Hig Herbert, Enoch, Ed Umphrey, and I tent together I wood like to get a pass today to go over to the city it is about a mile and a half I heard Planey was coming over tomorrow to pay the town bounty to us We have not been examined yet The sergeon is sick and cant but their will another come soon and we shall hav to try the test I am glad that I enlisted becus every one who is able to cary a gun will be drafted soon 2 more days and enlisting is over with them It is a butiful morning and Drums are beating up lively write all the news you can think of you may find a letter in the offis writ the 12th direct I think to Box 2171 pleas direct to Box 2171 & 20 regiment PO.E. that I think will come safe Tim fitch is hear to cary this home to you cis Crofford for me just now will you I wish I had more cloths for I cant tell when we shall be uniformed the 17th is not more than half uniformed yet so it will be some time before we shall be.

YOURS TRULY
A. HATCH

Arlington
Sept 9th/62

DEAR WIFE I feel it a pleasure to sit hear on my knapsack to write a few lines to let you know that I am well or better of my cold my head is dizzy yet. It is a rainy day hear for the first rainy day we hav had since we left Portland Well Helen I will tell you how we tent hear we have rubber blankets & to of us tak them & make a tent like the roof of a house it is about 6 ft long & 4 ft wide & 3 ft from the ground to the rigpole which rests on to crutched ones about 3 ft high & hear I am on the ground with my knapsack for a seat. Well that will do for that our boys went out yesterday for some water & found one of Jeffs Pills that he fired a twenty four pounder yesterday I was on gard. We are on the advancd line their is a Rifle pit right in front of us We moved day before yesterday about a quarter of a mile we can see the white house from hear wich is about six miles to the east Noth east from hear the Rebels are concentrating above & some think they will cross over into Maryland Gen Mclenen had got a forse of 250 thousands he will give a charge of Abes pills I hope and drive them into the bag & take Stone Wall. We are strongly fortifide as I wrote you before with forts & rifle pits we expected contact night before last but they went up by us they would throw rockets up as their was two brigades so as to keep in hail of each other I think we shall not be atacted hear because we are so strongly fortifide a man told who belongs to the secont Maine regt that it is as strong as it is at richmond he said he has ben in eight battles & onley gained one the last battle of bull run was an offle one Mcdowell had I think 120 thou and Jackson 70. Oh he is a bad man I fear. I want you to give my love to Father & Mother & horace and ciss baby every day for me I want you to keep up good spirits for I trust the Lord will bring me back in the corse of 1 or 2 years we may stay hear to or three months or more we shall be attached to Porters Core under Gen Mclenan I expect I have wrote you this makes three times since I got to Washington & want you to write me how many letters you receive from me

I will write againe how to direct to me for fear you do not get them & for fear they wer not right back them as follows till further orders. Washington D C. Co. E. 20th Me. Regt. Vol.

YOUR TRUE FRIEND & HUSBAND
ALBERT HATCH

I WANT YOU to excuse my bad writing and spelling. We have heard that Gen Jackson is in Pensilvina our tents are come just now

Battlefield
Sept 18th 1862

DEAR WIFE I will write a few lines to let you know that I am well & Enoch is not very well he got his hands poisond som at arlington hights and marching so far it het his blood & yesterday he went to the hospittle Tom Foster & the rest of the boys are well except John Pool We stayed back under the hills at the rear of the battle it was an oful one our force drove them its som whear above harpers ferry I saw Gen Mclenan yesterday I have not received any letters since I left Portland I got Enochs last night & opened it I cant find out whear to send it yet I think he will be back in the ranks again in a few days you will get the nuse about the battle & particulars as soon as I shall it has ben a glorious victory anyhow as near as I know I want you to write two sheets in a letter & write often this makes five letters I have writ since I left Portland & have received none I got one the night before I left Portland I have to write on my cartriage bocks sitting on the ground I think you must have received but the post office is so far you can't get them Enoch is better so Laine Fitch tells me he is over the hill I must cary this letter to him it seems to be quyet this morning I must close

YOUR FAITHFUL HUSBAND
ALBERT HATCH

Sept 27th, 1862
Near Sharpsburg

Dear wife
It is with great pleasure I take my pencil to write a few lines to you, this is a very fine saturday after noon I hav ben washing my shirt & Stockings & hav them drying hear on my tent I think it look a little like rain. I hope it will not rain much before we get into winter quarters. when it duz rain here it rains all the time most & is very muddy we have all got the dirhear i have got some better and I crave for something good to eat & I cant help bying some cheas & cakes of the butter sometimes for we dont get nothing but coffee & hard bread fresh beef and salt pork we have not had one potato since we came to washington nor any fish nor tea nor brown bread well we shall have to make the best of it.

Trusting in the God of battles for a Speedy settlement with the south acording to the constitution. I think I can say that religion is good here & of a truth we need it here. O the sin that is in the army. the people ought to fast and pray for a Speedy Settlement with the south you must pray for me in earnest & tell Father & Mother to, give my love to them & tell them I hope to see them in a few weeks Tell Horace to be a good boy & write to me soon & I will thank him a thousand times. you dont know what pleas it gives me to get letters from you I love to read whear you write about little Crofford tell him I love him & tell I think of him every day this paper is about played out I will write some more tomorrow

Antietam Md
Oct 18th/62

We was on picket Sunday night & it rained but we had a barn to lay in as providence would hav it. we are on picket today & my post is up on a hill to look over the river to see that the rebs dont come in a force on us. it is a pleasant place their is but four of us up hear the rest is down by the river or under the hill.

US Army Hospital
Stewart's Mansion, Md
Jan 7/63

Thair wer three died here last Sunday in the hospital & one of the indiana men was shot by one of the gards of a conneticut regt the man had his pass but did not halt as soon as bade to the bulet went right through his stomach & he is alive yet and may live but no thanks to a green sentinal who don it

Frank Farrin, 1848–1916 2nd Regiment, Maine Cavalry. Lynne Drisko

Frank Farrin enlisted in 1863, and served for two years before being mustered out in November 1865.

The granite Civil War monument for which John Goudy successfully sought contributions. It stands in Walpole's West Bristol cemetery, in sight of the school that gave seventeen students and a teacher to the war effort. A paper, "Bristol in the Civil War," in the possession of Eugenie W. Cole asserts that, "... it is apparent that almost every [Walpole] man who was able, was in service...." Author photo, 1998

The European War, as it was referred to in South Bristol, stirred the town's deep feelings of patriotism. In 1918 a town hall celebration of South Bristol's recent incorporation reflected the fervor: refreshments, flowers, and tokens were sold to raise money for the Red Cross; the crowd joined in as renditions of patriotic songs were led from the stage. In the *Damariscotta Herald*, a front page article related:

Off at one side the delightful game of "hit the kaiser" was in progress and many relieved their feelings by plugging the ugly visage most successfully. This satisfactory sport brought the Red Cross some fifteen dollars or more. Horace Kelsey was the general in charge of the attack.

Miss Lasker came to the front and with enthusiasm sang a number of war songs in which all the people who knew them joined. Miss Lasker's vigor and "pep" in singing charmed everybody into singing, "Over There," "Pack Up Your Troubles in Your Old Kit Bag," and "I'm On My Way to Berlin."

Mention should be made of the effectiveness of Mrs. Ropes' song, "Keep the Home Fires Burning."

Graves of Civil War soldiers: "It has passed away like a dream." Many lines from an 1887 essay were brought to mind by this November scene in the Rutherford Island cemetery. "… the first snows of winter whiten the graves of those who wore the blue and those who wore the gray…." "… wondering whether perchance they might not lie, colder than ice, with calm faces set for eternity, under the snow…." AUTHOR PHOTO, 1997

SOUTH BRISTOL lost two young men in the First World War, both of them from Christmas Cove. Richard Rundlett Wells, son of Captain Frank Wells, was a student at the University of Maine when he enlisted in the Navy and was commissioned as an ensign. He was an officer on board the USS TICONDEROGA when she was torpedoed by a German submarine. Wellington Jordon was one of the thousands of soldiers who died from influenza without ever having left American soil.

MY UNCLE WELLIE died of the flu at Fort Devens during the epidemic of 1918. There's a bronze plaque on a boulder in front of the Union Church to commemorate him. The marker changed the name of the road to Wellington Road, but people still call it the Middle Road.

—Catherine Jordon Walker

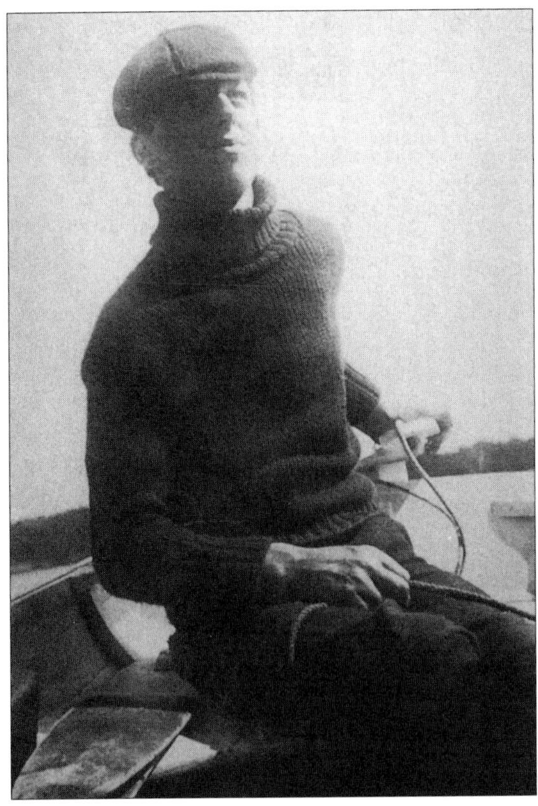

Wellington Jordon, 1891–1918. Co. M, 74th U.S. Infantry. CATHERINE JORDON WALKER

IN 1918 HALF a million Americans died from influenza. That year, more soldiers died of the flu than on the battlefield. According to one account, they got the sniffles one day, and were often dead the next.

Lewis Stanley Alley, Jr. ELIZABETH ALLEY HOUSE

LEWIS STANLEY ALLEY, "Junior," was the only soldier from South Bristol who lost his life in World War II. He was buried where he fell, in Holland.

I WAS ELEVEN years old then. We used to come home for lunch every day—the school was right up here, you know. The minute I walked in the house I knew something was wrong. We had a woodbox built into the corner of the living room, and I remember clear as day: Mama was in the woodbox. They sent a telegram, and then later someone came out from the War Department. I'll never forget it. —Elizabeth Alley House

War time Song of 1916
1

Oh! This is a brave loyal Country
When you butt up against us look out
We can lick all Thats set befor us
And we'll put the hun to rout
= 2 =

Oh we are not boasting or bragging
We are telling you only whats true
For we are the good old Yankee's
And our flag is the red, white And blue
= 3 =

Oh we are the boys with the Courage,
The spirit that nothing can kill
We'll make you set up and take Notice
And swallow Each nice little pill
= 4 =

Now if you dont wish to get damaged
Would like to see daylight once more
Come off with your hat dont act insane
When Sammie is passing your door.
Lura E Holman

1920

"War Time Song of 1916," from the notebook of Lura Holman, who lived with the Rapelyes on Clark's Cove Road. Mervin Rice

This lookout tower, photographed in 1943, was high atop a hill on Rutherford Island where civilian spotters could look out across John's Bay to the sea.
MARGARET FARRIN HOUSE

THIS WAS THE *lookout during World War II. Volunteers went there, and it looked right over onto the ocean. We watched and we reported if any planes come over, and submarines. If we saw any out there we reported it to an office in Brunswick. We saw B-24s, and the bombers, and we had to identify them. We think they were all our own, but you never know. And we would see a lot of whales also come up and spout. We had powerful binoculars to watch.* —Margaret Farrin House

AFTER GERMANS *were supposedly found coming ashore at Mt. Desert, they would have patrols here all night, ride 'round and around the island with the car lights off to discover anyone who might have come ashore. I would sometimes go with my father on the 3:00-6:00 A.M. shift.*

Two maids from Europe, working for summer people, became especially anxious about the idea of Nazis appearing in John's Bay. Mackerel fishing near shore with seines and lights sent them into a real panic. —Arletta Thorpe Rice

IN WORLD WAR II *we had to have these ration books. Each member in the family had to have one. You'd take it up to the grocery store and there were coupons they'd tear off for sugar and meat and butter. You'd be glad when the next book came. You'd run short. You had to be careful, you know. You'd only get them once a month.*

—Katherine Poole Norwood

BEFORE THEN, *not many people left home to do anything, but when the war came almost everybody did. Lots of people went away then to either work in the shipyard or be in the service.*

—Arletta Thorpe Rice

DURING THE LAST *part of the war, when we first moved to South Bristol, we were on Ram Island—my dad was the keeper down on Ram Island Light. My father and my brother and myself rowed our dory in from Ram Island into Christmas Cove early in the morning and walked up the road to the house behind the S Road Schoolhouse. That's where we owned, and we were getting it ready to move into. And so we worked on the house all day, and all day long—we'd anchored the dory down Christmas Cove—and all day long the army, and the sheriff's department, and the state*

INSTRUCTIONS

1 This book is valuable. Do not lose it.

2 Each stamp authorizes you to purchase rationed goods in the quantities and at the times designated by the Office of Price Administration. Without the stamps you will be unable to purchase those goods.

3 Detailed instructions concerning the use of the book and the stamps will be issued. Watch for those instructions so that you will know how to use your book and stamps. Your Local War Price and Rationing Board can give you full information.

4 Do not throw this book away when all of the stamps have been used, or when the time for their use has expired. You may be required to present this book when you apply for subsequent books.

Rationing is a vital part of your country's war effort. Any attempt to violate the rules is an effort to deny someone his share and will create hardship and help the enemy.

This book is your Government's assurance of your right to buy your fair share of certain goods made scarce by war. Price ceilings have also been established for your protection. Dealers must post these prices conspicuously. Don't pay more.

Give your whole support to rationing and thereby conserve our vital goods. Be guided by the rule:

"If you don't need it, DON'T BUY IT."

16—32209-1 ☆ U. S. GOVERNMENT PRINTING OFFICE : 1943

UNITED STATES OF AMERICA
OFFICE OF PRICE ADMINISTRATION

538323 EW

WAR RATION BOOK No. 3 *Void if altered*

NOT VALID WITHOUT STAMP

Identification of person to whom issued: PRINT IN FULL

Ralph P Spier
(First name) (Middle name) (Last name)

Street number or rural route 1 (Res: Durham)

City or post office Auburn State Maine

AGE	SEX	WEIGHT	HEIGHT	OCCUPATION
15	Male	1?0 Lbs.	5 Ft. 2 In.	Farming (At Home)

SIGNATURE Ralph P. Spier
(Person to whom book is issued. If such person is unable to sign because of age or incapacity, another may sign in his behalf.)

WARNING

This book is the property of the United States Government. It is unlawful to sell it to any other person, or to use it or permit anyone else to use it, except to obtain rationed goods in accordance with regulations of the Office of Price Administration. Any person who finds a lost War Ration Book must return it to the War Price and Rationing Board which issued it. Persons who violate rationing regulations are subject to $10,000 fine or imprisonment, or both.

OPA Form No. R-130

LOCAL BOARD ACTION

Issued by .... (Local board number) (Date)

Street address ....

City .... State ....

.... (Signature of issuing officer)

Book # 4.

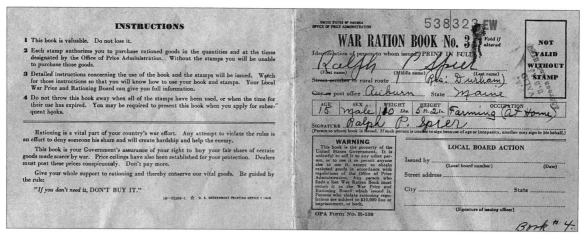

World War II ration book. AUTHOR'S COLLECTION

police were going up and down the road with sirens, you know—a lot of commotion. And we never thought much of it.

We had to leave in the middle of the afternoon to get back to the lighthouse because my father had to light the light before dark. So we headed down the road again walking, and this deputy sheriff stopped us and asked who we were—'cause we were strangers in town, see—asked who we were, where we were going, where we'd been. So Father explained it all out to him. The sheriff said, "Well, you can't go any further. We've been looking for you people all day." He says, "We got a report that Nazi spies had landed in Christmas Cove." In a dory! And the funny thing is, in the stern of that dory on the inside was a little bronze plate that said, "This dory property of the U.S. Coast Guard" and a number on it that identified it. And nobody bothered all day to look in the dory and see anything about it. And Father said, "I can't. I've got to get back and light that light. I can't go with you." So the sheriff gave up on him 'cause he refused. And we had an article in the paper—"South Bristol Spies"! —Ralph Norwood

It's changed, all right.
—Robert Woodward

This artist's rendering of the new Wawenock Club was made into a postcard, and also illustrated an August 1926 article in the *Lincoln County News* describing the club's gala opening. William A. Kelsey

All those windows on the north side, and that dining room, was added on. The roof in front, those tall pillars up the front of it—when we lived there, they only went up one story.

The rooms inside haven't been changed. As you go in off the front porch, the one to the right was our parlor. The organ was in there, and the good furniture was in there. On a Sunday, if they wanted to do singing or anything, that's where they gathered. Next room below it was a living room. Then there was a little room off that was a bedroom. If anybody was sick they always slept in there, down near the kitchen. A great big kitchen was in there. And back then there was an open shed which you'd use in the summertime for cooking, to keep the house cooler. Upstairs of that is where a locker room is now. One of the bedrooms upstairs, that my brother and I always slept in, a smaller bedroom, that is a shower room for the ladies today. We had a stove out in the kitchen, and then the living room had a big heater stove in there, with wood. There was a fireplace in the parlor but I don't think we ever used it in our time. As long as my folks lived there they always heated the place with the two stoves. —Robert Woodward

In a place like South Bristol, the history and the character of the town is rooted in its houses as surely as in the people and the landscape. Some buildings have been lovingly restored while others abide under layers of "improvements"—indications of endurance as well as of change. Tales told about a few of these have become part of the local lore.

Before becoming the Wawenock Country Club in 1926, the house and farm were the homeplace of Robert Woodward's grandfather, William T. Kelsey—the same Kelsey who had run the town poorhouse—and his wife Sarah Hodgdon. The house was built in the 1840s by William's father Samuel Kelsey, a well-known Walpole shipbuilder. Owned in the 1870s by Edward, another of Samuel Kelsey's sons, it was sold to William and Sarah in 1892. By the time of William's death in 1911, their daughter Angie was living on the Gut in South Bristol, married to Robert H. Woodward. With their little son Robert K., the Woodwards moved to the farmhouse to take care of Angie's mother.

Remember the old house up the west side of the hill that we used to call the haunted house? We just named it haunted because it was a rundown old house; I mean, it was old, and they were decrepit when they were empty. Us kids would walk up there and we'd get close together—hug each other. Oh, it was scary, you know, and there was no street lights then. You know, now you're lit up a little bit, but the way it was then you had to, oh, hang on to each other and go!

—Beatrice Plummer Rice

The Solomon Cavis house, on the West Side Road, Rutherford Island. Author photo, 1997

The Cornell's art colony building, as it stood—and still stands—on a spit of land that forms the western shore of Long Cove. J. Douglas Thompson

The Solomon Cavis house was built in the 1820s. Early in the twentieth century it stood empty for many years, and earned the nickname "Ghost House." After the death of his wife, one of the later residents bricked up one of the chimneys to keep evil spirits away.

Long Cove Point made out on the edge of Long Cove from the West Side Road. There was a house there, an old Cape, and there was a building out there that was used by Charles Cornell and his sister as a art colony. They used to have people come there for the summer and study art. That building was built by Morris Hall around 1908 from plans by A. G. Randall. —Doug Thompson

A SUMMER RESIDENT, now in his eighties, gleefully tells stories of boyhood spying from his parents' cottage across the Gut on the Shipyard Road—the art students often went skinny-dipping.

MRS. CORNELL OWNED IT. *I worked for her—I used to go over and lug water for them after school. They had a black cook, and I used to go over there—for a quarter a night—after school and lug water from a well they had up the road a little ways, drinking water. And I always got a piece of pie or something out of it from the cook—she was a nice old girl.* —Bill Kelsey

The Davis house. This photograph is undated, but what appear to be bird cages on the table at left have a decidedly Victorian look to them.
MARGARET FARRIN HOUSE

SOMETIMES REFERRED TO as the Davis House, John Otis built this house in the 1820s for his daughter Mary Ann and her husband Samuel Davis; it is one of the earliest houses on Rutherford Island. It remained in the same family for 130 years.

Robert Merrill's Federal-style house; James Sproul II moved it to its present location in 1833. From this angle, the ell of Robert Sproul's attached Cape is blocked from view by the larger portion of the house.
AUTHOR PHOTO, 1993

IN THE LATTER HALF of the 1700s, Robert Sproul purchased 200 acres of land from one of the original proprietors of the Pemaquid Patent and built a cape-style house on it. In 1833 his grandson moved this house from across the road—today's State Route 129—and attached it to the cape, creating an ell.

Local lore has it that a hidden chamber was built in behind the fireplace in the old Sproul homestead so the owners could hide during Indian attacks.

William T. Kelsey's dwelling, built in 1810 by Bedfield Plummer, Jr., on what later became the town poor farm. AUTHOR PHOTO, 1997

IN 1873, WHEN William T. Kelsey became overseer of the poor for the town of Bristol, he purchased the 1810 farmstead built by Bedfield Plummer, Jr. Here, on land overlooking what later became known as Poorhouse Cove, he ran the town poorhouse. The elegant house that still remains there was his own dwelling place; the separate building in which the poor lived has been gone for many years. The current owner notes that the two large ash trees still standing by the front door have traditionally been called the "marriage trees."

THAT WAS THE town poorhouse years and years ago. When anybody was so poor they couldn't take care of themselves they went up there to live.

When they was digging the foundation for the poorhouse, they found the skeletons of two Indians, sitting bolt upright. —Katherine Poole Norwood

BACK IN THE old days that's what they did with the old people. The town supported them instead of supporting individual households—they put them all in a place like that. Mostly old people—'cause if anybody could work, they'd give 'em a clam digger, tell 'em to go to work. —Ralph Norwood

TOWN OF BRISTOL. 9

"	"	"	"	"	"	15	.0287
"	"	"	"	"	"	16	.0075
"	"	"	"	"	"	17	.0155
"	"	"	"	"	"	18	.0195
"	"	"	"	"	"	19	.0226
"	"	"	"	"	"	21	.0174

W. C. THOMPSON,
H. H. GOUDY,
A. A FARROW, } Assessors of Bristol, Me.

SELECTMEN'S ACCOUNT.

Appropriations voted at Annual Meeting, March 5th, 1894, and Special Meeting, March 28th, 1894 :

For Town Expenses	$3700.00	
" Roads and Bridges	2200.00	
" Winter Roads	1800.00	
" Common Schools	2800.00	
" Repairs on School buildings	350 00	
" Free High Schools	175.00	
" Memorial purposes	30.00	
Total Appropriations		$11055.00

Support of Poor.

C. C Robbins, wood furnished Jane West, 1893	$4.00	
J. M. Bryant, taking S. Sherman to Augusta, 1893	25.00	
W. S. Brainerd, certificate of insanity, S. Sherman	1.00	
Insane Asylum, board of Sewall Sherman 1893	3.21	
N. W. Gamage, goods furnished D. P. House, 1893 and 1894	37.00	
Reform School, clothing and board for Frank Carter and W. Bradley	26.00	

10 ANNUAL REPORT

W. H. Prentice, going to Warren after Josie Peters	4.50	
W. T. Kelsey, last quarter, 1893, Support of Poor	162.50	
Town of Bremen, goods furnished S. Richardson	9.00	
Insane Asylum, board of S. Sherman, 1894	43.81	
E. W. Fossett. sending tramp out of town	4.50	
Reform School, board of Frank Carter and W. Bradley	26.00	
J E.Nichols, goods furnished Wealtha Thompson, '93	4.50	
W. T. Kelsey, first quarter, 1894, Support of Poor	125.00	
Insane Asylum, board S. Sherman	32.86	
Arad Hatch, burial expenses of Geo. Peters	21.00	
C. C. Robbins, wood furnished Jane West, 1894	5.00	
W. S. Brainerd, medical attendance, Town Poor	20.00	
H. H. Goudy, trip to Bath on acc't of Chas Little	2.60	
Reform School, board of F. Carter and W. Bradley	22.86	
Arad Hatch, burial expenses, Jane West	24.00	
Wm. T. Kelsey, 2nd quarter, 1894, Support of Poor	125.00	
H. H Goudy, wood furnished Mrs Keyes	8.00	
Insane Asylum, board of S. Sherman	41 45	
Geo. Bearce, digging grave of Jane West	4 50	
Mrs. Bertha Redonnett, nursing Jane West	6 50	
James H Little, services rendered Jane West	5.00	
W G. Loud, supplies furnished Jos Munro	9 00	
J. E. Nichols, " " " "	13.00	
A A Farrow, trip to Bath, on acc't C. Little	3.60	
Dr. F. C. Hall, medical attendance, Mrs. S Richardson	8 00	
Dr W. S. Brainerd, medical attendance, ~~Mrs S Richardson~~	7.00	
Wm. T Kelsey, Support of Poor, 3rd quarter	125.00	
		$960.49

Bristol Town Report for Year Ending February 20th, 1895: Selectman's Account.
LALEAH CONDON KENNEDY

A PAGE FROM THE 1894 Bristol town report illustrates how the town took care of its own, not only showing the $537.50 given to William Kelsey for "Support of Poor," but listing appropriations for items such as clothing and reform school board for two boys, transportation and insane asylum board for an S. Sherman, and for goods furnished to individuals by various store proprietors like South Bristol's Nelson Gamage. It is also a bleak record of the final year of Jane West, an eighty-eight-year-old widow: first listing the cost of supplying firewood to her, then wages for someone to nurse her, followed at the last by expenditures for burial expenses and the digging of her grave.

My children and grandchildren both were christened here …

—Donald Hunter

Walpole Meeting House, as it appeared on a card postmarked 1913. The text, lower left, erroneously dates it at 1776 rather than the true date, 1772. CATHERINE JORDON WALKER

… MY SON AND DAUGHTER *were married here. This summer, my granddaughter's going to be married here—she'll be the ninth generation of Hunters.*

—Donald Hunter

BUILT IN 1772, Walpole Meeting House has been offering continual worship services longer than any other church in Maine. The Hunter family has been involved in the meeting house since it was first built on the land given by their patriarch, Henry Hunter.

I'M DONALD HUNTER. I was born in Bristol in the year 1927 and my family had to do with this church here since its origin. And in 227 years there's always been a Deacon Hunter.… I am the one now.

Interior of the Walpole Meeting House, showing box pews and pulpit. In the nineteenth century, family pews were passed down through families as an inheritance; they can be seen listed in deeds and wills of the time. For example, in 1838 Martha Plummer Poole inherited 100 acres, a small island, and half a pew in the Walpole Meeting House. CATHERINE JORDON WALKER

I'LL TELL ABOUT *Doris Goudy. She was very active in this church, and she worked her head off to keep things maintained. Kinda funny, the first meeting we went to. She ran things with an iron hand because she was a matriarch of the thing, obviously, for years and years and years. The first annual meeting that we went to, I thought was rather humorous. Robert Woodward was the president of it and he would sit down and everybody would gather 'round when the proscribed time was, and she would come along with this master sheet and the whole order of the meeting, and the way it was to be voted and so forth—it was all in print, and she'd slide it in front of him. It was kinda comical—there it would be, all cut and dried. At one of the first meetings we went to they wanted to have an election of officers; Robert said he thought he'd been president long enough, and he'd like to change. And Doris said, well, she was awful sorry, but everyone would have to keep the same office that they held. We all looked at everyone else. "Because we still have two thousand 'Order of Services' to give out." So we couldn't change—'til those brochures were gone you had to keep your office.* —Debbie Hunter

SOLIDLY BUILT from local timbers, the meeting house has withstood the ravages of Maine winters for well over two centuries. Of the many meeting houses in the state, it is the only one that remains unchanged; it appears to us today much as it did to worshippers in the eighteenth century.

THE EAST SIDE *was so bad that we had to replace the shingles ten or twelve years ago. But the other three sides are the original shingles, hand-split shingles of white pine. Back in those days they had better wood—that helped. It's post-and-beam construction, with very heavy timbers in the attic. And the nails are handmade nails. So it kept someone busy an awful long time making nails.*

The panels in the balcony here are thirty inches wide. There's not very many thirty-inch boards today. In Revolutionary times they weren't supposed to cut anything any larger than twenty-four inches—the king wanted all the big trees for his masts. We separated from England shortly after this building was built so I don't think they bothered with it. Some of these natives were rather … set in their ways. They probably found a tree and they didn't measure it. They just would not.

It was a problem making glass—they couldn't get big pieces. That was why they had all these small panes. They came from England, and they each cost the price of a cow. We don't know how much a cow cost in those days, but I imagine it was a fair sum. Cows were a valuable commodity, too, of course. —Donald Hunter

At the time *it was built central heating was unknown. They had box pews because they would bring these metal containers full of hot coals and set them on the floor, and throw a robe over everybody in the pew, and see, that kept 'em warm.*

—Donald Hunter

There is a pew *in front there and that's where the deacons sat. You know what they did? What their job was? You're supposed to set up there and read the lines out of the hymnbook and then the congregation sung the lines. That was your job. You see, in those days printed material was hard to come by. The deacon would have the only hymnbook and he would tell them what to sing.*

—Debbie Hunter

When Thomas McClure came to Walpole in 1797, he established a prosperous trading post near the meeting house, and built himself a residence of such grandeur that it included a ballroom that took up the entire top floor. He kept innumerable slaves, and it's likely that these were the people confined to worship in the upper gallery of the meeting house.

There was slaves here—*indentured servants they were called—but you can't find out much about it—it was very hush-hush. Of course, then abolition came along. Maine became a state in 1820 as a compromise—Missouri came in as a slave state and Maine came in as a free state and I think probably at that time there were a few slaves around but I have an idea they were here earlier than that. They used to set upstairs. They must've been tortured to set on those seats. I don't know why they'd do that to anybody, seats like that … to keep them awake, they said. And the floors are sloped. You couldn't fall asleep in the service, could you? You'd fall over.* —Donald Hunter

The 1687 pewter communion set, made in London by Thomas Cary and still owned by the Old Walpole Meeting House. TRUSTEES OF THE OLD WALPOLE MEETING HOUSE

Reverend Lewis D. Evans, from the 1876 marriage certificate of Charles B. Woodward and Mary Albertina Sproul. Reverend Evans was the last settled pastor of the Walpole Meeting House. EUGENIE WOODWARD COLE

I CAN SAY *that it disappeared from a church in England. They thought that the early Walpole brought it over here. Yes. They thought the Walpole family brought it from England—without permission, it sounds like. 'Course we keep that in the bank, in the vault. It is quite valuable. But we have it on display here in the summer.*

—Donald Hunter

DON'S UNCLE USED TO *carry them, he kept them in the house down here and he would come over every Sunday with them in a Schlitz beer box. And Don's father carried them, during his tenure, in a Schlitz beer box. So when we gained "custody" we decided that they needed something a little more in keeping, although they were probably safer in there. Except that I'm not sure—Schlitz beer might be attractive, too—wouldn't a fella be some disappointed to find those old plates in there instead of beer! Anyway, Don made them a proper box, so now they have a proper box. Oh, dear, but it was kinda comical to see Don's father come carrying—and his uncle as well—carrying a Schlitz beer box with that perfectly gorgeous pewter in it from 1687.* —Debbie Hunter

IN 1886 HARVEY GAUL began construction of the Walpole Union Church. He finished the exterior that year—it is said that the bell in the bell tower came from an abandoned railroad locomotive—but he took seven more years to complete the interior. In 1888 he donated the land that it stood on to the Walpole Sewing Society. On the portion of the deed where the conveyor would normally fill in the amount of the sale, he wrote "in consideration of the love and affection which I have for the cause of religion, I give a piece of land for the location of a Chapel." Shortly before his death in 1896 he donated the

Walpole Union Church, before a recent restoration.
AUTHOR PHOTO, 1996

CARD.

The Ladies of the "West Bristol Circle" feeling their indebtedness to Rev. L. D. Evans for the interesting lecture he delivered at Centennial hall last Wednesday evening for the benefit of their chapel, earnestly tender to him their sincere thanks. Also to Mrs. Robert Hysom of Boothbay who so kindly lent her aid to the cause, by rendering some very fine music, during the evening; to Mr. and Mrs. J. H. Goudy who so generously and willingly opened their hall and gave the free use of it to the society, and who, in every possiable way, helped to make the evening, socially as well as financialy, a success; and also to Mrs. William Clark who so ably managed the affair, would they extend their heart-felt thanks.

Excerpt from the *Pemaquid Messenger,* October 1886.

church to the community, deeding it over to its first trustees Enoch Goudy, Gilbert Curtis, and Elden Oliver. The trustees were charged with holding "the chapel for the use and benefit of any Christian denomination that may desire to hold services therein...." In the latter part of the twentieth century, services lapsed in the church and the chapel remained unused; in the years since this photo was taken in the mid 1990s, a local group has restored the building and reopened it for worship and special events.

Undated photo of the South Bristol Union Church in its original position, with the Lincoln School at left.
William A. Kelsey

We, the Ladies of South Bristol, believing a church or place of public worship needful in this place, bond ourselves together to labor and solicit money for the purpose. This building to be a Union Church for all Denominations or ordained Ministers to preach in. To have a bell in a steeple or Belfry in some suitable manner for the building, and to be located near the island school house. October 1, 1880.

Twenty-one "Ladies of South Bristol" signed this document, paying 25 cents, and two dollars every year thereafter, which entitled them to their own pew. Thanks to their efforts the new Union Church was built in 1887 on land donated by Lois R. Otis, and incorporated in 1898.

In 1907 the Ladies raised more funds by selling cookbooks for 35 cents each, and in 1908 were able to build a parsonage.

And then, *it must have been in the twenties, maybe, they moved the church. They turned the church enough so's to put a basement in underneath. Evidently it didn't have a basement before. And then the Ladies' Aid and us younger folks—us young mothers that couldn't go out much in the daytime—when our husbands were home at night to take care of the kids, why we had "Progressive Club," and we would meet every Monday night up there in the Memorial Room, they called it. That's where we used to have our Ladies' Aid and our Progressive Club meetings, and had our summer fairs there, too; and in the wintertime kids would have socials and things there.*

It was called "Memorial" in memory of one of the old ministers that was here. There was a minister by the name of Dunnells, Minister Dunnells. And I know when they turned the church around and made the room underneath they called it the Memorial Room, and I think it was in his memory.

—Nellie McFarland Frey

FRIDAY, OCTOBER 21, 1921. LEWISTON EVENING JOURNAL

Some South Bristol People Declare It's Only a Tempest in a Teapot

Alleged Assault Upon Parson Wm. H. Jackson, Culmination of Series of Troubles—One Pastor Already Has Resigned—School Principal Retired—Each Side Tells Its Story—Some of Town's Best Known People Involved

Headline from a lengthy article in the *Lewiston Evening Journal*, October 21, 1921. MARGARET FARRIN HOUSE

I REMEMBER the scandal with Reverend Jackson. I was only five or six years old, so the things I remember are mostly hearsay. A lot of the ladies of the congregation were involved, my mother included. They "pulled his coattails," as I remember.

—Doug Thompson

The Eastern Star Lodge and the Ladies' Aid was the entertainment that womenfolks had then.

—Nellie McFarland Frey

The house known as the "Community House," was once used for Ladies' Aid Society meetings and activities. At the time, the house was owned by local philanthropist Samuel Miles, who donated its use to the community.
AUTHOR PHOTO, 1997

IT WAS THEIR LIFE, you know, that's what they looked forward to for their entertainment. When I first started school—first, second, third grade—they used to meet up in the building across the road from the church. That's where they had their Ladies' Aid meetings, and of course I was in school in the schoolhouse just in the next building there. We always called it the Community House because that's where they used to have their fairs, and Ladies' Aid and everything before they moved the church. —Nellie McFarland Frey

THE LADIES' AID was organized in 1886 to raise money to build the church. "When I joined the Aid in 1902," Josie Gould recounted in 1964, "we had no regular place to meet and we met anywhere we could. We didn't have electric lights to sew by in those days. We had eighty members then...." By 1964 their numbers had shrunk to fifteen, and she had been a member for sixty-two years, Alice McFarland for fifty-five years, Mona Farrin and Annie May Farrin for fifty-two years, and Maude Tibbetts for fifty years.

Installation at the Pogonia Chapter, Order of the Eastern Star. This particular picture is notable because it includes women from three generations of the same family: Lucinda Gamage, her daughter Annie May Farrin, and Annie May's daughters Margaret House and Charlotte Eugley. MARGARET FARRIN HOUSE

OF COURSE THEY *had their Ladies' Aid—Sewing Circle they called it. A group of women sewed—sewed things, made things for their fairs; they had a fair in the summer and made money for the church like we have our church group now. My mother always called it Sewing Circle. They used to go ten o'clock in the morning and sometimes they'd be there 'til four o'clock in the afternoon—make a whole day of it. But they used to do so much different kind of work for the fairs than what we do now. Mother, and Catherine's mother and Gerry's mother, they used to make fancy pillowcases, and of course aprons, and mittens—stuff like that. They just kept busy the year 'round.*

—Nellie McFarland Frey

THE POGONIA CHAPTER of the Order of the Eastern Star opened with twenty-nine charter members in 1912. Included among these were Sisters Lizzie Gamage, Helen Jordon, Carrie Turner, Frances Tibbetts, Lettie Kelsey, Sarah Thompson, Idella Seavey, Nellie Smith, and Angie Gamage, and Brothers Everett Gamage, John Turner, Mark Thompson, Frank Jordon, and Elliot Brewer.

POGONIA CHAPTER, *Eastern Star. That's always been going up here. Had a big lodge up here at one time, for a small town. I think it was eighty members. It's the ladies' part of the Masons, you see. Every year they had election of officers in March. Every year the officers changed. That is, sometimes the same ones took their offices over and over. They'd elect new officers like Worthy Matron and Worthy Patron, Secretary, and the Treasurer, and Conductress. Yes, they'd elect officers, and they'd have the installation ceremony. Install the officers into their offices. And we used to visit all around to different meetings in the other towns around. We'd go to Bath and Rockland and Rockport and Thomaston, places like that. It's a wonderful lodge; it's a wonderful thing.*

—Nellie McFarland Frey

Upstairs they used to have the town meetings.
—Katherine Poole Norwood

Second floor of the old South Bristol town hall, where the March town meetings were held for many decades. AUTHOR PHOTO, 1997

THEY'D MEET all morning, and then the women would fix dinner. They would cook beans and brown bread at home and take them along. Then they'd have the dinner downstairs, and then everybody'd go back upstairs and meet all afternoon. Just about everybody'd go. Mama and Daddy used to leave me home with my sister and she'd take care of me. —Katherine Poole Norwood

A large crowd attended town meeting Monday. More money was raised than last year, so the tax rate will be higher The Ladies' Aid served a fine dinner in the hall below. They wish to thank all who patronized them.

THE TOWN MEETING would always be the second Monday in March. People from South Bristol used to come up to the meeting in their boats to where the icehouses were—they called it the town landing—and they'd walk up the hill to the town meeting. Town meetings were a get-together. People would see people they hadn't seen all winter. They'd have a baked bean dinner, brown bread, and pies. Ladies' Aid used to put these on. And it was an all-day affair pretty much. There'd be some real arguments on appropriation of money, but in general it was a real good day. —Robert Woodward

Excerpt from the *Lincoln County News*, 1930s.

The old Clark's Cove wharf, adjacent to the American Ice Company wharfs, used to be referred to as the town landing. WILLIAM A. KELSEY

Proposed Constitutional Amendments

Official Ballot

For the Town of

SOUTH BRISTOL

September 10, 1917

Frank W. Ball

Secretary of State

Those in favor of any, or all, of the following proposed amendments will place a cross (X) in each, or any, of the squares marked "Yes" devoted to the amendment, or amendments, for which they desire to vote; those opposed will place a cross (X) in the opposite square, or squares, marked "No."

PROPOSED AMENDMENT NO. 1.

YES

NO

WOMAN'S SUFFRAGE.

Chapter 4 of the resolves of 1917 submits the following Constitutional amendments to the electors for their approval. First it is proposed that the following Article be appended:

'The right to vote or to hold office shall not be denied or abridged on account of sex; provided, however, that citizens by marriage only shall not be allowed to vote or hold office until after a period of residence in the United States equal to that required by law for the naturalization of men in this State. In the construction of this Constitution the masculine pronoun shall be construed as including both men and women.'

Second, that Article II of the Constitution be amended by striking out the word "male" in the first line of section one so that said section one, as amended, shall read as follows:

'Sec. 1. Every citizen of the United States of the age of twenty-one years and upwards, excepting paupers, persons under guardianship, and Indians not taxed, having his residence established in this State for the term of three months next preceding any election, shall be an elector for Governor, Senators and Representatives, in the town or plantation where his residence is so established; and the elections shall be by written ballot. But persons in the military, naval or marine service of the United States, or this State, shall not be considered as having obtained such established residence by being stationed in any garrison, barrack, or military place, in any town or plantation; nor shall the residence of a student at any seminary of learning entitle him to the right of suffrage in the town or plantation where such seminary is established. No person, however, shall be deemed to have lost his residence by reason of his absence from the State in the military service of the United States, or of this State.'

"SHALL THE CONSTITUTION BE AMENDED AS PROPOSED BY A RESOLUTION OF THE LEGISLATURE GRANTING SUFFRAGE TO WOMEN UPON EQUAL TERMS WITH MEN?"

Portion of a South Bristol ballot, 1917, to decide the fate of women's suffrage. KATHERINE POOLE NORWOOD

THURSDAY, SEPTEMBER 5, 1918

FLAG RAISING AT SOUTH BRISTOL

Grand Celebration of the Incorporation of the New Town

South Bristol, the new town, truly had a most successful christening on Friday afternoon, August 30. A beautiful new flag-staff, a splendid new flag, a town-hall made all new and fresh from what was formerly the old Centennial Hall, a new spirit of friendship between the mother-town of Bristol and the daughter, these marked this day in large red and many relieved their feelings by plugging the ugly visage most successfully. This satisfactory sport brought the Red Cross some fifteen dollars or more. Horace Kelsey was the general in charge of this attack.

PROGRAM

The formal celebration began with a band concert under the direction of

Photo by J. D. Lindsay

SCENE AT THE TOWN HOUSE

Banner headline, *Damariscotta Herald*, September 5, 1918. Although the town was incorporated and elected its first officers in 1915, the official celebration wasn't held until two and a half years later. EUGENIE WOODWARD COLE

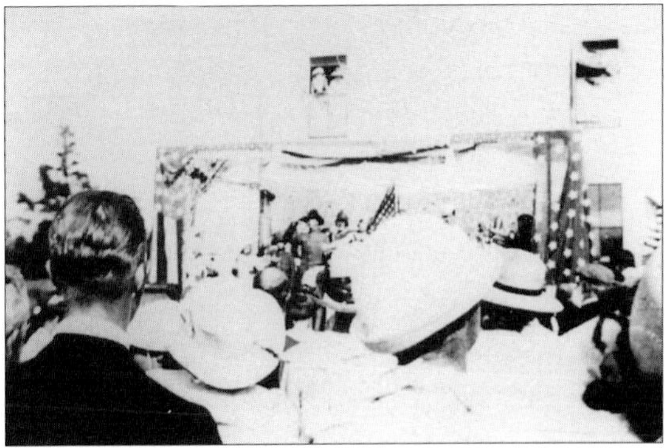

Incorporation Day celebration, August 30, 1918. The photograph was taken by someone standing in the crowd: women watch the ceremony from a second-story window in the new town hall; throngs pack the yard; a cavalry-hatted soldier salutes on a bunting-draped platform. MARGARET FARRIN HOUSE

UNTIL 1915 SOUTH BRISTOL was part of the town of Bristol. No one knows for certain why, or by whom, the separation was instigated. Some claim that people in South Bristol were unhappy with the poor roads and ramshackle bridge; others say that the opinions of residents from South Bristol were being rudely ignored at town meeting; still others claim that S. A. Miles was behind the split.

Many people in Bristol bitterly opposed the separation of the two towns, but on March 19, 1915, the law declaring South Bristol an independent town was passed through the state legislature, with only twenty-six legislators voting against division. Ten days later, in the Bristol town meeting, the clerk recorded a resolution denouncing the legislature's Committee on Towns for their "injust decision," i.e., allowing South Bristol to become a separate town.

In 1917 Burton B. Blaisdell wrote in the *Lewiston Journal*:

IF EVERY DIVORCE could end as happily for all concerned as did that of South Bristol from the town of Bristol, this would, indeed, be a more joyous world. As is usually the case in matters of this kind, it took a big fight to win the separation; but the majority of the people of the new town seem to be well satisfied with the results and feel that they have been fully rewarded for their indefatigable efforts during the six years of strife, which was carried into three sessions of the legislature.

The Damariscotta Herald's front page account of the new town's incorporation celebration was decidedly more upbeat:

Thursday, September 5, 1918
South Bristol, the new town, truly had a most successful christening on Friday afternoon, August 30. A beautiful new flag-staff, a splendid new flag, a town-hall made all new and fresh from what was formerly the old Centennial Hall, a new spirit of friendship between the mother-town of Bristol and the daughter, these marked this day in large red letters in the calendar of the town's history.

Shortly after noon people began to gather at the Town Hall at Clark's Cove. They came on foot, in automobiles, in carriages, and by boat. All of the surrounding towns were represented, Wiscasset, Edgecomb, Newcastle, Southport, Damariscotta, Boothbay Harbor.

The former "Centennial Hall," recently purchased by the town for a Town Hall had been thoroughly renovated within and without. Outside the hall flags and banners were displayed in great profusion. Within, a new set of signal flags decorated the walls.

Attractive young women greeted each newcomer with appeals to buy tags for the Red Cross at his own price. No one was seen to refuse these appeals and soon every one had a Red Cross token dangling from a button hole. Flower girls offered bouquets which found many purchasers.

The formal celebration began with a band concert under the direction of Mr. John Monroe of Round Pond. At the conclusion of this Mr. S. A. Miles appeared upon the platform and was greeted with great applause.

While the band played "The Star Spangled Banner," Mr. Elijah Woodman, escorted by three children in red, white, and blue decorations, came to the front and raised the flag, while the audience led by Mrs. James Ropes and a chorus of girls sang "The Star Spangled Banner." As the flag rising, gracefully unfurled, many small flags fell from its folds and were eagerly seized by those fortunate enough to be where they fell. Then Mrs. Ropes sang the "Battle Hymn of the Republic," the audience joining in the chorus.

The first meeting of the new town was called December 15, 1915 at Centennial Hall, Clark's Cove. The meeting was organized by Everett Gamage, justice of the peace.... Everett Poole was elected town clerk and duly sworn. Everett W. Gamage was elected town treasurer; Wilbur Bearce, Robert H. Woodward, and Frank Wells were elected selectman.

The whole meeting was marked by a sense of union and a spirit of concord. Every vote was unanimous and while perhaps a tinge of sadness over the separation yet everyone appeared desirous that the new dispensation should prove to be good for all of this section. It is safe to say that few town meetings of this state ever adjourned with better satisfaction over the good results achieved.

—Nelson W. Gamage,
A Short History of South Bristol, Maine

The earliest drawbridge that I remember swung like the present one, although it was hand operated. —Doug Thompson

My grandfather used to operate that because his business was close by. I can remember that it was opened by just inserting a crank—a huge long bar—down in there and walking around and around, pushing the bar—and it swung that bridge open. Once, he got his coat caught in the gears, and had to shed it to escape.

—Doug Thompson

But there were earlier bridges:

The bridge is so crooked
It is hard to cross at night
Unless you take for your compass
The post that holds the streetlight...."

The poem of an anonymous South Bristol woman echoed her neighbors' sentiments about the village bridge in the late 1800s.

Repairing the old stone bridge. This photograph is undated, but the building at right was constructed in 1894.
William A. Kelsey

In the settlement's earliest days, Rutherford Island was reached by a dugout or log canoe ferry, operated by pulling a rope that stretched from shore to shore. The first bridge, built some time before 1815, was no doubt wooden, as by 1822 it was reported to be "rotten and impassable."

Subsequent wooden bridges were built and maintained until the early 1890s, when a stone bridge with wooden planking was constructed by J. N. Fossett, a bridgebuilder from Pemaquid. In the local community much was made of the poor quality of this structure. In his history of South Bristol, Nelson Gamage refers to the bridge: "Tradition informs us that one barrel of rum was used by the workmen while building the present stone bridge. We have no reason to doubt this story. The work is in evidence and speaks for itself...."

An unusual view of the stone bridge, reproduced from an undated cyanotype. The 1894 store on the west side is not yet there, although Nelson Gamage's can just be seen on the east side. Note the stonework in the center, possibly the vestiges of an older bridge, and the ox in the center of the photograph. MARGARET FARRIN HOUSE

The first swing bridge. This photo shows it in the open position; the island is on the left and mainland on the right. MARGARET FARRIN HOUSE

THE FIRST SWING BRIDGE, built in 1903, was a hand-cranked span; its tenders were men whose businesses were nearby: Charles Clifford, Dan Berry, and finally Eliphalet Thompson.

THE LAST BRIDGE before the present one, completed in 1925, was a "bobtail" drawbridge and lasted only five years. Evidently, not enough people paid heed to the "Stop—Look—Drawbridge" sign:

LATER ON, A BRIDGE was built which became widely known as pretty much of a monstrosity. Huge concrete blocks, full of iron, as square as this table; huge chains, and two great high towers and a series of gears that operated the thing; and the weights would come down the track. The tracks were made of iron, started out straight, then curved down to be level with the end of it and those blocks would come down and the end of the bridge would go up. There were some funny incidents in regard to that, such as people not noticing the warning that the bridge was open and driving up onto that bridge as it was up in the air. That happened on several occasions. And I've heard that there was only one other one built like it in the state—it was a bad piece of engineering, I'm sure. I can remember it. When they took it down they put up a temporary bridge and the boats couldn't get through—there was no opening. Started out near Everett Gamage's building and came in over by the other end of where the bridge is now.

—Doug Thompson

BACK IN THOSE DAYS, the '20s and '30s, there was a bridge that we used to call the "little bridge." There was a little bridge and a big bridge. Passage could be made through that when the tide was halfway up. There was a big mussel bed there that you had to clear, but small boats could get through.

—Doug Thompson

The "monstrosity" drawbridge, looking north from the island sometime between 1925 and 1930. Note the sign on a pole in front of the dry goods store, warning motorists to look for the bridge. DAVID W. ANDREWS

The fixed "little" bridge. The pumper of the town's new fire engine is being tested as an interested crowd looks on. MARGARET FARRIN HOUSE

This early photograph shows the houses and barns that were completely destroyed when a fire swept up the west side of the road in 1917. These substantial buildings are rarely seen in photographs of South Bristol. The buildings on the east (right) side of the road escaped destruction.
MARGARET FARRIN HOUSE

WE USED TO take our skiffs and row around the Gut, and at that time—it still occurs—the current runs through the drawbridge and it's not always governed by the incoming and the outgoing tides totally. It's determined as to whether there was a bigger bore of water into the river or a larger bore into John's Bay; whichever is the larger creates more water and a higher situation so the water would flow away from that direction. And we used to go out there wherever we could get the current going in the right direction, and just sit in the stern of these little skiffs we had, steer 'em with an oar and go zipping through the bridge propelled by the current—and usually there was a chop at the end that would be created by the current going against the wind. That was great fun.

—Doug Thompson

THE SECTION of the road immediately north and south of the bridge was, and continues to be, the commercial center of the village. Successive photographs, looking north from the island, show the changes over many years and can be dated approximately by the structures and businesses that appear in them.

Standing in the middle of the road, looking north from the island. The road appears to swing more westerly than it does now, the Eastern Gut reaching further west. On the far left is the small building destined to be a dry goods store, then a lunch room, and even a poolroom. Next to it is Merritt Thompson's grocery store, and across the road, with the proprietor standing on the porch, is Alice Pierce's dry goods store. Margaret Farrin House

Another view north towards the mainland shows the main street of the village before the road and bridge were moved to their present locations. The buildings identify this as having been taken sometime between 1890 and 1894.

Numbered identifications were handwritten on the back of the photo by Annie May Farrin. "Merritt" no doubt refers to Merritt Thompson, who owned the village grocery store at the time; "Chittenden" would most likely refer to Dan Chittenden, who lived at the top of the hill. Albert Thorpe and Nelson Gamage both had general stores; Alice Pierce, the first dry goods store in town; Milton Thompson was a local inventor; and Pearly Spear, whose rocky front yard the three men are sitting on, was a fisherman.

The camera here is placed in nearly the same spot as in the previous photograph, but is moved slightly northward and westward, probably onto the wooden sidewalk. We can see the structure of the first swing bridge, pegging this as 1903 or later; A. A. Pierce's sign still hangs on the store, indicating that it is no later than 1911. Notice that another store has appeared on the right: Nelson Gamage's store, built on pilings at the edge of the Gut. In the middle distance the first swing bridge is visible. PEMAQUID HISTORICAL ASSOCIATION

Main road, 1914 or 1915. On the left, women chat under the awning of Ada McFarland's dry goods store; across the road Lois Otis now owns Alice Pierce's shop. In the middle distance, a couple spurns the wooden sidewalk and strolls across the bridge. CATHERINE JORDON WALKER

Automobiles are "rafted up" in front of J. R. Little's grocery store and Lois Otis's dry goods store on the east side of the road, indicating that this photograph was taken in the summer: some things never change. The bobtail bridge is gone. MARGARET FARRIN HOUSE

Yup, lot of things come in barrels those days, and wooden boxes and so forth.
—Afton Farrin, Jr.

IRISH BARRELS *we called them—I think we called them that. Crown Pilot come in barrels. Molasses, I think, vinegar, sauerkraut—it was quite popular then. You brought your own container—they had a faucet on the bottom of the barrel and they turned a spigot to get what they wanted. Then they had these pumps, too, on top, they used to pump it a little bit. Usually the end of the season they'd have a barrel, there'd be all these flies in there—they'd get in somehow. That bothered me. Oh, boy.*
—Afton Farrin, Jr.

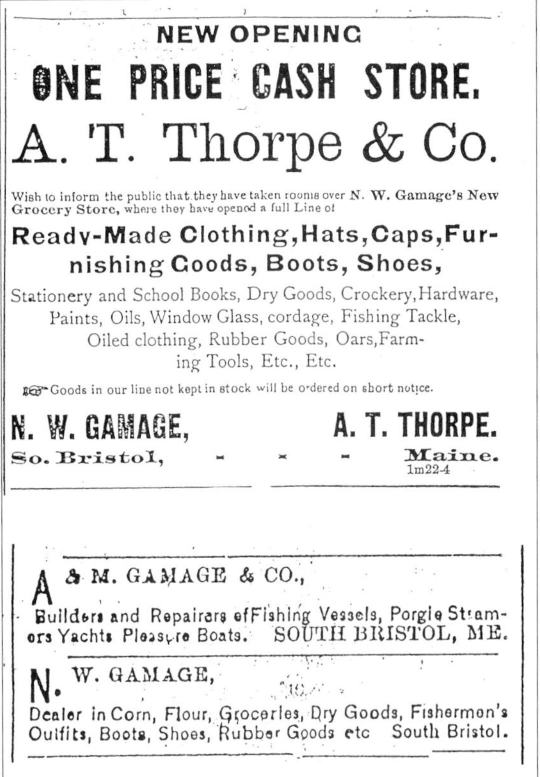

NEW OPENING

ONE PRICE CASH STORE.

A. T. Thorpe & Co.

Wish to inform the public that they have taken rooms over N. W. Gamage's New Grocery Store, where they have opened a full Line of

Ready-Made Clothing, Hats, Caps, Furnishing Goods, Boots, Shoes,

Stationery and School Books, Dry Goods, Crockery, Hardware, Paints, Oils, Window Glass, cordage, Fishing Tackle, Oiled clothing, Rubber Goods, Oars, Farming Tools, Etc., Etc.

☞Goods in our line not kept in stock will be ordered on short notice.

N. W. GAMAGE, **A. T. THORPE.**
So. Bristol, - - - Maine.
1m22-4

A & M. GAMAGE & CO.,
Builders and Repairers of Fishing Vessels, Porgie Steamers Yachts Pleasure Boats. SOUTH BRISTOL, ME.

N. W. GAMAGE,
Dealer in Corn, Flour, Groceries, Dry Goods, Fishermen's Outfits, Boots, Shoes, Rubber Goods etc South Bristol.

Advertisement from the *Pemaquid Messenger*, December 1888. A. T. Thorpe's store was in the center of the village, on the south side of the bridge.

The building that housed the grocery store, at the head of the South Bristol steamer wharf. The rolling doors indicate that this photo was probably taken after Horace Kelsey and Will Alley had begun operating their boatbuilding business there in the 1930s. MARGARET FARRIN HOUSE

THEY'D BUY STUFF IN BULK, *cut it up. I remember they used to have big wooden boxes of dates and prunes and stuff; they'd pull them out of the wooden box—they'd have these little tools. Everything was that way—by bulk. I think most of it was in wooden boxes and barrels. You had to have everything handled by hand, that's right. I think most people probably had a grocery list, but they went in to see what was available. They didn't have the variety in those days, I think, just the staples. Sugar, geez, I think even sugar came in barrels for a while there.*

Oh, cheese used to be popular. They'd come in these big round boxes—even those were in wooden boxes in those days, wooden round containers. Every store used to have this big cheese, cut off a slice, you know. Apples come in barrels. Fruit, you didn't see too much fruit in those days. People depended on apples pretty much locally; 'course they could barrel those. Strawberries was quite a seller. Most stores had strawberries and raspberries. A lot of berries. Salt fish was a big item. Salt pollock—we always had those in the store. Salt cod. We used to put—maybe they still do—salt cod in little wooden boxes; smoked herring were in these little square boxes. I think a lot of that was happening during the '20s, late '20s, I think. Of course I was born in 1916, so I don't recall too much of it, but everything was changing about then.

—Afton Farrin, Jr.

THERE WAS A *building where the town parking lot is now. Used to be a library upstairs in it, and a barbershop. Chester Clifford ran the store for a while, and then Kelsey and Alley ran the store for a while, and then they turned it into a boatshop, wooden boats.*

That was a large store, and Merritt Thompson—I don't remember Merritt Thompson myself—but he owned it at one time. He owned that big building there and that store and that was the chief supply of all the surrounding area for groceries and so forth.

Chester Clifford had the grocery store at the head of the steamship wharf, and he also had a candy store at the end of the drawbridge about where the bridgetender's is now. That building was moved from the north end of the draw across to the south end and used as a telephone headquarters building by Nash Telephone of Damariscotta for the experimental and first dial telephone in the area.

—Doug Thompson

ALICE AUGUSTA PIERCE, whose mother and stepfather lived in South Bristol, moved back to the town with her husband Robert to help care for Robert's aunt, Mary Pierce. In 1891 "Nannie Pierce," as Alice was known to her nieces and nephews, had a building constructed for her south of the bridge on the east side of the road, and opened the first dry goods store, "A. A. Pierce, Fancy Goods."

Alice Augusta Pierce, 1844–1934.
MARGARET FARRIN HOUSE.

Lois R. Otis, 1870-1940.
MARGARET FARRIN HOUSE

Lois R. Otis, 1870-1940, took over Alice Pierce's business in 1910 or 1911, and ran it for many years. It is her store that many of the tradition bearers recall visiting as children. Lois, who never married, was a member of one of the oldest families on the island; her father was the local character Eben Otis. It was she who donated the land for the Union Church.

AT ONE TIME *there was two dry goods stores here in the village. A lady by the name of Lois Otis ran one. She had just about anything you'd want. And then across the road, that was a dry goods, too—Mrs. Emery's—but we usually went to Lois Otis's. It always used to be so much fun to go up there, because she'd always have the things that you'd love to see.* —Nellie McFarland Frey

I WORE HAIR RIBBONS THEN, *and my sisters did. In Miss Otis's store they had this little cabinet, a wooden cabinet with a door on it, and shelves inside all filled with rolls of pretty hair ribbons. And that was something we always wanted for Christmas—two or three new hair ribbons.*
—Catherine Jordon Walker

WHEN WE MOVED *back here in '41, there was still the little dry goods store owned by Lois Otis, and across the road was another dry goods store owned by Charlotte Emery, Sarah's mother.* —Catherine Jordon Walker

Catherine and Helen Jordon, c. 1918.
CATHERINE JORDON WALKER

The building on the west side of the road where Ada McFarland and later, Charlotte Emery, had dry goods businesses. AUTHOR PHOTO, 1997

Martha Farrin, wife of proprietor Bob Farrin, c. 1935 or '36. After Charlotte Emery gave up the dry goods store, one of the businesses in the same building was "Bob's Lunch"; another was a poolroom which Doug Thompson recalled as being "quite the hangout." MARGARET FARRIN HOUSE

1890s advertising card for J. P. Coats thread. AUTHOR'S COLLECTION

ED GAMAGE lived upstairs of his drugstore. He sold everything in there from boots to clothing to drugs; he was a druggist. But the drugstore also had hardware and miscellaneous items and clothing and a soda fountain—one of the old-fashioned soda fountains where he made ice cream sodas. It was a gathering place for many people.

In addition to many drugs he had shoes and hardware and candy, and they also had an ice cream fountain. It was somewhat of a joke as to the size of the ice cream that one purchased there—in many instances we'd go across the street to the Everett Gamage ice cream parlor, perhaps got a little larger dip of ice cream for our money.

Looking south onto Rutherford Island, from the end of the bridge. Ed Gamage's drugstore is the building on the far right; Everett Gamage's is the building with the Moxie sign on the far left. The large building next to Ed Gamage's is Merritt Thompson's grocery store, with a library on the top floor. CATHERINE JORDON WALKER

Ed was known far and wide. There was no doctor in town and if anybody had a cut or took a fall or something of that nature they'd go to Ed and he'd patch them up in some manner, perform first aid the best he could. He'd take care of them 'til they could get to a doctor, or perhaps they didn't go at all.

During the evenings after supper, the men would gather in the grocery stores downtown. They would gather in the store that was operated by Chester Clifford and later then that by Kelsey and Alley, or over in Gamage's drugstore, and they'd talk over the local politics or the happenings of the day.

If they were in Ed Gamage's store, when a certain time came during the evening, Ed would get up—he'd be participating in the conversation, but he'd get up and he'd walk over and start turning out the lights. He'd go over and pull the chain on one of the lights that was hanging from the ceiling, one of those old-fashioned electric lights with a chain on it, he'd pull that and say, "Well, boys," and they all knew what the signal was, that it was time for them to go home. And I can remember when I was a kid when my father would be one of the men there. Before he went home he would go to the candy counter and buy a little bag of candy. They always had a whole lot of what we called penny candy in those days—quite a sizable chunk of good candy for a cent. So he'd buy a bag of candy for a little treat before we went to bed.

—Doug Thompson

J. R. Little and his store, 1935 or '36. His summer clerks sit on the porch: Doug Thompson, left, and Vern McFarland. J. DOUGLAS THOMPSON

J. R. LITTLE and his wife Augusta lived up over the store. I worked for them all the summers that I was going to college at that store next to L. R. Otis. I clerked for him. Vern McFarland also worked there. Those days, you waited on customers, you know. They came in with their list and you went to the shelves and got them. They stood at the counter and waited, or perhaps just looked around and said, "Well, I'll have one of those," in addition to the list. You went and got all the goods and packed it up and added it up and took their money.... I drove a delivery truck every day down to Christmas Cove. People would telephone in their orders or I would take orders after the deliveries and bring them back. I'd put up the orders, except for the perishable items, in the afternoon and then the next morning early complete the orders, load them in the truck, and away I would go. It would take me about half a day to deliver the groceries. J. R. Little was a real nice man to work for, and his wife was a very fine person.
—Doug Thompson

WHEN AFTON PASSED, Frank took the store over and it became Farrin's Lobster Pound, which was a well-known source of lobsters. He bought directly from the fishermen and he also sold fishing supplies and groceries. He served as a sort of neighborhood store. —Doug Thompson

THERE WAS A FLOAT out there with a little house on it, and a huge tank on cribwork right behind the building. This was a gasoline tank. And my grandfather had pumps down on that float and he pumped gasoline into boats. All pumped by hand. I used to work for him—you'd pump a hundred, hundred and fifty gallons into a huge yacht that came in in the summer. It was quite a long, tiresome job. —Doug Thompson

In back of Farrin's, with work boats tied up to the float. William A. Kelsey

Doug Thompson (in white shirt) buying lobsters for Farrin's Lobster Pound, summer 1951. Note how few boats are moored in the Eastern Gut.
J. Douglas Thompson

Eliphalet Thompson's gasoline float, on the Eastern Gut. Beyond it, on the mainland, is the French House, Thompson Inn, and Sumner McFarland's boatbuilding shop. William A. Kelsey

After his son-in-law Horace Kelsey took over the big store, Chester Clifford ran a store next to his house on the West Side Road. This store was later taken over by Ernest Alley and called Alley's Store; still a popular spot, it's now known as the Island Grocery.

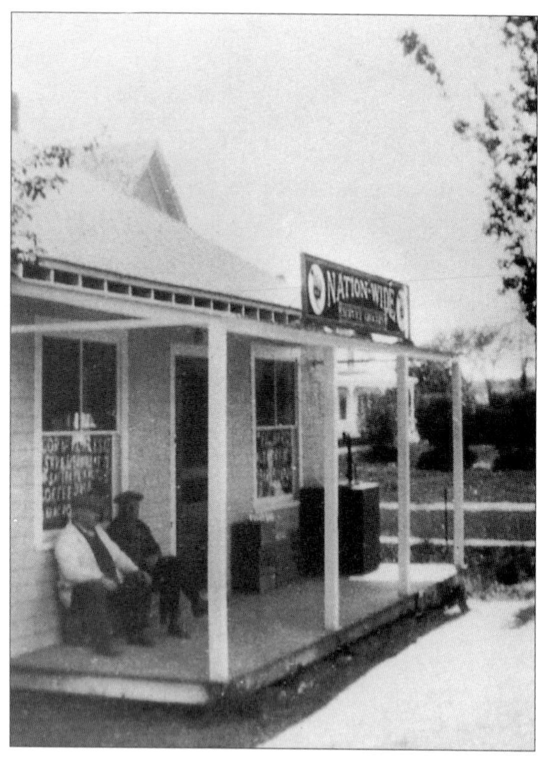

Chester Clifford, 1871–1940, and friend on the porch of his West Side Road grocery store, Nation Wide Market, c. 1930s. Clifford ran a succession of grocery and candy stores in the village; this was his third, and last, one. MARGARET FARRIN HOUSE

THERE WAS A *man named Chester Clifford who had a store up here where the Island Grocery is now. My father worked for him when he and my mama were first married. He taught my father to make wafers and Needhams. We always went down there from school at noontime. We'd have a nickel or so and go down and buy penny candy down there.* —Nellie McFarland Frey

OF COURSE *I walked home every day at noontime, and we would stop to the store. If my father was home he'd say, "Well, here's a nickel for you, a nickel for you, a nickel for you"—for all the kids. Or once in a while it might be just pennies.*
—Beatrice Plummer Rice

OVER ON THE *Shipyard Road, back in the '20s, long before Harvey Gamage's shipyard was even thought of, there were coal sheds on that site and in one of these buildings Plummer Leeman and his son Elliot had a little candy factory there where they made wafers, the type of wafers that we remember as Necco wafers. He manufactured them for the stores and shipped them out of there and we kids could go down there and get some of the broken pieces at bargain prices. We kids did that, and got a good quantity for a penny. Every penny counted then. Nobody wasted many of them, so candy was a luxury.* —Doug Thompson

AT MARK RUSSELL'S HOUSE, *Mark Russell's wife used to make wafers. Daddy used to tell how the kids at the school on the S Road would be allowed to go over and buy wafers up there, homemade wafers, at her house. They told about how she had this big rolling pin that she'd roll 'em out with and make them. They'd go up there and buy wafers.*
—Katherine Poole Norwood

E. W. Haley's Store, Clark's Cove Road. Even after the decline of the ice business, it continued to operate as a general store. MERVIN RICE

THAT'S THE STORE *that was down at Clark's Cove, where the Haleys were—that's the store. That burned. Gas pumps there, and a grocery store. And there was a post office where that store was—it was in that building. And the house sat over to the side of it. That was one of the houses that the ice crews stayed in. They called that the American Ice Company, in Clark's Cove there. That was one of the houses—they had three, maybe four houses.* —Mervin Rice

THAT STORE WAS MOVED *from the ice company boardinghouse complex up to the top of the hill, to where the Brunner's garage is now, and they turned it into a store. It was a general store. That was Earl Haley's. He had everything there.*

As a young boy, when I got old enough to have a license—fifteen, I guess it was in those days—I used to work for him in the summertime. We had a little delivery truck. Used to go 'round and take orders, and then deliver groceries to the houses around the neighborhood. —Robert Woodward

Back in those times, 'bout all roads had stone walls on each side.

—Robert Woodward

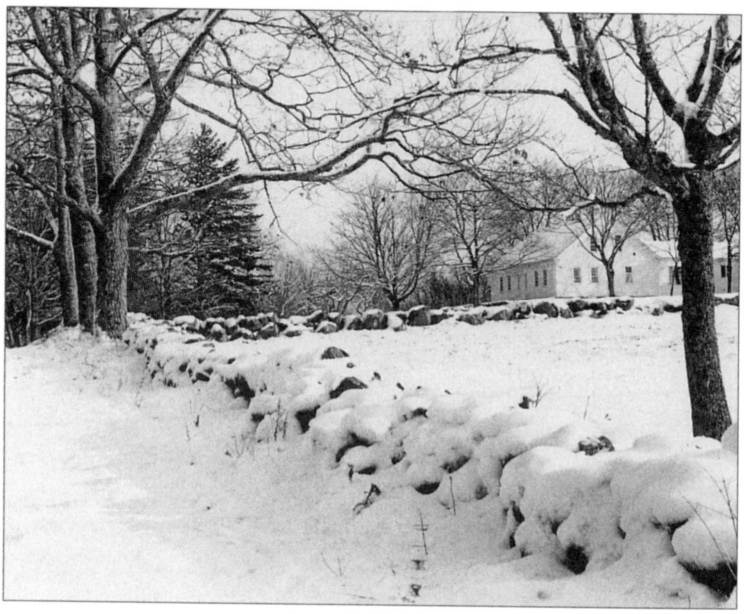

A stone wall borders Clark's Cove Road opposite the town hall. Although this was the first snowfall of the winter, drifts had already started to pile up against the walls. AUTHOR PHOTO, 1997

...AND THEY *used to fill in with snow. They didn't shovel them out, didn't break 'em out in those days. They used to take a big sled, logging sled, with a round log underneath it. Put two pair of oxen on it, hauling it. They'd just go through and beat the snow down. Packed it down. Horses drove over it with sleighs. Then sometimes there'd be so much snow packed down you'd go out in the field where there wasn't so much snow, and use the field for the roadway that winter. That was particularly true on this hill up by the town hall. That was all hayfield where the bushes are now. That road would fill right up with snow. There were cars around here by about 1918, but come September, you put them in the garage and jacked 'em up.* —Robert Woodward

THERE'S A LONG HILL *which used to pose some problems in the wintertime because the snow used to drift on it so badly that even the horses hauling a sleigh would have trouble getting up it. The mail carriers used to go down to Clark's Cove—that was their stop off—and they had a difficult time getting up that hill; they usually had to make their own road out through the fields.*

A card postmarked 1909 shows Sam King's first car on Main Street in Damariscotta.
KATHERINE POOLE NORWOOD

During those days people did not leave South Bristol during the winter very often. All the goods were brought in by horse and sleigh, and unless they had their own horse and sleigh they didn't go up to Damariscotta to do their shopping. The roads were in pretty bad shape. They tried to keep them plowed; they had an old Oshkosh tractor that would go about four miles per hour. When we had a heavy storm it was quite a job to keep the roads clear. —Doug Thompson

WE WENT FROM South Bristol to Damariscotta, met the train, got a load of freight. My father worked for S. A. Miles, and he kept the horse to home. We'd leave South Bristol about four o'clock in the morning. Pitch dark, snow on the ground—you know, in the wintertime. Do it on the end of the week when we didn't have to go to school. Go with him to Damariscotta, get a load of freight on the sled—horse sled. It'd be hardware, stuff they was working with down there in them camps. They were building camps all over. The lumber come another way—I don't know how the lumber come—but all the hardware stuff come in on the train. 'Course, we walked half way to keep warm—colder than hell. We wouldn't get back home 'til dark. That was a long trip for a horse—walked all the way. —Mervin Rice

THAT'S SAM KING'S CAR. He was the first one to bring a car to South Bristol. He lived on McFarland's Cove Road. He was the first one to come, just about, to South Bristol with a car and he'd stop at the S Road School and take all the children for rides in his car. —Katherine Poole Norwood

Mudhole on the causeway between "little" bridge and the swing bridge.
William A. Kelsey

Mudholes existed every spring until they dried up. People with cars were very anxious, of course, to get their cars on the road after having them jacked up in the garage all winter. There were several of these mudholes where somebody either with a little truck or horses would pull people out of the mud.

Fred Foster had horses, and he was one of the people who carried the mail, hauled mail with sleigh and wagon in the wintertime—fall and winter when the mail wasn't going on the river, to and from the station in Newcastle. He had some cows and sold milk, delivered milk, and in the spring of the year Fred's horses were put to work because there was a big mudhole in the road out front of his house. Cars would get to certain places where the mud was so deep they couldn't get through, and there would be somebody at each mudhole hauling them through, and Fred did this at the one in front of his house. —Doug Thompson

Wilder Kelsey owned the garage north of the bridge and lived above it. Wilder was a strapping, burly man who had wrestled semi-professionally, and more notably, saved my life one night. Returning the family car to his South Bristol garage after a Christmas Cove dance one night (of course, I had to use the car to pick up my date although she lived almost in sight of the Casino), I paused in one of the large garage doorways, as a large dark car came down the hill and stopped with me in the headlights. A voice invited me to move, but emboldened by my first drink of Prohibition rum, I pointed to the other garage doorway. The car door opened and a figure unfurled taller and taller as Wilder raced down the stairway—picked me up to move me aside as Gene Tunney drove his car into the garage.

—John Howland, *Heron Island Memories*

Kelsey's Garage in South Bristol village, just north of the swing bridge. Many Heron Island families parked their cars here when they were on the island.
William A. Kelsey

When I was a kid there was an old building they used to call the Klondike Building where Kelsey's Garage is—the building right across from Clifford's, there. I don't know why it had that name, but I know once as kids we went in there. There was a summer kid called Billy Wilder—he was older than I. We found an old one-cylinder Harley Davidson motorcycle in there. The tires were cut, and we sewed them up. We got the thing going; I got on it and I went up over Kid Hill. And my father was out in the yard—he saw me and he almost died! And then there was an old car in there, just a two-seater—old Buick or something. We got that going and went up to the flat up above Raymond Poole's and we got that thing up to sixty miles an hour—we thought we were doing something! And I guess we were, in that time, in that thing.

—Doug Thompson

In early days the mail came both by water and by horse and buggy from Newcastle. —Nellie McFarland Frey

Robert Hanley Woodward took over driving the mail when his brother-in-law, Arthur Kelsey, fell ill. EUGENIE WOODWARD COLE

THERE WERE MANY drivers over the years, Gene Wiley, Arthur Kelsey, and Sam Page being among the first. During World War I there was no regular driver and the menfolks of the town took turns going to Newcastle two or three times a week with horse and buggy to bring down the mail.

—Nellie McFarland Frey

THE FIRST POST OFFICE in what is now South Bristol was at a landing on the Damariscotta River, close to the Walpole Meeting House. Thomas McClure had established a trading post there in 1795, and in 1800 he became the first postmaster. This was the start of more than a century of mail delivery by horse and by water.

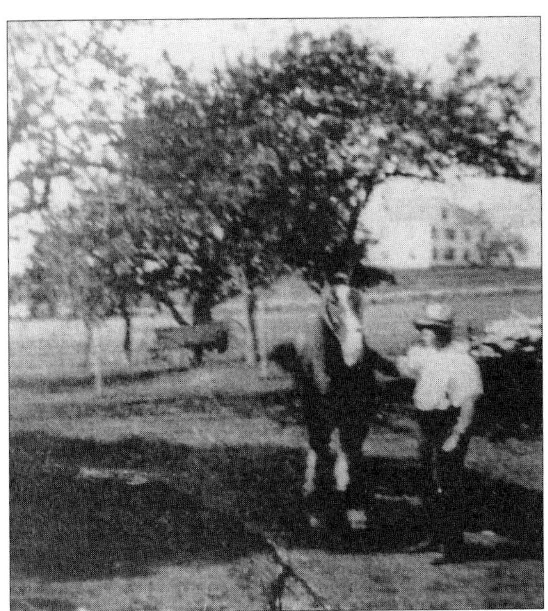

William T. Kelsey, 1847–1911. This is the same William Kelsey who ran the town poorhouse. EUGENIE WOODWARD COLE

Brooks McFarland at the Walpole post office. AUTHOR PHOTO, 1995

MY GRANDFATHER, *William Kelsey, used to drive the mail with horse and buggy from South Bristol to Damariscotta. Year 'round, I guess he did, at that time. Then later on, when boats got more prevalent, the summertime mail used to go on the boats a lot. I think the overland mail still had to go because they had to stop at all the mailboxes along the road.* —Robert Woodward

EUGENE WYLIE had the mail "stage route," as it was called, for years, going from South Bristol to Newcastle to pick up the mail. He had eight horses in his barn and used to rotate the teams every day, so that no pair ever went two days in a row.

THE MAIL CAME *that way, too, by horse. He went every day with a sleigh, but they went in around Clark's Cove. There was a post office there, and they changed horses there; then they took another horse, went from there to Damariscotta. Got the mail—took it off the train there—got the mail, then they'd come back, and they'd come back in around Clark's Cove, and change back to the horse they'd come up on and left in the morning. They'd change and take him and leave the other horse there—they'd swap back, go from there to South Bristol. But in the summertime they went by water. They made two trips a day by water, two mails a day. They'd go quite early in the morning to Damariscotta, pick up the mail in Damariscotta, and they'd come back as far as Pleasant Cove—there was a post office there; then they come down, left mail at Clark's Cove, come down through the narrows to East Boothbay and left mail at East Boothbay, then 'cross to South Bristol, post office there, then they took it by horse or car from there to Christmas Cove. That was back when I was just a kid, but I can remember it easy; probably I was nine, ten years old—probably '25, something like that.*

—Mervin Rice

The first driver that we remember having a truck for bringing the mail was Bill Foster, who drove for several years, after which time Anthony Eugley took over; then came Brooks McFarland, who held the job for over thirty years.

—Nellie McFarland Frey

Uncle Benny

Summer visitors and residents of Christmas Cove will be deeply grieved to learn of the serious illness of Captain Benjamin Andrews, otherwise known as Uncle Benny. For many years this fine old man carried the mail in his rowboat from South Bristol to Christmas Cove, and then to Heron Island. No matter what the weather Uncle Benny was always faithful to his trust and as the bow of his dory scraped the piles of the old wharf his dog would bark. "Hello, Uncle Benny!" many a voice called out, "Hello! Hello!" A merry voice with cheery eyes, a mailbag over his shoulder all crashed together with fishhooks. "Hello!"

—*The Clamdigger*, probably 1917

These launches they talked about—the Pilgrim was one them, and the Celia E. They serviced East Boothbay, Heron Island in the summer, Christmas Cove, and South Bristol with freight, passengers, and mail. They carried the mail in the summer. The mail came on the train to Newcastle. My uncle had the contract to deliver it from the station to the boat which was only about a mile and a half. And then he came down the river and there were stops in Clark's Cove, Poole's Landing on the other side, and leave mail there.

—Doug Thompson

My mother was the Christmas Cove postmistress beginning in the '30s. When I was twelve I clerked there. I had a punt which I rowed about the Cove; frequently, I delivered mail or telegrams

The Christmas Cove post office, with Albert T. Thorpe standing on the porch. Thorpe was the second postmaster at "Christmas," after Captain Frank Wells.
Arletta Thorpe Rice

from the post office to the west side of the Cove. In the summer my "route" included Flora McFarland's dining room, where fresh-baked cookies were my "pay."

It was a summer office only. The office was open from the first of June to the end of September. We needed it when the Holly Inn was here—people wrote letters then—they didn't send faxes in those days, or email. And we had a telephone in the post office because we also had a Western Union agency.

A lot of people would send their Christmas cards and ask to have them done, and she'd bind them all up and pay postage to send them back. She wouldn't gyp them by sending it from South Bristol—she sent them back. She wasn't allowed to postmark them—they all wanted them postmarked December 25, but she couldn't do that because her office was closed.

A big time was when a summer girl made her debut in Middleburg, Virginia, and her mother, out of kindness to my mother, brought all her coming out invitations here to be mailed. Maybe it was a kindness to my mother, or maybe she thought

One of the earliest Walpole post offices was the Hatch house, at the bend on Clark's Cove Road. PHILLIP HATCH

The Rapelye farmhouse, where the Walpole post office was located when Carrie Rapelye was postmistress. It was on the upper section of Clark's Cove Road, partway between the Darling Center and Wawenock Country Club. MERVIN RICE

Christmas Cove was a prestigious postmark to be sending her coming out party invitations from. And that was a big day. We had that rolling cart full of invitations. That was a big deal, because she got paid according to the flow of mail through her post office. —Arletta Thorpe Rice

I USED TO GET a lot of letters from schoolchildren because somehow one year there was an article in a teacher's national magazine mentioning Christmas Cove, and that it might be a good idea to have the schoolchildren have their letters postmarked Christmas Cove at Christmastime. We had so many boxes of letters, and of course the post office was closed in the winter. We had to send them back. But I do remember one woman who always addressed her cards and had me send them the last day of September, that was the day the post office closed—just to get the postmark on the envelopes. —Catherine Jordon Walker

THAT'S WHERE the post office was for a long time. They had a little ell thing built onto the house, kind of a little room. Carrie Rapelye had a little store there, sold candy bars and a few little things. Post Office was in that little room there. She had that for years. She finally got so old she had to give up the post office and it was moved up here at Koch's, right over here where the orchard is. That's where it moved to. They had it in the ell part of the house, had the post office in there. She give it up or she died, and then they moved it up here where it is now. —Mervin Rice

THE FIRST POSTMASTER in the village was John Otis, who operated out of a building adjacent to where Union Church now is, serving from 1863 through 1885. He was followed by a succession of shopkeepers: typically the post office would be located inside of the general store, and so we also recognize these names as proprietors of local mercantiles and groceries: Nelson Gamage, Julius C. Gamage, Merritt Thompson, and Daniel Berry.

Farrin's Store, probably about 1951. Doug and Jo Thompson's gift shop is at right. J. DOUGLAS THOMPSON

The building that housed the last village post office before the present one, across the road from Farrin's store. AUTHOR PHOTO, 1997

IN 1917 EVERETT GAMAGE became postmaster and the post office was back in one end of where he had his store. Mail wasn't delivered then and we'd walk up and wait for the mail to come in. Everett served for sixteen years, after which Afton Farrin became postmaster and the post office was moved across the bridge to Farrin's Store. After Afton Farrin's death in 1949, Charles Frey was appointed and served for almost thirty years. Most of this time the post office was located in the small building just north of Wilder Kelsey's garage. On August 6, 1973, it was moved a final time to the new parish house—on church property, within 200 feet of where the first post office was located.

—Nellie McFarland Frey

By 1888 these people were all involved in boardinghouses. —Arletta Thorpe Rice

"Greetings from South Bristol." An early tinted postcard produced for the tourist trade. WILLIAM A. KELSEY

ELIPHALET'S WAS A boardinghouse, the Brewers' was a boardinghouse, Aunt Arletta took in boarders. It didn't take very much to take in boarders then. They didn't eat very well and they didn't have fancy rooms or bedding. Didn't have any running water, no electricity.

—Arletta Thorpe Rice

AS THE OFFSHORE fisheries declined in the 1880s, natives up and down the coast of the South Bristol peninsula turned to the newly burgeoning tourist trade as a source of income. Summer visitors came by steamer from Boston and New York, often spending the entire summer at the shore. In Christmas Cove and South Bristol village, hotels were built to accommodate them; homes were converted into summer boardinghouses even as far up as Walpole. On Heron Island and in Christmas Cove, cottages were built by local craftsmen; these summer colonies still thrive, and many of the cottages are to this day summer retreats for family members of the original owners.

TEN YEARS AT PEMAQUID.

Not many years ago Christmas Cove was one of the many fishing stations located along our coast from which sailed large and substantial fishing vessels, with sturdy crews on long voyages to the banks of Newfoundland and other places. The Thorp brothers owning two vessels, one called the "Mountain Laurel" sailed by Capt. Edward, and the "Twilight" by Capt. Loring Thorp, used to belong here. They made two trips to the banks for codfish each spring, being gone from six to eight weeks; then during the latter part of the summer visited the Bay of Chaleurs and British coast in pursuit of mackerel. Large buildings were required to store and salt the fish they caught; flakes covering much land were built to dry and cure them on. A store was provided to furnish with goods the families of those hardy men who manned their vessels. This is one of the "passing industries" of our sea coast. Steamers now land passengers where old bankers landed codfish. The old storehouses protect the freight and baggage of the summer visitors, and the descendants of the fishermen cater to their wants.

J. Henry Cartland, *Ten Years at Pemaquid*, 1899.

FROM A VERY SMALL *beginning and fairly soon, every fisherman's house, or many of them, took boarders, additions were built to the houses, and boat shops were turned into dining rooms. Fishermen became masons and carpenters and built cottages, and some took sailing parties in the summer in the boats they had made in winter. Women took in washing. In short, the whole community of people was glad to take in summer boarders and the money they spent.*

—Henry Seaver, letter to his nephew, 1937

BACK IN THOSE DAYS *practically everybody in the summertime rented rooms and took in boarders. All of these were boardinghouses, and in the summer they were filled up.* —Doug Thompson

THE MOST WELL KNOWN, and largest, of the local hostelries was the Holly Inn, first opened

A card showing the first Holly Inn from the John's Bay side, postmarked 1906. The message reads, "This house burned last Saturday night." WILLIAM A. KELSEY

in 1903 by Albert T. Thorpe. Situated on a high bluff that overlooked John's Bay on the east and the Christmas Cove harbor on the west, it drew summer visitors with its spectacular views, cool ocean breezes, and fresh seafood. In 1906, however, it burned to the ground, becoming the first of South Bristol's "summer flammables."

Not to be deterred, Thorpe rebuilt; this time it was a much larger structure, with ninety sleeping rooms. Guests by then could make use of the recreational facilities across the road at the Christmas Cove Improvement Association: the Casino, tennis, swimming, and boating, among other pleasures. Unfortunately, this inn, too, was destroyed by fire in 1923. In 1924, with the financial help of three investors from the CCIA, Albert Thorpe rebuilt one last time; the "New Holly Inn," was an enormous structure, with more than a hundred sleeping rooms and a large dining room overlooking John's Bay. Alas, this burned in 1940, seven years after Albert Thorpe's death at age sixty-five. It's no wonder that mere mention of the Holly Inns to many natives calls forth the memory of a spectacular blaze.

The second Holly Inn. At first, the fire was slow to spread, and volunteers and hotel employees had time to rescue some items from inside. WILLIAM A. KELSEY

The town firetruck, parked on the Bar, pumps water up to the fire. The Bar is a low, narrow neck of land, nearly at sea level; parked in the middle of it the pumper could be within a few yards of the water on either side. WILLIAM A. KELSEY

I CAN REMEMBER *one burning that I went to the fire. We were there all day—every man, I guess, in town. They had hand-pumpers operated by the firemen themselves, a group on each side of these handles, pumping up and down, pumping salt water onto that fire. That fire burned all day long.*

—Doug Thompson

I REMEMBER THE *Holly Inn burning—it was 1923, and I was thirteen. I was helping out at the Russell House when they were so busy; we lived right behind it so they'd ask if I'd come down and help with the waitressing. This happened right after noontime and everybody left from everywhere and went over to get closer to it. I've got a little souvenir that I picked up off the grounds—two egg cups that fused together. Think how hot that must have been! They rarely saved a building in those days.*

—Catherine Jordon Walker

I WAS OUT PLAYING *one day when Dad came running down the road. I was only three or four years old. And he came running by the house and he kept right on going and hollered at Mama and says, "The Holly Inn is burning!" and he kept on going to help fight the fire. Mama and I went down by the water and watched the old Holly Inn burn.*

—Nellie McFarland Frey

I CAN TELL YOU, *this made some fire when that burned. It was right in our bedroom windows over there—we could actually see the flames from Christmas Cove, my brother and I. My dad was fire chief.* —Bill Kelsey

The second Inn succumbs to fire, 1923. Albert T. Thorpe is the large man in a white shirt, in front of the steps. Wilder Kelsey, the fire chief, is to Thorpe's right, holding his hat down at his side. PEMAQUID HISTORICAL ASSOCIATION

THE RUSSELL HOUSE, today's Coveside Inn, was built in the 1880s, and was at first run as a boardinghouse. Around 1900 its owners Albion and Hannah Russell Gamage enlarged it to become a hotel. With a large dining room and space for a hundred guests, it was another popular spot. Christmas Cove House, Rutherford House, the French-McFarland House and numerous boardinghouses also welcomed summer visitors.

DURING THE SAME PERIOD, guest accommodations were also being expanded up in the village. The Thompson Inn was opened by Eliphalet McFarland in 1905 on the mainland side of the Eastern Gut. It had been a Thompson homestead, built in 1840 by Ada Thompson McFarland's grandfather. She and her husband Eliphalet bought it in 1903. They began by taking in boarders, then enlarged it with the addition of a two-story wing and

Russell House. Local lore has it that the storage building, on the right, was moved to its location by sliding it across the ice from the other side of the cove. CATHERINE JORDON WALKER

This unusual view of the Summit House is a private photograph taken in July 1908. The visitors are sitting beside today's West Side Road, with the camera looking east up the hill towards the hotel. WILLIAM A. KELSEY

verandah. Its 1905 brochure describes it as "... not a hotel, but a select house for about thirty people who are looking for a restful place to spend the summer...." The nearby French House was built in 1882 by "Wash" French, a pogy boat captain, and was later operated in conjunction with the Thompson Inn.

IN 1892, NELSON GAMAGE, a civil war veteran and one of the town's postmasters, opened the elegant Summit House on Rutherford Island. He sited it on a choice spot high above the village. Many postcards of the day show the view from its cupola: a sweeping panorama of the harbors of both the Eastern and the Western Gut, and across to the Damariscotta River. It proved to be such a popular hotel that guests were reputed to be willing, when all the guest rooms were filled, to sleep on cots on the porch.

Like its Christmas Cove counterparts it, too, succumbed to fire. In 1917 Summit House escaped harm in the disastrous fire that swept up the hill on the west side of the main road. In 1918, however, spontaneous combustion is believed to have sparked in the hotel's lamp room—where maids had been cleaning and filling kerosene lamps—starting a fire that destroyed the hotel. All that survived was "Brambletye Cottage," the Gamage's home and sometime annex to the hotel.

FOR THE first half of the twentieth century, the hotels and boardinghouses provided a source of summer employment for many of the natives, particularly young women, who would often board at the place where they were working.

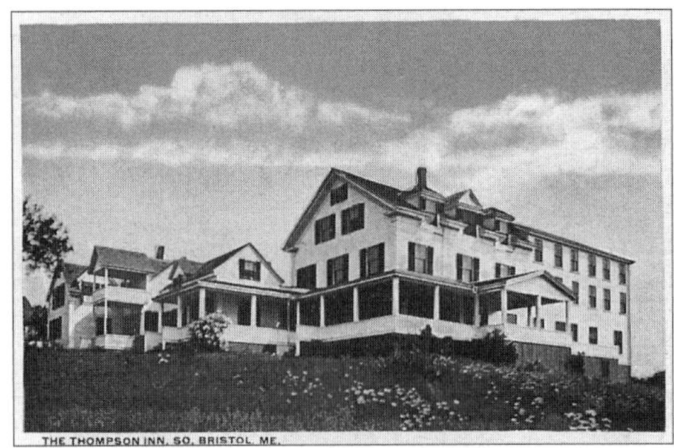

Undated postcard of the Thompson Inn addressed to Helen Russell, 1907. Catherine Jordon Walker

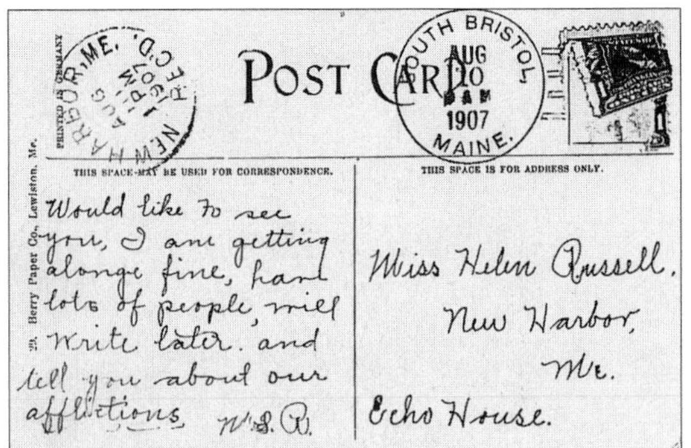

South Bristol, Maine. August 10, 1907
Would like to see you, I am getting along fine, have lots of people, will write later and tell you about our *<u>afflictions</u>*. *—W. S. J.*

Postcard of the "New Holly Inn" dining room addressed to to Ella Burton. William A. Kelsey

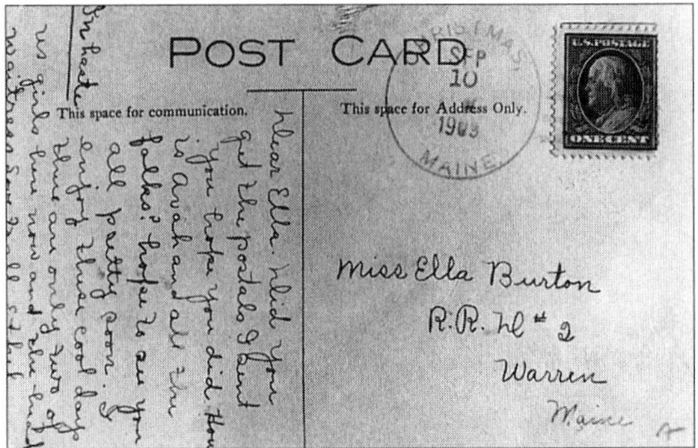

Christmas, Maine. Sep. 10, 1903 *<u>In haste.</u>*
Dear Ella. Did you get the postals I sent you hope you did. How is Avah and all the folks? hope to see you pretty soon. I enjoy these cool days there are only two of us girls here now and the head waitress. Love to all

Postcard of Summit House addressed to Mrs. Wotton in Friendship. Author's collection

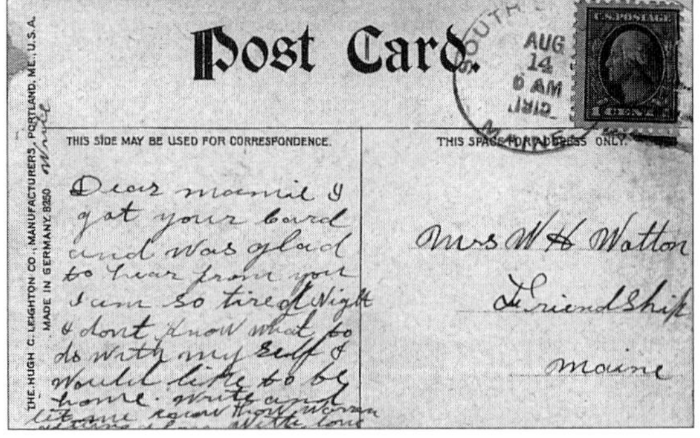

South Bristol, Maine. August 14, 1915. Dear Mamie I got your card and was glad to hear from you. I am so tired at night I don't know what to do with myself & would like to be home. Write and let me know how Warrens getting along. With love, Olivia.

"Fête Day" at the Christmas Cove Improvement Association, 1913. Crowds throng the steamer wharf and Casino grounds. Catherine Jordon Walker

In those days before the advent of the telephone, Winnie Jordon and Helen Russell, later to become sisters-in-law, were just two of the many who went off to work in the hotels, and kept in touch with each other by postcard.

Christmas Cove, encompassing the southernmost part of Rutherford Island, became a popular destination for summer visitors near the end of the century yet it still retained a year-round native population. In the early part of the twentieth century, young people from up in the village were drawn to its summer attractions.

Down on the wharf at Christmas Cove—it was a lively place during the summertime down there. We used to go down there; that was our entertainment. Right there on the wharf there were large buildings which housed a bowling alley, a pool room, ice cream parlors, a general store that employed several people ... and that was the place to spend the evenings—lot of excitement going on down there. It sure was a lively place there, where we kids used to love to hang out evenings during the summer. And in the evening there was always either a New York or a Boston yacht club anchored in there, or a big steamer coming in. Just alive, y'know. —Doug Thompson

Yacht club at anchor in Christmas Cove harbor. William A. Kelsey

Christmas Cove Casino about 1916, photographed by Goldwin, the teenage daughter of Captain Frank Gilbert. Marian Coughlin

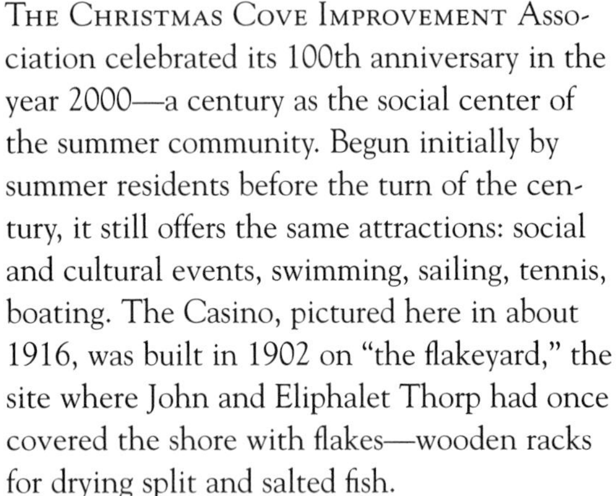

The Christmas Cove Improvement Association celebrated its 100th anniversary in the year 2000—a century as the social center of the summer community. Begun initially by summer residents before the turn of the century, it still offers the same attractions: social and cultural events, swimming, sailing, tennis, boating. The Casino, pictured here in about 1916, was built in 1902 on "the flakeyard," the site where John and Eliphalet Thorp had once covered the shore with flakes—wooden racks for drying split and salted fish.

The first backstops at the CCIA tennis courts, back in the days when women still wore long dresses to play, were made of fishnets strung between wooden posts. From a card postmarked 1906. William A. Kelsey

Christmas Cove Land Company: *this is a project that never amounted to anything, thank heavens. Someone had the idea of developing this whole part of the island. I remember the man who had something to do with it. His name was William Nash.* —Catherine Jordon Walker

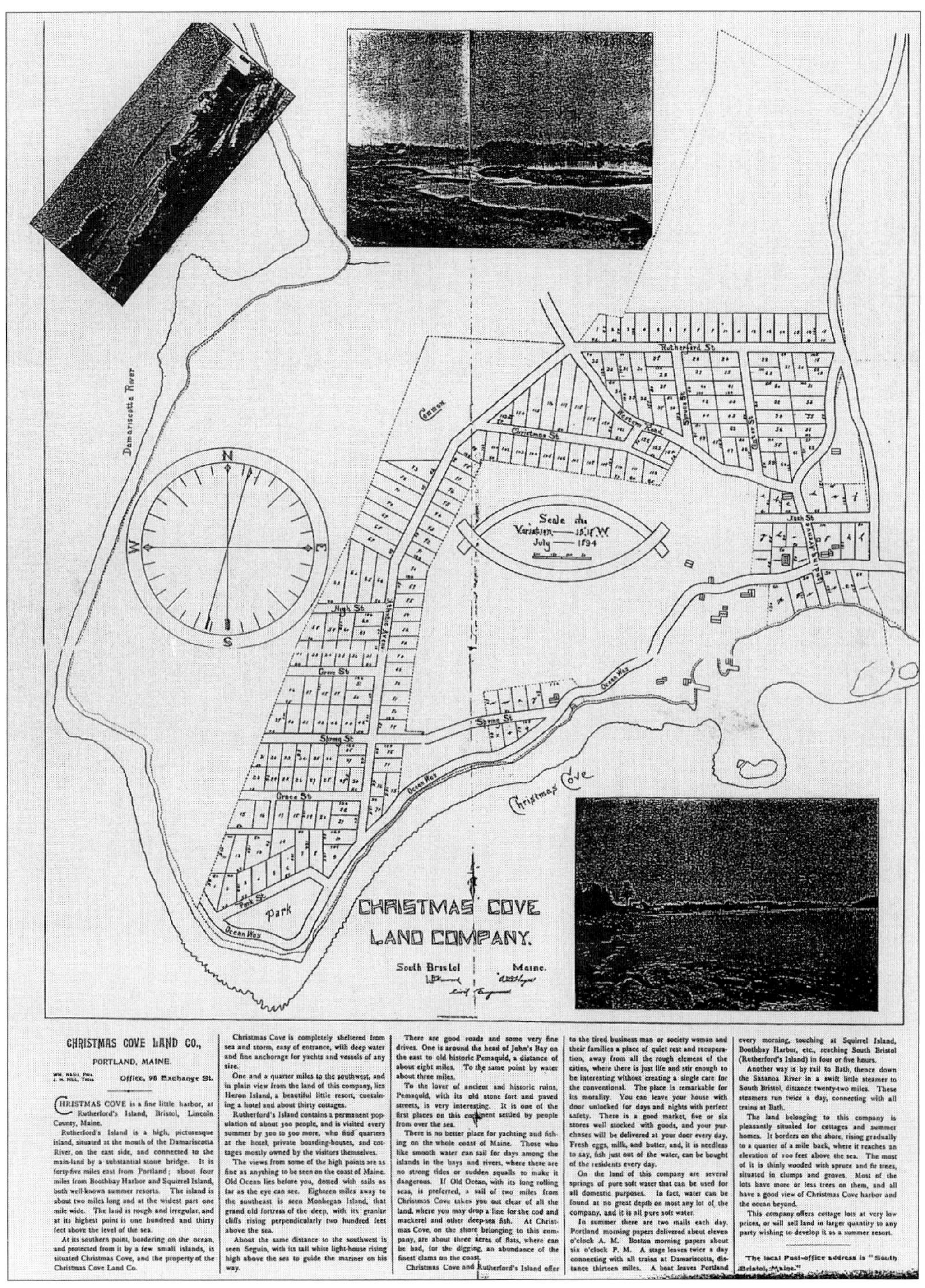

CHRISTMAS COVE LAND CO.,

PORTLAND, MAINE.

Office, 98 Exchange St.

CHRISTMAS COVE is a fine little harbor, at Rutherford's Island, Bristol, Lincoln County, Maine.

Rutherford's Island is a high, picturesque island, situated at the mouth of the Damariscotta River, on the east side, and connected to the main-land by a substantial stone bridge. It is forty-five miles east from Portland; about four miles from Boothbay Harbor and Squirrel Island, both well-known summer resorts. The island is about two miles long and at the widest part one mile wide. The land is rough and irregular, and at its highest point is one hundred and thirty feet above the level of the sea.

At its southern point, bordering on the ocean, and protected from it by a few small islands, is situated Christmas Cove, and the property of the Christmas Cove Land Co.

Christmas Cove is completely sheltered from sea and storm, easy of entrance, with deep water and fine anchorage for yachts and vessels of any size.

One and a quarter miles to the southwest, and in plain view from the land of this company, lies Heron Island, a beautiful little resort, containing a hotel and about thirty cottages.

Rutherford's Island contains a permanent population of about 300 people, and is visited every summer by 300 to 500 more, who find quarters at the hotel, private boarding-houses, and cottages mostly owned by the visitors themselves.

The views from some of the high points are as fine as anything to be seen on the coast of Maine. Old Ocean lies before you, dotted with sails as far as the eye can see. Eighteen miles away to the southeast is seen Monhegan Island, that grand old fortress of the deep, with its granite cliffs rising perpendicularly two hundred feet above the sea.

About the same distance to the southwest is seen Seguin, with its tall white light-house rising high above the sea to guide the mariner on his way.

There are good roads and some very fine drives. One is around the head of John's Bay on the east to old historic Pemaquid, a distance of about eight miles. To the same point by water about three miles.

To the lover of ancient and historic ruins, Pemaquid, with its old stone fort and paved streets, is very interesting. It is one of the first places on this continent settled by people from over the sea.

There is no better place for yachting and fishing on the whole coast of Maine. Those who like smooth water can sail for days among the islands in the bays and rivers, where there are no strong tides or sudden squalls to make it dangerous. If Old Ocean, with its long rolling seas, is preferred, a sail of two miles from Christmas Cove takes you out clear of all the land, where you may drop a line for the cod and mackerel and other deep-sea fish. At Christmas Cove, on the shore belonging to this company, are about three acres of flats, where can be had, for the digging, an abundance of the finest clams on the coast.

Christmas Cove and Rutherford's Island offer to the tired business man or society woman and their families a place of quiet rest and recuperation, away from all the rough element of the cities, where there is just life and stir enough to be interesting without creating a single care for the conventional. The place is remarkable for its morality. You can leave your house with door unlocked for days and nights with perfect safety. There is a good market, five or six stores well stocked with goods, and your purchases will be delivered at your door every day. Fresh eggs, milk, and butter, and, it is needless to say, fish just out of the water, can be bought of the residents every day.

On the land of this company are several springs of pure soft water that can be used for all domestic purposes. In fact, water can be found at no great depth on most any lot of the company, and it is all pure soft water.

In summer there are two mails each day. Portland morning papers delivered about eleven o'clock A. M. Boston morning papers about six o'clock P. M. A stage leaves twice a day connecting with all trains at Damariscotta, distance thirteen miles. A boat leaves Portland every morning, touching at Squirrel Island, Boothbay Harbor, etc., reaching South Bristol (Rutherford's Island) in four or five hours.

Another way is by rail to Bath, thence down the Sasanoa River in a swift little steamer to South Bristol, distance twenty-two miles. These steamers run twice a day, connecting with all trains at Bath.

The land belonging to this company is pleasantly situated for cottages and summer homes. It borders on the shore, rising gradually to a quarter of a mile back, where it reaches an elevation of 100 feet above the sea. The most of it is thinly wooded with spruce and fir trees, situated in clumps and groves. Most of the lots have more or less trees on them, and all have a good view of Christmas Cove harbor and the ocean beyond.

This company offers cottage lots at very low prices, or will sell land in larger quantity to any party wishing to develop it as a summer resort.

The local Post-office address is "South Bristol, Maine."

Plat map and prospectus for the Christmas Cove Land Company, 1894. CATHERINE JORDON WALKER

A FAMILY OF INDIANS spent summers in tents off John's Bay curve in Christmas Cove. They came to Heron several times during the season, in birch bark canoes, to sell handcrafted sweetgrass baskets, toy canoes, and tomahawks carved of wood, delicate canoes fashioned in birch bark, sturdy ash and birch bark "boxes" useful by the hearth.

—Floyd Humphries, "Boyhood Memories"

THERE WAS A HUGE ROCK there alongside of the road, at the head of Christmas Cove. When I was a kid at home, the Indians used to come down from Old Town. They would set up their housekeeping there in a camp that was on that big rock, right by the side of the road on what we called the Bar. They had a shack there on that ledge and they stayed there all summer—gathered sweetgrass and reeds and so forth, and made and sold their baskets. They knew where all of the good stuff grew. Their name was Ranco. Members of the Ranco family are still living up in Old Town. It was right there on that bar. —Doug Thompson

Summer guests promenade on the Bar at Christmas Cove; the Ranco's camp is in the center foreground. Courtesy WILLIAM A. KELSEY

THE SOURCE OF the sweetgrass was always a well-kept secret. The Indians kept it well to themselves.

—Norman Hamlin

SWEETGRASS GROWS IN THE FIELD—it's a hay. It grows where it's kind of swampy. But the baskets—you could smell it—it has a sweet smell. Mama for years had a big hank of sweetgrass hanging in her bedroom; you could smell that all over the house.

—Nellie McFarland Frey

I was born in 1910, and we spent seven summers there on Heron Island...

—Catherine Jordon Walker

...NOT THE YEAR I WAS BORN, *but starting the next year. There were two large rooms up over the store. It was so pleasant, I loved it. I have such happy memories of those days.*

—Catherine Jordon Walker

Catherine Jordon sitting next to the Heron Island steamer wharf, c. 1914.
CATHERINE JORDON WALKER

UNLIKE MOST OF South Bristol's other islands, Inner Heron Island was uninhabited until late in the nineteenth century. It was owned by the state of Maine until 1884, when it was sold to a land speculator from Boston. It passed through other hands in subsequent years, and the first four cottages were constructed in 1887. By 1910 the summer-cottage community of twenty-five cottages, clubhouse, and post office was virtually complete, with only three additional cottages added in the twentieth century. Nearly half of these buildings were constructed by Will Jordon or his son Frank.

Similar to the summer community at Christmas Cove, many of the original summer residents were from the clergy or the teaching profession; also like the Cove, many members of today's thriving summer community are descendants of the original cottage owners.

The Heron Island store and post office. Frank Jordon was the storekeeper as well as being the island's first postmaster. It was here that the steamers delivered the mail, foodstuffs, and supplies on which the islanders depended. CATHERINE JORDON WALKER

THE STORE CARRIED *everything that anybody could want. The produce and the meat and everything came on the steamboat; there were usually two trips a day. There were two mails a day. Imagine it—when letters cost two cents for a stamp, and a penny for a postcard.* —Catherine Jordon Walker

HELEN JORDON'S ACCOUNTS on a 1913 page of the store's ledger reveal the variety of goods and services offered, as well as their prices:

1 basket peaches	.10
2 mackerel	.18
1# Pilot	.10
1 pkg Cheese Sandwich	.10
2 cans deviled ham	.10
1 ½# cod to fry	.15
1 jar bacon	.22
1 loaf bread	.12
6 Lobsters	.60
Lugging 1 box water	.15
Trip to Cove	.50

A short distance beyond the end of the bowling alleys stood an icehouse and nearly opposite the icehouse, across the road, a stable for the island horse. Filled in the spring from Thompson's icehouse in South Bristol with 100-pound cakes, carried by barge to Heron, the island icehouse supplied the needs of hotel, store, and cottages. About once a week, Frank and Wellie Jordon drove the nag hitched to an old underslung Maine wagon to deliver ice. Each cottage, or many cottages, had a large, handmade, zinc-lined rectangular icebox. To us lads, the trick was irresistible. Mischievous, perhaps, mean really. When Frank or Wellie left the horse to graze on the center path while delivering with tongs a cake of ice to someone, a couple of us brats hopped in the wagon, drove it 500 yards north, then escaped in the woods to watch patient Frank walk to his abandoned four-wheeler cart.

—Floyd Humphries, "Boyhood Memories"

The steamer ENTERPRISE at the Heron Island wharf, from a card postmarked 1910. The jackstaff and bow of a smaller steamer can just be seen to the left of the wharf. WILLIAM A. KELSEY

SEE THE SIGN? THAT POST? *If that were this way, the boat would go by. If it was this way the boat came in. If it was horizontal the boat would come in—they had some people or some mail. It was a flagstop.* —Bill Kelsey

The footbridge from Davis Point to Gem Island, about 1904. The house on the left was later torn down and replaced with a more modern structure. J. DOUGLAS THOMPSON

Postcard of Witch Island, postmarked 1910. The –message on the back: "Tell them all hello. I pass this island tomorrow...." WILLIAM A. KELSEY

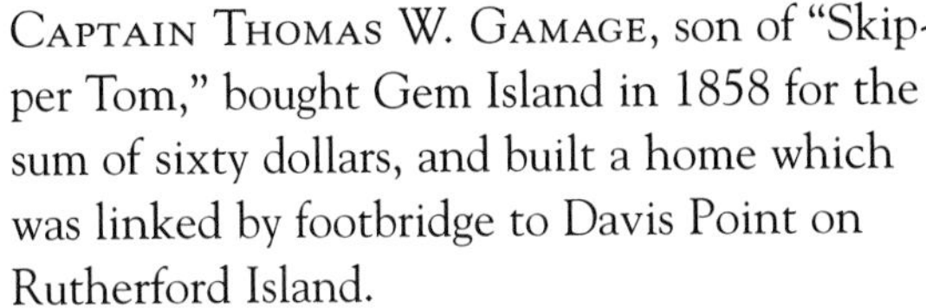

CAPTAIN THOMAS W. GAMAGE, son of "Skipper Tom," bought Gem Island in 1858 for the sum of sixty dollars, and built a home which was linked by footbridge to Davis Point on Rutherford Island.

MY MOTHER USED TO *take me out there somewhere on Davis Point to pick blackberries; we used to walk down there. She caught me one day about twenty feet out on the bridge, and it was all rotten. Didn't I get scolded. "Get off that _____ bridge!"* —Bill Kelsey

FORMERLY KNOWN AS DAVIS ISLAND, the island was purchased by Daniel Chittenden in 1867, who came there with his wife Grace Courtland Chittenden to occupy it as a summer residence.

"Uncle Dan," as he was known, and his wife were indeed very strange and remarkable people. They came from New York City, where Grace Courtland Chittenden was the financial editor of the *Wall Street Daily News,* a sort of predecessor of the *Wall Street Journal.* As financial editor, she began to attract unusual attention. With some sort of uncanny judgment, her evaluations and predictions about the value of all investments, became so accurate that she became known far and wide as "The Witch of Wall Street."

The fame and reputation of this woman followed her to South Bristol, Maine, and it began to be a common expression that Davis's Island was the home of "the Witch," so much so that the name was actually changed and it has been called such to this day.

—Harold Castner, "The Castner Papers"

GENE TUNNEY'S HOUSE -- JOHN'S BAY -- PEMAQUID BEACH, MAINE
AS SEEN FROM CAP'N ELIOT WINSLOW'S "ARGO" B281

Gene Tunney's house on John's Island. Tunney's mother-in-law, Katherine Rowland Lauder, bought the island in 1926, and built a Bar Harbor-style cottage on it. Her brother Henry had owned nearby Witch Island since 1916. WILLIAM A. KELSEY

AFTER THE BIG FIGHT *with Jack Dempsey, Tunney flew here and he went on to John's Island. He was married to a girl—Polly Lauder—and her mother owned the island. She was here, of course, and he come here and went on the island. Well, it seems 'bout daylight that there was all these reporters around trying to get a picture of him. He came out of that house bare naked, run down and jumped overboard. 'Course he didn't think anybody was around, you know. Jeez, they got pictures of it. He says, "If I ever hear tell anybody's seen one of them pictures, I'll hang each and every one of you." Boy, was he ugly. They got pictures, but I don't believe anybody ever seen 'em.*

—Mervin Rice

PRESIDENT KENNEDY *was coming up there for a visit, and they of course cordoned off the whole island. They wouldn't let boats anywhere near that island when he was coming in there. They even made the Tunneys leave. That whole town was full of Secret Service people. Every available room that could be rented, they had them.*

They brought him in with a helicopter. They had a caretaker out there, of course, on the island— Alex Ropes—and he had a nice garden out there. And when they came in with that helicopter there were squashes, cucumbers, tomatoes—everything—all flying through the air.

—Doug Thompson

PRESIDENT KENNEDY left the Tunneys two gifts in thanks for his visit: the White House telephone, and the American flag that had flown over the house during his three-day visit.

IT WAS ON THRUMCAP that Edward Cornelius Holmes took up his abode by the old "Squatter's Rights," after the disaster of the burning of the $10,000 plant at Damariscotta Oyster

TEN YEARS AT PEMAQUID.

As we pass out of Christmas Cove continuing our passage toward Pemaquid Beach, we leave Inner Heron Island on the south. That large island which the steamer now heads for, whose highest part is covered with spruce trees is called Thrumbcap. It is owned by Mr. Edward C. Holmes (a relative of Oliver Wendell Holmes) who with his family and friends have occupied it for several years, using steam and sailing yachts for conveyance to different places of interest. One of the prettiest little beaches to be found in this section extends across a cove at the south end of this island which consists entirely of finely broken and bleached mussel shells. Mr. Holmes has shipped many barrels of them for hen food. At one time he had a mill at one of the oyster shell heaps above referred to on the eastern bank of the Damariscotta River where he made a business of grinding up the shells for the same purpose.

J. Henry Cartland, 1899.

Summer visitors watch a steamer cut through the Thread of Life; from a card postmarked 1908.
Author's collection

Shell heaps in 1896, in which he lost his entire fortune. He continued to ship ground shells from there for poultry uses but the venture was of little profit to him. He later removed to Damariscotta Mills and died there in a humble shack, alone and destitute.

—Harold Castner,
"The Castner Papers"

O. W. Holmes *and his mother lived on Thrumcap Island. He told me that they moved ashore around the twenties. There used to be the shell of an old house on Thrumcap Island when I was quite young, and the night before the Fourth of July, 1929 or '30, this thing went up in flames. I remember standing out on this porch and seeing it—flames going up on Thrumcap Island, and that was the shell of the old house.* —Norman Hamlin

Thrums are rope yarns, which old-time sailors used to weave into skullcaps for themselves. Hence, any round, bare island was called a thrumcap.

They'd camp out on the islands, go lobstering—Turnip Island and Thrumcap. Afton Farrin, Ted Farrin, used to camp out on Thrumcap just in shacks, spend a week or two at a time out there fishing. They didn't have to come up to bring their stuff to market every day—they'd bring it once a week, whatever; they didn't get much for lobsters, five cents apiece—something like that. They'd be right there tending their traps every morning, every day, and I imagine they were probably close to their bait supply because they probably got their bait off of the different pogy boats. —Bill Kelsey

On Turnip Island, there had been kind of a shack when I was young. We used to row out there and explore the island, and there was this kind of shell of an old house. About that time there was a period when a fisherman and his wife and newborn baby used to live out there, and they used to row their dory up to this beach and come ashore because there was a spring down here. They would get fresh water there, fill up demijohns. It was only a temporary place; it was a shelter during the summer. —Norman Hamlin

TEN YEARS AT PEMAQUID.

Here we change our course; abruptly sweeping around the red spar buoy on our left, we enter a narrow passage called the "Thread of Life," which is formed by a part of the smaller islands, which extend in nearly a straight line between the two larger islands, Thrumbcap on the south and Birch Island on the north. The little huts seen along this passage upon either side of it, are occupied, a part of the year, by fishermen who come from a distance to catch lobsters, finding a safe and convenient harbor for the pursuit of their occupation.

J. Henry Cartland, 1899.

The TOURIST steams through the Thread of Life, on her way to Pemaquid. WILLIAM A. KELSEY

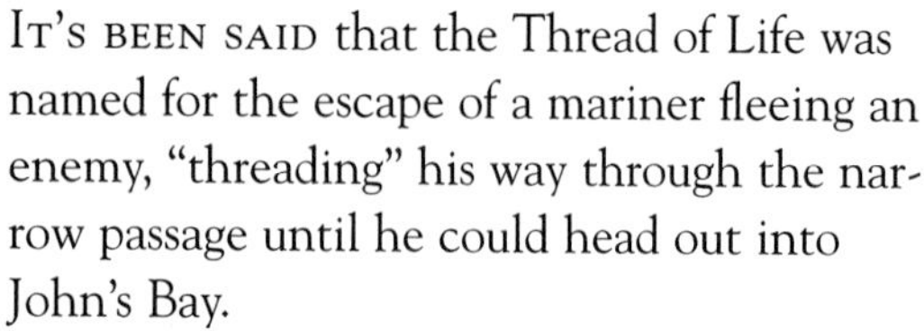

IT'S BEEN SAID that the Thread of Life was named for the escape of a mariner fleeing an enemy, "threading" his way through the narrow passage until he could head out into John's Bay.

YOU COME BETWEEN Crow and Thrumcap, and up the Thread of Life around the point. That's where the shipwrecks were, and that was a way to get safely into harbor. You come between Crow and Thrumcap, and up the Thread of Life around the point. —Arletta Thorpe Rice

HERE ARE STEAMBOATS going through these passages. This one would go over to Pemaquid. Instead of having to go around Thrumcap they'd cut up through the Thread of Life: somewhere in here there's a little spot called the "Needle's Eye." You have to know where you're going to go through the Needle's Eye. —Doug Thompson

My grandmother made the best cookies...
—Margaret Farrin House

. . .JUST SUGAR COOKIES, but she had a little bush of caraway—she had caraway seeds growing outside and we used to pick caraway. I used to gather them when they'd get dry, go out and gather them for her. And then she'd sprinkle it on the sugar cookies. Make it good—kinda different.

—Margaret Farrin House

Martha Marden King, born either 1843 or 1845. She is pictured here sitting in the doorway of her father's house on the Bar, with an in-progress rag rug on her lap. ARLETTA THORPE RICE

I COULD NEVER come up to my mother's or my aunt's cooking. Never. Biscuits, yeast bread. Old-fashioned fruit cakes. Yellow cake, with cream filling and white frosting. Coated with colored caraway seeds—always put 'em on my birthday cake.

—Nellie McFarland Frey

OF COURSE ALL the mothers had different things that they made special. Catherine's mother used to have—oh, she made the most delicious molasses cookies. Of course everybody used to roll their cookies out and cut them with a cookie cutter. And then she made thin sugar cookies—oh, so good.

—Nellie McFarland Frey

104 RUTHERFORD COOK BOOK

DOUGHNUTS

1 cup sugar
1 cup sweet milk
2 eggs
2 tablespoons thick cream
2 teaspoons cream tartar
1 teaspoon soda
Salt and nutmeg

—*Edna Pool.*

DOUGHNUTS IN RHYME

One cup of sugar, one cup of milk,
Two eggs beaten fine as silk.
Salt and nutmeg (lemon will do),
Of baking powder, teaspoons two.
Lightly stir the flour in,
Roll on pie board, not too thin;
Cut in diamonds, twists or rings,
Drop with care the doughy things
Into fat that swiftly swells
Evenly the tiny cells;
Watch with care the time for turning,
Fry them brown, just short of burning;
Roll in sugar, serve when cool.
This is a never failing rule.

DOUGHNUTS

1 cup sour milk
2 eggs
1 cup sugar
½ nutmeg
1 teaspoon soda
¾ teaspoon salt
4 teaspoons melted lard
Flour to make soft dough

Fry in very hot fat.—*Alice O. Gamage.*

MOLASSES DOUGHNUTS

1 cup molasses
½ cup sugar
1 cup milk
1 tablespoon butter
2 eggs
2 teaspoons cream tartar
1 teaspoon soda
Spice, salt and flour

—*Macie Foster Oliver.*

Recipe page and poem from the *Rutherford Cook Book*, originally published in 1930 by the Ladies' Aid.

She cooked on a woodstove, always, that's right. One thing she used to make was nice doughnuts. Oh, I used to like those. She used to have hot doughnuts, you know. Make a whole batch of doughnuts and we'd come in when she was frying them up and have a hot doughnut. Right wonderful.

—Robert Woodward

I never had much luck with doughnuts—they'd come out so hard—but my mother's doughnuts were so good. And I remember her using a fork like that, turning them over. It browns on one side and then turn it over to brown on the other side. Oh, it's fun to make them.

—Beatrice Plummer Rice

Martha Marden King, daughter of master mariner Simon Marden, was known as "The Rag Artist." She lived in the little sea captain's house on the Bar, just below the Holly Inn. She sold her rugs—intricate images of local scenes—to summer visitors at the Inn and the Christmas Cove boardinghouses.

What my mother and some of the ladies her age used to do, if there was a big family and the parents didn't have much money, they'd go to that family and sew. They'd have certain days of the week they'd go and sew for the children in the big families.

My mother always sewed—her sister had a big family of children, and so she sewed and knitted mittens and sweaters for them the year 'round. Mama always had an old treadle machine, and she did a lot on that, and I'm sure she did some by hand, too. She would go and buy yard goods, make aprons for her sister and Dad's sister and different ones, and make clothes and knit mittens and sweaters and caps for her sister's family all the time. They had quite a family of children and not much money. She made just about all my clothes, and she made clothes for my older children, too. And she still kept on knitting mittens, just about as long as she was around here.

—Nellie McFarland Frey

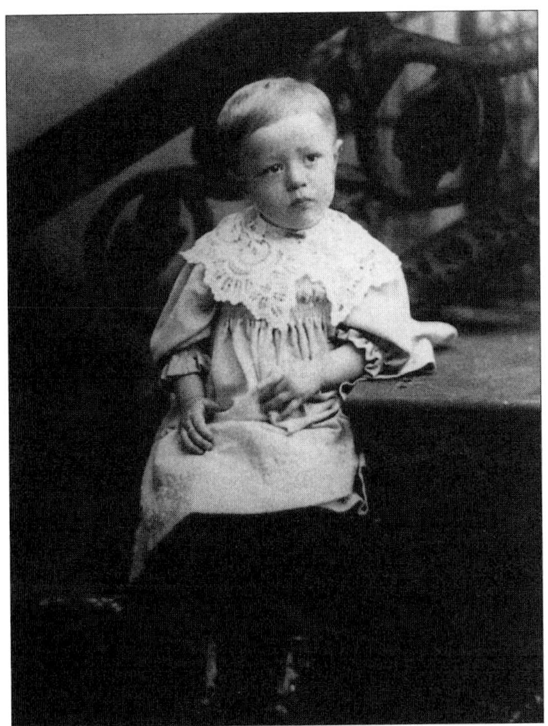

Elliot Gamage Leeman, about 1889.
MARGARET FARRIN HOUSE

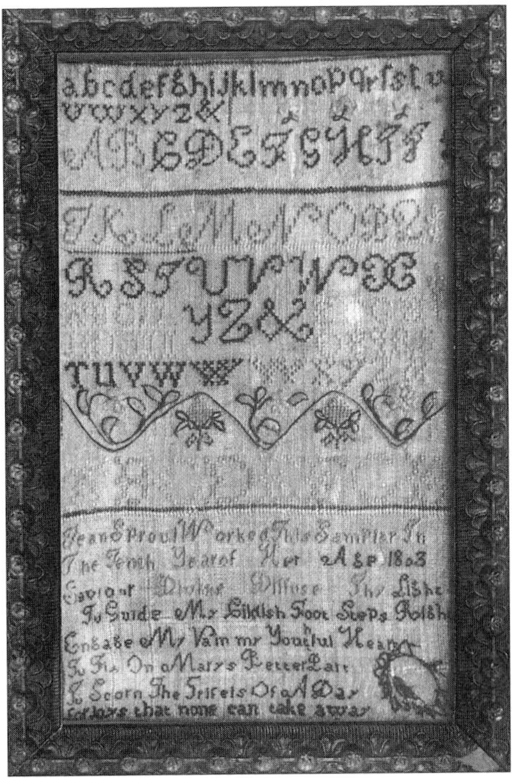

Sampler by Jane Sproul of Walpole, worked in 1803 when she was ten years old. Married to Thomas Foster in 1812, Jane Sproul and her husband were the progenitors of many of the families still found on the peninsula. EUGENIE WOODWARD COLE

"Jane Sproul Worked This Sampler In
The Tenth Year of Her Age 1803
Savior Divine Diffuse Thy Light
To Guide My Cildish Foot Steps Right
Engage My Vain My Youthful Heart
So Tis On Mary's Better Part
To Scorn The Trifels Of A Day
for joys that none can take away."

MY MOTHER *did a lot of tatting and I remember when we'd start school, we had one good dark navy blue or black dress, and we used to get collars, you know. My mother would make collars. She'd tat. I know one collar that I had to go with it—she had tatted a collar quite wide; and then, you used to be able to buy collars to go with that one dark dress that you had.*

For crocheting you use a small steel hook, and with tatting, it has what they call a tatting shuttle. Did you ever see a tatting shuttle? My mother had several and she used to try and teach me. I was crocheting and knitting and everything and she used to try to teach me to tat, and I could not learn. It was a shuttle thing like this and her hand would go just like that—picking up the stitches, going just—oh, she could tat so fast—but I never did learn to do tatting. —Nellie McFarland Frey

EMMA GAMAGE *used to do laundry for the summer people; Mama used to help her. And Mama would take me down there when she'd do some ironing and stuff. Mama used to spread her pillowcases and towels out on the ground, whiten 'em right out.* —Nellie McFarland Frey

Grandmother Lucinda Norwood Gamage, c. 1938. MARGARET FARRIN HOUSE

Margaret Russell Thorpe, 1837–1901. Her son, Albert T., was the proprietor of the Holly Inns in Christmas Cove. ARLETTA THORPE RICE

I CAN REMEMBER when I used to go over to my grandmother's and she'd do laundry; of course she scrubbed it by hand and everything. She'd put sheets and things out back on the ground to whiten them out. She had clotheslines, too, but if she wanted it to really whiten out she'd do that.

—Margaret Farrin House

WELL, THEY ALWAYS wore a hat, no matter what. And they always had a hatpin sticking through to hold the hat on. They all had long hair done up in a bun on the back—they used to have their hair in pugs, they called them, in the back. They put their hat on and put the pins right through the hat.

—Nellie McFarland Frey

THEY SAVED THEIR combings and they put them in that little thing called a hair receiver, and then when they were doing their hair they put the ball of hair in and combed it over it: in those days they wore the big pompadours and the rats, as they called them, to hold the pompadours up.

—Arletta Thorpe Rice

WHEN MY MOTHER would take her hair out of the bun her hair would be 'way down on the bottom part of her back. I can remember seeing her sit on the side of the bed and braid her hair. My gosh, she could braid it and then twist it around, then pin it up with her hairpins, you know. She used to have these combs, you know, celluloid, we used to have celluloid, now they call it plastic, and she always had those in the side of her hair, holding her hair. —Nellie McFarland Frey

Myra Clifford and an unidentified friend with pompadour hairdo. MARGARET FARRIN HOUSE

Alice McFarland holds her little daughter Nellie, 1919. NELLIE MCFARLAND FREY

MAMA USED TO *start in the spring with dandelion greens. Of course they grow like everything around here in April—wild, you know. Oh, she used to spend hours and hours digging dandelion greens and then canning them. They were bitter, but we always loved them. We always soaked 'em a lot in cold water, and got the sand off. Sometimes you felt you could chew on a little grit, but that was part of it.*

Well, they used to eat all these different things. You know, on the spruce trees the new little tips that would come out in the spring—we'd eat those. Just kind of pull the sprill, you know—pull the little sprills off and eat those. Oh, yes, they were good. And Mama used to take, too, the stalks of the raspberry bushes when they were real young and tender, and pull the skin off of them and eat the inside of that.

Bog onion, that turns into the pretty ferns used to grow by the side of the road. Oh, yes, in fact when they're up just about like this, the top curls over like a fiddlehead—I supposed that's why they got their name! I never did eat fiddleheads, but we used to dig 'em up and eat them. Mama used to show me about these fiddleheads—when they just come through the ground they called them bog onions and she'd pull them up—the whole thing. And there was a white core thing in the middle, chewy and good as it could be. She called them bog onions, for some reason.

After they got a car and I was big enough to go with her, they'd go over on the Harrington Road—this side or the other side of Harrington Church—and pick, and get something that Mama called tongue greens. Tongue greens. Well, they were quite big leaf things—I guess maybe the shape of tongues or something. I don't know where she got that name from either, but she used to cook them.

Well, you know back years and years ago, that was good for you. It is now. They used all that stuff for medicinal purposes. That was the beginning of natural food; it's much better than the natural food is you get nowadays.

—Nellie McFarland Frey

Van Seiders readying shrimp for processing at Farrin's, probably late 1960s or early 1970s.
RED BOUTILIER PHOTO, AUTHOR'S COLLECTION

DURING THE WARTIME, shrimp began to come in around here. They were very reasonable at the time, seems to me a few dollars a bushel. We bought a bushel and my poor wife had to process 'em—break their heads off, put 'em in jars, process them in boiling water. When I got home from work at 1:30 in the morning she was still working. God, that was awful. We never had that many shrimp again in our lifetime, I'll tell you that. But they tasted so good the next year. Beautiful shrimp.
—Robert Woodward

THERE USED TO BE a crabapple tree at the house down below here. And in the fall Mama would gather the crabapples, and she made some kind of syrup. Cooked them some in the syrup, and then she'd put them in jars and saved them for the winter. Then Sunday nights she'd make hot biscuit and we'd have hot biscuit and canned crabapples.
—Nellie McFarland Frey

WE ALWAYS HAD a pig or two we raised during the year and then they was killed off in wintertime, fall time. We didn't have refrigeration back in those times—winters were cold enough that you could hang a lot of meat up. And they used to pickle a lot of meat in salt brine—hams and things like that. When you killed an animal you always shared some with a neighbor, and when he killed his he'd share some with you. —Robert Woodward

DAD USED TO buy a side of pork—there used to be farmers around that would sell joints of pork in the fall for people to have through the winter—probably someone over in Pemaquid or somewhere.

The fishermen used to go and catch pollock; they'd catch these pollock and they'd split 'em and salt 'em. Oh, was they ever good.
—Nellie McFarland Frey

MY FATHER AND MOTHER *used to go to Barney Fossett's farm on Harrington Road and buy fruits and vegetables and apples from him for the winter, store them in the cellar.* —Doug Thompson

ANOTHER THING *my mother used to do was to make spruce beer in the spring. Did I ever love that stuff! I thought, so many times, I wish I had written down how she did it. This spruce beer, it had a taste—you'd never find anything else that tasted like it.*

My father would go into the woods and collect the stuff. I suppose there must have been some pieces of spruce tree—branches of spruce, that's probably how it got its name. And I think he used fir balsam branches, and yellow birch—the bark from yellow birch. And they used to gather those little things, we always called 'em ivy pips; they were little peppermint things that used to grow around here. Little tiny plants that had little red berries on them. Oh, it tasted so good, and the leaves tasted so good. Well, anyway, Dad would go out and gather all this stuff and then Mama had a big kettle and she'd cover that with water and steep it for two or three days on the back of the old cook stove. I wish I knew how to do it. They'd steep that a certain number of days, and after it was all done as much as they thought it should be, why then they'd take all that stuff out, and save the water it was cooked in, and then they mixed in so much sugar, and yeast cakes. And then she'd have that simmer for a while, I don't know how long. Mixed it all together somehow. And then she had regular crocks or jugs that she would put it in and you would have to wait a week or two before it was ready to drink. But was it ever good. It just had a taste—you'd never get a taste like that again.

My father used to make what they called home-brew. You've probably heard of that. He and Frank Jordon used to do that, and then Frank Jordon used to make elderberry wine. Up above their house the elderberries grew, and somehow or other he made elderberry wine. But everybody around was doing stuff like that.

During Prohibition, I guess there used to be some men that had boats. They used to say that they would go out to the three-mile limit off the coast and meet boats of people bringing in liquor from some other place; and they would bring it in and sell it around. In fact, I think my father used to get in on that every once in a while. I think he didn't go out to bring it in, but of course the fellas that would go out and meet the big boat from somewhere else, they had to go out to the three-mile limit. Evidently those boats couldn't come in closer than three miles of the coast. So the fellas had those big boats and they'd go out there, and bring it in and sell it—I don't know where they would sell it, but—rumrunning, that's what they called it. —Nellie McFarland Frey

How did they make a living? They subsisted.

—Arletta Thorpe Rice

Children mending fishing nets, c. 1920s. ATLANTIC FISHERMAN MAGAZINE

IN THE LATTER PART of the 1800s, a living could rarely be made from either the land or the water alone. Men raised animals or crops and perhaps worked at the brickyards, quarries, ice ponds, or shipyards. Women took in laundry, mended nets, and worked in the canneries and pogy factories. Many families took in summer boarders; others dried fish on dooryard flakes to augment their income. Young boys and girls helped doing chores, cleaning nets, clamming, and fishing. Life was hard, and for many not much above subsistence level. Few could look upon fishing, farming, or work in the factories as a full living.

CAPTAINS OF THE ICE SCHOONERS went to South America or New Orleans or wherever they had to go to sell ice, and then came back, and you traditionally got your hay in around the Fourth of July. You didn't set your traps until people got their hay in, and then you did. The same people who were lobstering, were farming—they got their hay in first.

—Edward Myers

Fosters, Otises, Thorps, Tibbetts—they all fished for the Boston market, but they also tended to their cows and flocks of sheep between trips to the Banks. Cows and sheep grazed where the tennis courts are now, and all the way down to Thorp's Point. —Arletta Thorpe Rice

What we might now call "multi-tasking" is a way of life that persisted well into the twentieth century.

I fished for forty-five years, I guess, maybe fifty. Even when I was going to school, I still fished in the summer. In the winter I worked in the woods somewhat—I cut a little pulp, and sawlogs and stuff. And then I had chickens, too—broilers, mostly. Then I had a few gardens, trying to raise some things. I used to sell corn, I remember, and strawberries, I had strawberries. I had some sheep at one time, too. I think I had forty of 'em for a while. I used to shear them, and people would call me once in a while to come shear theirs.

—Afton Farrin, Jr.

Ervine Hatch worked in Gamage's shipyard for twenty-eight years, as a carpenter and painter. He went by boat in the summer, and hauled lobster traps going down and coming back.

—Edward Myers

During the depression when things were really rough, the WPA was in the process of operating, and one of the projects they had was to build an athletic field. Out back of that school it was nothing but rock, and I can recall the men out there working with pick and shovel and wheelbarrows, digging away on those rocks trying to break it open and trying to level it off in order to make an athletic field. —Doug Thompson

Works Progress Administration logo from a poster of the 1930s.

Toward the end of the depression they started these work programs, and my father was somehow lucky enough to be foreman of the local WPA—somehow or other my father got the job. We were one of the lucky families.

They did little projects around in the area. Down back of the school they built a big field for the kids to play ball. That was a WPA project. There were several. —Nellie McFarland Frey

After I graduated, jobs were pretty scarce, and I stayed home during the winter. It got pretty boring without a job and we—another fellow and I—went into the woods cutting logs. We cut logs and firewood. We got two dollars a thousand for the logs we cut, and three dollars for a cord of the firewood. —Doug Thompson

PEOPLE IN MY *husband's family lost all their savings when the banks closed. His uncle had worked hard all his life and they were frugal and saved up money, and I don't think they ever got much of it back. People did whatever they had to do to get by.*

—Catherine Jordon Walker

MONEY WAS *very scarce in those days; jobs were very, very scarce, and people had to figure very closely. Fortunately, fish were more plentiful then. In the winter, even, we could go frost fishing, or spearing eels, or hooking sand dabs in the freshwater streams that were open—we hooked them through the ice. Clams were plentiful, and some people would shuck them out and sell them to various people who were unable to go clamming; they were selling them for maybe fifty cents a quart or twenty-five cents a pint.* —Doug Thompson

YOU COULD ALWAYS *catch cunners if you couldn't catch anything else. Go right down here and throw a line in the water, catch cunners, bring them in, and Mother would fry 'em up—and that was lunch.*

—Norman Hamlin

WE GOT ALONG *very well, we didn't starve, we didn't anything, we had everything that we would want, didn't we? We'd can everything from the garden. Have to put it through boiling water, and cool it down, get the covers clapped on so there's no air in there, no leakage. Lot of work to that. We went through the whole process of it. Vegetables, jams, and jellies, oh, everything.*

—Eugenie Bang Woodward

TIMES WERE PRETTY HARD. *Cigarettes were sold in stores one at a time, a penny apiece. Money was scarce.* —Doug Thompson

Walpole was quite a busy place at that time, when they cut ice and shipped it out on schooners.

—Catherine Jordon Walker

Gussie Wiley was a Kelsey and she grew up there in Clark's Cove. She used to tell me about the schooners coming in to get ice when she was young, in the 1870s or '80s, I suppose.

—Catherine Jordon Walker

The schooner ALICE M. DEERING at the Clark's Cove wharf of the Bristol, later American, Ice Company. Between the camera and the enormous icehouses is the Clark's Cove town landing, where two women stand next to a freight shed. MARGARET FARRIN HOUSE

JUST LIKE FISH had been, ice ponds and riverbank brick clay were valuable natural resources on the Bristol peninsula, and in the last decades of the nineteenth century became a lucrative source of income to offset the waning fisheries and farmers' winter hiatus.

In 1880 the Bristol Ice Company began the construction of two large icehouses and a two-hundred-foot wharf in Clark's Cove. By 1882 they were a thriving business, shipping 14,000 tons of ice to southern destinations; in 1890 they loaded more than ninety vessels with cargoes of ice bound for ports around the world.

Bristol Ice Company ice slide. Diagonal poles were used to brace the ice house walls against the weight of the ice. William A. Kelsey

WALPOLE

Business is very lively at the Bristol Ice Works. They have been the past two weeks filling their houses and loading vessels.

The second mate of a vessel loading ice at the Cove had his leg broken by a bale of hay rolling on to it last Friday. The leg was set by Dr. Brainerd, and the man was sent to the hospital at Portland, Saturday.

Sch. Eleanor, Capt. Poole, is expected in to the Cove to load ice. A number of other vessels are also expected right along.

John Shroder engineer on Sch. Jonathan Bourne was home last week for a few days. The Bourne loaded ice at Clark's Cove for Norfolk and sailed Saturday.

Excerpts from the *Pemaquid Messenger,* 1888 and 1889.

It was quite a big operation. They used to have teams of horses; they had a stable there where they'd put the horses when they came to work there on the ice. The ice came out of the water onto a belt. There was a conveyor belt from the pond, underneath the roadway there, that went over to these icehouses, to haul the ice when they cut the ice into blocks. They rode it up onto this conveyor belt, and then there was a steam engine about halfway between the road and the storage houses that was used to power this conveyance belt. As the houses filled up they had to move the conveyance belt up so the ice would slide off of the belt right into the right level in the ice house. They'd slide them right into the icehouse, and they packed the ice with sawdust around the outside edges and meadow hay which kind of insulated it. In the summertime coasting vessels would come in and load up with this ice and they'd haul it to Boston, and New York, the Caribbean, maybe even South America—all over. —Robert Woodward

That house there belonged to the American Ice Company. Men lived in that through the winter. They cut the ice and they had a big, well, call it a railway or a sluiceway went 'cross the road over to the shore and schooners come in and they'd ground 'em out and load 'em there with ice. And they cut that pond about three times through the winter. And when they was loaded, they'd ground 'em out but a good high tide they'd float, of course. They'd sail; sailed 'em in there.

The ice crew boardinghouse on Clark's Cove Road, next to the old ice pond. The earliest part of the structure dates back to 1780. AUTHOR PHOTO, 1997

During the war it all fell down. It had an endless chain that went around, see, and we took that chain and hauled it to Portland for junk—had a whole truckload of chain—that's what happened to it. —Mervin Rice

THEY USED TO *call it the boardinghouse. It was part of that boardinghouse complex there. In the wintertime they'd get a crew of men from all around—South Bristol, New Harbor, Bristol, wherever—they used to come there and live in the boardinghouse and cut ice. I can remember as a kid going into that house; in the dining room, there was pine floors in there. The men never took off their boots—they always had on studded boots, sharp boots to walk on the ice with. They never took them off, and that floor was all full of holes. They always walked right in the house there with their boots on.* —Robert Woodward

WHEN THE ROAD *was over there, the house was a story-and-a-half central-chimney Cape. Evander and his father, probably, cut right around the top of the first floor, and jacked it up, and put a second floor in. And when we got here there were eight nine-by-eleven bedrooms, four on the top floor, four on the next floor. Each had a double bed, and a bureau and a pitcher and bowl, and they had a six-holer privy behind what is now our garage. So this was a boardinghouse for the ice company. Two to a bed, so there were sixteen people on the second floor and third floor. Edna Kelsey cooked on the woodstove in her kitchen for a lot of people. Then, when the ice company went, they turned it into a summer boardinghouse.*

—Edward Myers

MY GRANDMOTHER *Edna Kelsey ran the boardinghouse in the Kelsey homestead. My father, Norman Kelsey, was the sixth generation to live there. Edna ran the boardinghouse before 1911, the year Norman was born, until I was maybe five or six in the 1940s. She cooked three meals a day for sixteen boarders plus her family of four children. Food was from the garden, lobsters Everett caught, and eggs from the chickens.*

—Carolyn Edna Kelsey

EVANDER AND ERVINE *[Hatch] took the dock building off the ice company dock, cribbed it up, and moved it over. Lowered it down onto the ice in the winter of 1917, and they took a capstan and put it in the ice each day—walked around it and pulled the building across. It took them a month. The building is up there on the other side of the River Road. They were offered the two islands or fifty dollars. Didn't see much use in a couple islands, so they took the fifty dollars.*

—Edward Myers

Ice-cutting crew in front of the Thompson Ice House. Thompson Ice House Preservation Corporation

Herbert Thompson wields a saw at the annual ice harvest. Thompson Ice House Preservation Corporation

In 1826 Asa Thompson, a descendant of one of the earliest settlers of South Bristol, dredged the bed of a spring-fed stream on his property, dammed it up, and built an icehouse there. That was the beginning of an ice business that was handed down through three more generations of Thompsons: Melvin, Melvin's son Walter, and Walter's son Herbert, who many in town still recall. The W. W. Thompson Ice Company wagon was a familiar sight in town, delivering ice both to the hotels and to private homes and cottages.

In 1974, while still in active operation, the icehouse was placed on the National Register of Historic Places. The last commercial ice harvest there was in 1984. Today, it has been given new life by the Thompson Ice House Preservation Corporation, which rebuilt the deteriorating icehouse and sponsors yearly ice harvests, once more a community event.

I remember the annual harvest and the grooving with horse-drawn groover, the sawing mechanism, mechanical sawing, hand sawing—and the ability of the men in the icehouse—the ice cakes came down the chute at great speeds and had to be swung into place with a pole hook.

My father, along with many able-bodied men, participated in the annual harvest. A call would be put out by Melvin Thompson or Melvin's son Walter, and then Walter's son Herbert would put out the word that the ice was ready. The time would vary, determined by the temperatures over a period of time necessary for it to freeze. The pond was a shallow one, but spring-fed. It produced the best of ice. Whenever the ice was ready, people would even get released from work so that they could harvest the ice and harvest it while it was in good shape and before it melted. Almost everybody at one time or another worked in harvesting the ice.

The ice-cutting was an important winter event. Timing was of great importance. When the ice was "right," it had to be done. —Doug Thompson

Herbert Thompson claimed that a fishing boat heading offshore for some days might load up with five tons of manufactured ice to ensure that its catch would remain chilled until the boat returned. But, Thompson said, if that same boat was loaded with his natural ice, the skipper needed to take only two tons on board.

I used to go *up to my grandfather Woodward's, about halfway between here and Damariscotta. Go up there when they were getting hay in in the summertime. He always had a bucket of water out in the summer kitchen with ice in it so you could get a drink of icewater. Oh, that was something to me as a kid. We never had ice at home. He had a little icehouse out back of his property and he had ice all summer—cut his own ice.*

We had a very deep well out in front of the golf course house, and it was cold down in the bottom of that well—always. In fact, my mother used to put cream down there to keep—or milk, or anything else you wanted to put down in there—lower it down to the bottom of the well, and it would keep her cream sweet and nice.

—Robert Woodward

Of course *for a long time, we didn't have any refrigerator or anything. We had an icebox set out on the porch, and Herbert Thompson, he used to come once, twice a week and bring us a big cake of ice and put it in that icebox; we'd keep our milk and stuff in that. Milk, and butter, and anything perishable. Sometimes the ice would last and sometimes it wouldn't. And then my mother and father got a refrigerator before I did, they got it long before I married and moved over here, and when my older kids was little we kept milk and butter and stuff over there in their refrigerator—so we'd have to run back and forth across the road for our milk and butter!* —Nellie McFarland Frey

There are three new brick-yards to be built this spring, beside two new cook houses for boarding the men, this will make seven brick-yards on this side of the town.

Excerpt from the *Pemaquid Messenger*, 1888.

Evander Hatch's *story, that he told to me, was that they brought bricks over from the brickyard and put them out on that little point there, and they brought the scows in on neap tides and loaded them, and on spring tides floated them off and they sailed them to the Back Bay. Loaded with brick, an enormous mainsail, a jib or two, they sailed them to Back Bay and that's why you see all that Damariscotta River brick on Beacon Hill.*

And he told me the story about completing his load, and spending the night. It was the fifth of June, one of the longest days of the year, and at four o'clock they made sail in a light northerly to Thatcher's, the lighthouse off Boston, and then came southwest—and he got back here before dark.

—Edward Myers

Brickyards first began to appear in Walpole in the 1840s; ultimately there were twenty-two brickyards on the Damariscotta River, seven of them in Walpole. West Bristol and Walpole farmers, many of them Civil War veterans, turned to brickmaking. Records of the time reveal brickyards carrying many of the family names associated with that part of South Bristol: Goudy, Bryant, Hatch, Clark, Feltis, Pitcher, Oliver, Kelsey. Demand for building materials from growing urban centers spurred the growth of the brickyards, which shipped hundreds of thousands of bricks up and down the Northeast seaboard from Nova Scotia to Boston. 1873, the year after the great Boston fire, was a year of notable profits.

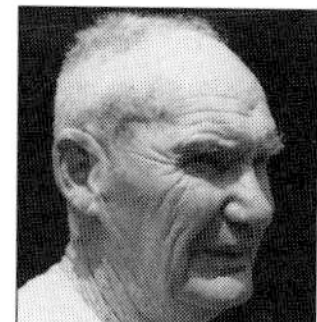

There's mineral in the water, and minerals in the ground. . .

—Mervin Rice

Applewood dousing rod. AUTHOR PHOTO

...AND THE ELECTRICITY in your body, that mineral in the ground draws that stick down. The dampness in that stick and you holding it, that's what makes it go down. You can't do it with gloves on. 'Course that vein can be going here, can be going there; come over the other way twenty feet and you won't hit it. Nobody knows what's going on underneath there. People stand and laugh at me and say, "You're just letting it fall down." When I hit a good vein of water, that stick I have, it works. I got a lot of electricity in my body.

I use either an alder or an apple tree—either one. You hold it like this. You cut it—it has a point out here, and then you come back with a fork, and then you bend the fork and you hold it tight like this, bend 'em 'round, see, get a good grip on it. Like you was making a slingshot. I hold it right up close to my body.

Up by the meeting house there's a triangle piece of land we used to call "the flatiron." Four or five houses right around, and they couldn't get no water. Some of 'em give up on it. Fella calls, says, "Could you douse a well for me?" I says, "Well, I'll go up, but I don't have any faith in it." I don't really believe in it. So I walked around there a little bit. I had a piece of apple tree I cut off that tree out there. Gee, that thing go down—I couldn't hold it—she go right down! Fella said, "What the hell is that?" I says, "Well, I can't hold it." "Aw," he said, "you're just foolin'." I said, "You take it." He take it and nothing happened. It twisted right off—I couldn't hold it. It go right down to the ground just like that—out of my hands. This other guy walked over and says, "You're wasting your time here. There ain't no water here anyway." I says, "I didn't say there was, I'm just telling him what I think." So I fooled around back and forth. This one place, boy, she go right down. So I put a stick in the ground. I says, "There's something down there. I don't know what the hell's down there, but there's something—I can't hold that stick at all." He went forty-five feet before he even hit the ledge. 'Twas all gravel. Finally got started—got down into the ledge, got down a hundred feet, he had a gallon a minute. Went down a hundred fifty feet, had three gallon a minute. So it does work for me. I don't advertise or nothing, cause I don't believe in it.

I doused one down at the Darling Center. Jeez, I got an awful signal on that one. They drilled two or three wells all around the house, but they kept getting gasoline 'cause a tank had leaked there. So they went right out by the road. Stick here, stick there. Dr. Dean says, "You ever do that?" I said if I get any signal I'll put a stick in the ground. Well, I went out there. I went down the woods, cut myself an alder, and I went out there and I fooled around. I did, and it took the bark right off of that. I couldn't hold it at all, and I put a stick in the ground. And I told 'em, "I put a stick in the ground, but I'd rather you drill on one of them other sticks." "No," he says, "we're going to drill right there," and they did, and I don't know just what it is, it ain't very deep, oh, maybe two hundred feet—and they've got over twenty-five gallons a minute. They're supplying the whole Darling Center with that one. So it does work.

Hell, no, I wouldn't advertise to find water. If I did, sure as hell wouldn't find any, probably. I just get a kick out of it, that's all. I like to do it. Been doing it quite a while. News spread, you know.

—Mervin Rice

There was a great deal of cooperation between neighbors in those days.

—Robert Woodward

The Robert Sproul farm was on a ridge overlooking John's Bay, at the top of what is known as McClintock's Hill. AUTHOR PHOTO, 1997.

IT WAS WONDERFUL. Back in those days you really knew your neighbor—he was your friend as well as your neighbor. You worked together, exchanged work. You'd go help him out for a day, he'd be back helping you out on some job you needed a hand on. That's the way it all went. When you killed an animal you always shared some with a neighbor, and when he killed his he always shared it with you. Somebody'd get sick in the wintertime, you'd gather up all the deadwood around, cut the man's wood for him. Gather together on a Sunday, have a bee. I can remember right back even in my time we were living here and I had a garden across the brook down here. I had a heart attack, and the whole neighborhood gathered here one Sunday, went up and planted my whole garden.

—Robert Woodward

THEY'D GATHER in their corn, the whole stalks, and bring it in the barn. Then they'd all come there some night, and take that corn and pull the ears off of the stalks, and then husk the ears, and they'd hang the ears up to dry. And then they'd have the corn to feed the chickens or the hens or whatever animals they wanted to feed it to, or grind it into some corn meal. It was a bee—they were having a little fun together. Probably there might be a little bit of cider come along on the side somewhere, something like that. But that was the idea—a husking bee. A little fun, a fun time at the harvest of the corn. —Robert Woodward

Austin Sproul's farmhouse on the West Side Road, Rutherford Island. AUTHOR PHOTO, 1997

Austin Sproul has purchased a new cow. We were sorry to hear he had to give up his lovely Guernsey cow that has roamed round his place for twelve years.

Austin Sproul is making quite an improvement by widening his driveway. This will be greatly appreciated by those who visit Austin during the evening as it will lessen the danger of backing into Mr. Seider's turnip patch.

Excerpts from the South Bristol personals column in the *Lincoln County News*, 1930s.

S. C. R. I. RED CHICKS

AND HATCHING EGGS

All Breeders State Tested and Accredited including Early Maturity and Heavy Egg Production.

HATCHES EVERY WEEK
ALL ELECTRIC BUCKEYE

AUSTIN V. SPROUL ***South Bristol***

Advertisement for Austin Sproul's chicken farm that appeared in the 1933 cookbooklet of a Damariscotta 4H Club, the Happy Home Helpers. BOURGOIN FAMILY

THERE WAS A MAN UP HERE *had a big chicken farm. Austin Sproul, his name was. He sold eggs, and he sold chickens to the summer people down around here. He had a lot of hen pens out the back of that house, way out into the pasture, quite a lot out through there. He'd send away late winter, early spring, for baby chicks—and they would come with the mail. And we'd go up to Everett Gamage's post office up here—you'd go in and you'd hear those chickies peeping. And we could look down into the boxes 'cause they had holes in the top. Little, tiny, yellow baby chicks. That was so much fun.*

That's when there wasn't all these regulations and stuff, you know. People could raise chickens. In fact my mother used to get chickens in the spring, just a few—like a dozen or so—and raise the chickens for Thanksgiving and Christmas. And she used to say, "After raising these chickens I hate the thought of killing them and eating them." But then all roasted up and with all the goodies along with it, I guess we just didn't think much about it. It was just one of those things you did and that was all there was to it. That's what everybody was doing. And you don't get a boughten chicken from any of the stores nowadays that tastes like those did.

That was a big thing every day to go out in my Mama's hen pen and collect the eggs. I loved it. She'd say, "Well, you want to go over in the hen pen and bring in some eggs?" and so I did. And that was fun—it was always kind of fun to see whether I'd get just two, or maybe eight or nine.

—Nellie McFarland Frey

Eugene Wylie's barn, with white rolling door, on the Thompson Inn Road. The "little" bridge can be seen in the left foreground; the French house is to the right. William A. Kelsey

See the barn? Right behind this house was another house where we used to take our milk can down and set it on the porch, and pick it up in the evening after he'd milked, full. No pasteurized milk—straight from the cow. Gene Wiley. Gene also had horses for haying and woodcutting and transporting the mail. —Doug Thompson

We had all kinds of cream, you know—we had our own cows. And my mother made her own butter. I can remember pounding the old churn up and down; I would help her out sometimes when she was churning—my father was hardly ever around in the daytime. We had there in the kitchen a milk separator; that was after a while. Originally we used to set the milk in round pans, pans that might be, what, three inches high, four inches. And in the morning she'd skim the cream off the top of it and put it into containers to save it for churning, and then the skim milk was fed to the animals. I don't know how she skimmed it off; I can't remember that but I think that it was stiff enough, heavy enough so she could slide it right off. And the little bit of skim milk that went into it didn't do any harm, I don't think.

And then we got the milk separator: then you just dumped the whole milk into that. It had a big crank on it and you cranked it through that, my father did. I can remember him now, winding on that for five or ten minutes. And out of one spout come the cream, and out of the other one come the skim milk. Yup, that was great.

—Robert Woodward

Deliveries were made down through South Bristol by horse and wagon. There were ice deliveries by the Thompsons: Herbert, his father Walter, and then Herbert's brother Melvin, they used to deliver ice to all the cottages and all the permanent homes down through the village and all the way down to the Christmas Cove area. There was Afton Farrin, Sr., who had a milk delivery, he delivered milk to the cottages and the people who lived in the town. He would be accompanied very often by some of his sons, Frank, or Afton Jr., or Robert, or Kenneth. And then there were milk deliveries by Fred

SOUTH BRISTOL, MAINE
Mr. Goudy will you please bring me
another small jar of butter when you come down. J.A. Leeman

1906 postcard to Dana Goudy, who farmed in Walpole. "Mr. Goudy will you please bring me another small jar of butter when you come down. J. A. Leeman." WILLIAM A. KELSEY

Foster and May. These people all had cows, and sold milk, and sometimes they'd sell some eggs along with it.

There would also be some trucks, go delivering certain types of goods, stopping from house to house. There was a fruit man in the summer from Bath. We used to call him "The Banana Man," and his name was Zack. He'd have all kinds of fruits and vegetables, stopping at every house, and people would look forward to seeing him. They'd plan on him being there a certain day of the week. Then there was a man who delivered extracts and house supplies and he came from Waldoboro. I can remember in the early days him coming with a horse and a boxed-in type of wagon to carry his goods; he specialized in Watkins products. Also from Bath was a man who came through town selling clothes, men's, women's, children's clothes. There also would be junk dealers. They would come along picking up junk—metal and paper and rags. Rags at that time were in demand as they were used in making paper. They'd come along shouting, "Rags! Rags!" —Doug Thompson

E. E. GAMAGE
HORSE SHOER AND JOBBER

Ernest Gamage in his village blacksmith shop, probably about 1896. The smithy was on the Eastern Gut, about where Osier's Wharf now stands; the mast and bowsprit of a sloop can just be seen behind the building. As a boy of sixteen, Ernest Gamage was on the deck of their lobster sloop SUPERIOR when his father was knocked overboard and drowned; he chose not to follow the sea. WAYNE AND AMY MCFARLAND

The infamous "horse cliff" can be seen from the S Road, just where it dips down to the head of Seal Cove. The high ledge is on the eastern shore of the cove. AUTHOR PHOTO, 1997

OF COURSE *Grampa used to sell milk when there was inns in town. Thompson Inn, Russell House, the Holly Inn. And they used to deliver it; Daddy went with him when he was a little boy, and he had butter and vegetables. They'd go down in horse and buggy and deliver it.*

—Katherine Poole Norwood

Duke, one of Mervin Rice's massive draft horses. Bud, the other horse in the pair, is standing on Duke's port side. MERVIN RICE

BELIEVE IT OR NOT, that high ledge over there on Seal Cove, I was told the story that when horses got old and they didn't want them anymore, they'd back them over that cliff.

—Katherine Poole Norwood

CIVIL WAR VETERAN Orville Clark lived on the farm later known as the Brittain place, just below Four Corners. He raised the trotter Pilot Knox, one-time champion of Maine.

Orville Clark, 1838–1899.
PEMAQUID HISTORICAL ASSOCIATION

THAT HORSE there weighed 2,400—he was a big horse. There's a mate to him; the mate was standing on the other side. That other horse behind him was just as big as he was—maybe didn't weigh quite so much, but it was about the same thing. They was a big pair. He was a dapple gray, we call it, and the other one was a bay horse—he was red with a black mane. The gray was Duke and the other one was Bud. They knew their names just as well as them horses that are trained.

I used them logging in the woods, hauling logs. Hauled a scoot—that was just wood runners, you know. We used it winter and summer. Just the same the summer as it was in the winter, just harder. That was a pair of big horses. I pulled them in the Damariscotta Fair—the last year of the fair, 1947. I pulled that team in a sweep-

George Atkinson with his team of oxen.
MARGARET FARRIN HOUSE

stakes. I got second place. Big drag, you've seen them, probably. They'd pile rocks on, and next horse to pull, if they was heavy horses they put on some more rock. They hauled two pound of rock to a pound of horse; that's the way they figured it.
—Mervin Rice

KATHY'S FATHER *used to tell a story about that horse and buggy—that he and his sister would go down to the village, down to South Bristol, and they'd buy hard candy—kids, you know, just kids. And that horse wouldn't leave town, he wouldn't start, unless they gave him a piece of this hard candy—so they had to give him a piece before he'd head home. And they come up over the top of the hill; when they got up to the top of the hill he'd stop, and wouldn't go again until they gave him another piece.*

When I was a teenager we didn't have no automobile. We bought this old horse, and his name was Jerry. And the only problem with the old horse was that he had been owned by a milkman and if you were driving down the road he wanted to go into every driveway you came to!
—Ralph Norwood

THERE WERE *a lot of horses on the road. Somebody behind you and he had a faster horse, he'd holler, "Want half the road!" he'd say, and you pulled over a little bit and let him go by. He'd let out a bellow, "Want half the road!" I can hear him now. You'd pull over and he'd go zinging by—good fast horse, you know. We had all kind of horses. Of course, horses were a big thing in them days—we raced them, and pulled them, and every damn' thing; rode them horseback, and every other damn' thing else.* —Mervin Rice

GEORGE ATKINSON *used to come with a pair of oxen and plow our garden for us.*
—Margaret Farrin House

WE HAD OXEN *for the heavy work. Eventually oxen were replaced with horses, but back in those days oxen was much more reasonable to have than horses.* —Robert Woodward

HERE'S DADDY *on the hayrake. There's a whole farming scene here. They raked it up with that before they put it in the hayrack.*
—Katherine Poole Norwood

Young Clifton Poole, seated on his father's hayrake.
KATHERINE POOLE NORWOOD

The Poole farm hayrack. KATHERINE POOLE NORWOOD

WHEN THEY USED TO *go cut hay they'd load it in a hayrack and we'd tramp it down, when we were kids. I suppose they did for generations. They'd back that into the barn with the horse, and then they'd undo the horse and hook him to pulling a great big haylift that come down from the scaffold, it would take great big bunches of hay up. And they'd pull the rope, and it would dump up on the scaffolds. They'd unhook the horse and hook him onto something that would pull the rope—just this single line, and it would pull this great big forkful of hay. The horse got so he knew what he was supposed to do, and they didn't have to handle the reins, usually. They'd just tell him to back and git up, and he'd go ahead, and they'd say stop when the load got up there and then they'd trip it—just a big fork. For generations that went on.*

—Katherine Poole Norwood

WE KIDS ALWAYS *had some of the animals to feed, and hens to pick up the eggs, and feed the chickens, feed the hens. And lug in wood at nighttime, fill up the woodbox so the woodbox was filled. When you got home from school those were the jobs that you had waiting for you. Kids were kept busy in those days, on the farm—the farm kids. There was no chance for this deviltry they get into today.*

—Robert Woodward

NEIGHBORS WOULD *all help each other out. It's the only way in the country. You've got to all work together. If you don't, you're the loser.*

—Eugenie Bang Woodward

The Voices

Afton Farrin, Jr.

Nellie McFarland Frey

Elizabeth Alley House

Margaret Farrin House

All photographs by the author

Donald Hunter

Bill Kelsey

Addison McFarland 1914–2001

Pete McFarland

Kathy Poole Norwood

Ralph Norwood II

Arletta Thorpe Rice

Mervin Rice

J. Douglas Thompson 1916–2002

Catherine Jordon Walker

Robert Woodward 1908–1998, and
Eugenie Bang Woodward

Notes and Credits

Fishing

PAGE 3 TOP Three men in a dory, 1960s; courtesy Afton H. Farrin, Jr. Alva Farrin is in the bow, Mel Farrin in the center.

PAGE 3 BOTTOM Panorama: untangling nets near Pemaquid Point, 1965; courtesy Afton H. Farrin, Jr.

PAGE 4 LEFT Damariscove Island Coast Guard station. Author's photo, 2001. Taken from the deck of Ralph Norwood II's wooden schooner, SHEKINAH GLORY.

PAGE 4 RIGHT Setting a mackerel trap off Pemaquid Point; courtesy Lynne Drisko.

PAGE 5 LEFT South Bristol fishermen; courtesy Catherine Jordon Walker.

PAGE 5 RIGHT Net reel on Farrin's Wharf; courtesy Lynne Drisko.

PAGE 5 BOTTOM Advertisement from the *Pemaquid Messenger*, late 1880s.

PAGE 6 Advertisements from *Atlantic Fisherman* magazine, 1924; author's collection. On its March 1924 masthead, *Atlantic Fisherman* subtitles itself "A 'Farm' Journal for the Harvesters of the Sea." A sidebar further explains:

> The *Atlantic Fisherman* is a paper for fishermen—producers—the men who actually fish for a living. It does not purpose [*sic*] to cover the fish trades; nor does it wish to be looked upon as a "trade paper." Rather do we like to think of it as a home paper for fishermen. Our first care is that its pages be readable, for we believe that matters of human interest and practical vocational help are more to be desired by our readers than stereotyped "trade notes" and dry-as-dust statistical matter. We want it to be regarded as a steady and reliable source of information, profit and entertainment by that vast army of 150,000 workfolk which constitutes our field.

PAGE 7 Handmade wooden knitting needle; author's photo. The use of this type of knitting needle is evidently still a widespread skill on the coast: one day at the Montsweag flea market I saw a young woman using one to repair a volleyball net; she told me that they always kept one around at her high school athletic department.

PAGE 7 RIGHT Junior Farrin, Anthony Eugley, and Ted Farrin; courtesy Lynne Drisko. The men are working at Farrin's Wharf, which in an earlier era was the South Bristol steamship wharf. In the background, a man is walking up the steep hill that leads to the main street of the village.

PAGE 8 Frank Jordon in a skiff; courtesy Catherine Jordon Walker.

PAGE 9 FISH HAWK IV at the float; courtesy William A. Kelsey.

PAGE 10 Irving Clifford at his fish market; courtesy William A. Kelsey.

PAGE 11 Fishing boat docked at Irving Clifford's wharf; courtesy William A. Kelsey. A. E. Merrill, a noted commercial photographer based for a time in Christmas Cove, took hundreds of scenic photos of the South Bristol area, many of which were made into postcards.

PAGE 13 Contemporary photograph of the building formerly used as a fish house by George Leighton; author photo 1997.

PAGE 14 George Leighton's herring factory on Gem Island; courtesy J. Douglas Thompson. This image is from a commercially printed photo booklet, published in 1904 by the Lakeside Press of Portland, Maine.

PAGE 15 Fowler, Foote, & Company pogy factory; courtesy Margaret Farrin House. Another photograph has recently come to light showing a pogy factory located on what is now known as the Sewall property on the Thompson Inn Road.

PAGE 16 Excerpt from the *Pemaquid Messenger*, December 18, 1887. It seems rather incongruous to imagine a picnic grove and eatery on the site where tons of menhaden were once processed into oil and masses of stinking chum.

PAGE 17 The WILLIAM A. WELLS; courtesy Maine Maritime Museum, Bath, Maine

Lost at Sea

PAGE 18 The wreck of the SADIE AND LILLIE; courtesy Laleah Condon Kennedy, Eugene B. Sproul Farm. This is the other vessel, that along with the GEORGE S. EDMUNDS, was shipwrecked on Pemaquid Point that same September night in 1903.

PAGE 19 Captain Willard Poole; courtesy Katherine Poole Norwood. Mertie Knipe Curtis's account courtesy of the Bristol Area Library, Pemaquid, Maine.

PAGE 20 LEFT Mary Pierce; courtesy Margaret Farrin House. Mary Pierce was cared for in her later years by her nephew Robert and his wife Alice A. (Gamage) Pierce, who moved back to the village from Southport to look after her. This is the A. A. Pierce who opened the first dry goods store in South Bristol village.

PAGE 20 RIGHT Rubbing of a portion of the Pierce tombstone in the Rutherford Island cemetery. All of the Pierce—or, as it's carved on the stone, Peirce—names are on one monument, with the three boys—James, Eliphalet, and Jonathan—on a single side. They, like their father, are obviously not buried there, having been lost at sea. Whether or not Elliott's body was returned for burial from the battlefield at Spotsylvania is a matter for conjecture.

PAGE 21 Captain Marshall M. Wells; courtesy Arletta Thorpe Rice. Reproduced from a carte de visite in the collection of Capt. Wells's great-granddaughter.

PAGE 21 Excerpt from "Capture at Sea," courtesy Katherine Poole Norwood. This account was written by Cleveland Poole, based on stories told to him by "Grandpa" Willard G. Poole, who was only twenty-three when he signed on as a seaman aboard the bark LAURAETTA. This is the same Willard Poole who later became captain of the GEORGE S. EDMUNDS, wrecked on Pemaquid Point in 1903.

PAGE 22 Painting of the bark LAURAETTA; courtesy A. Stanton Wells. Descendants of Captain Wells traditionally pronounce the vessel's name "Laurie-Etta." This painting on panel was passed down through the family and is now in the collection of Captain Wells's great-grandson.

PAGE 23 Handwritten account of the taking of the LAURAETTA by William Knipe; courtesy Bristol Area Library, Pemaquid, Maine. Listed as six years old in the U.S. Census of 1850, Knipe would have been eighteen when the LAURAETTA was captured.

PAGE 24 The doll Little Nell. Author photo, 1996.

PAGE 24–25 Newspaper articles from November 1889 and January 1890; courtesy Arletta Thorpe Rice, who transcribed these articles by hand from family copies. The sometimes treacherous ledges could give back, also. As alluded to in the newspaper article, salvage from wrecks would wash up all along the shoreline. Arletta has a beautiful old Thorpe coverlet which family tradition describes as woven from a bale of cotton that washed up onto their shore.

PAGE 25 Captain Manley S. Brewer; courtesy Arletta Thorpe Rice. Manley Brewer, born in Southport, was married to Eliphalet Thorp's daughter Lydia. They were one of the first families in Christmas Cove to open their home as a summer boardinghouse when the local fisheries began to decline.

PAGE 26 Crow Island and the Thread of Life. Author photo, 1997.

PAGE 27 Articles from the *Portland Evening Express*, March 4 and 5, 1947; courtesy Pemaquid Historical Association.

PAGE 28 Gerald Fossett and Roland LaBrie; courtesy Pemaquid Historical Association. This photograph was probably taken to illustrate an earlier newspaper article about the pair's record New Year's catch, for which they received the highest price per pound ever paid in Portland at the time.

Lobstering and Clamming

PAGE 29 Twenty-nine-pound lobster: *Atlantic Fisherman* magazine, 1929. The comparative size of the trap it's sitting on gives a sense of the scale of this behemoth.

PAGE 30 Lobster fisherman; courtesy Norman Hamlin. Traps weren't the only thing made from wood in those days. An advertisement in a 1924 issue of *Atlantic Fisherman* magazine touts "THE ONLY MACHINE MADE LOBSTER PLUGS," at $1.25 per thousand, asking "CAN YOU WHITTLE for 10¢ per 100?" These "plugs" were the small wooden wedges used to peg lobster claws in the days before fishermen learned to immobilize them with rubber bands. In the same issue, the Beetle Lumber Company of New Bedford advertises "Lobster Pot Buoys, Made of the best quality dry cedar in all sizes"

PAGE 31 Hook Lobster Pound; courtesy Norman Hamlin.

PAGE 31 Excerpt from *Atlantic Fisherman* magazine, July 1924. Nowadays it's these prices, rather than lobsters, that are quite "skurce."

PAGE 32 Lobster fisherman at the Tripod; courtesy Norman Hamlin.

PAGE 33 Bainbridge Young; courtesy Margaret Farrin House.

PAGE 34 Clam factory at Pemaquid Harbor; courtesy Pemaquid Historical Association.

PAGE 35 Recipe pages from the *South Bristol Cook Book*. The original title page subtitles it "The Ruther*food* Cook Book," probably a typographical error, but I prefer to think of it as a well-done pun.

Weather

PAGE 37 Bar Cottage, January 1933; courtesy William A. Kelsey.

PAGE 38 Thread of Life cove; author photo, 1997.

PAGES 39–40 Excerpt from "Summer's End," by Romilly Humphries. By permission of the author.

PAGE 40 House on Clark's Cove Road; author photo, 1997. The house stands just across the road from a path that leads down to the site of one of the old Damariscotta River brickyards. An excerpt from the June 1938 *Lincoln County News* gives an account of a woman surviving a lightning strike that is markedly similar to the events in Mervin Rice's narrative:

A Freak of Lightning

> Mrs. Dorothy Brown, wife of William J. Brown of Pemaquid Harbor, was struck by lightning Sunday and remains in a serious condition at her home.
>
> Mrs. Brown was standing by the sink in her kitchen cleaning her teeth when the bolt entered the room burning the back of her neck, one side of her face and her shoulder, and rendering her unconscious for several hours. Her back teeth were loosened and shattered by the stroke and she has spit out large pieces of enamel from them. She is suffering severe pains in her head which the slightest noise makes almost unbearable.... Her parents, Mr. and Mrs. Frank Dyer of Pemaquid Beach, were in the room at the time but felt no ill effects, and there was no damage done to the house....

PAGE 41 The Pierce house; courtesy Margaret Farrin House.

PAGE 42 Snow-covered Western Gut, 1934; courtesy Margaret Farrin House. Reproduced from an amateur snapshot. An excerpt from the local South Bristol column in the *Pemaquid Messenger* on February 22, 1888, reported that "The western gut is frozen over more now than it has been for a number of years...."

Steamers and Launches

PAGE 43 Ladies on a steamer; courtesy William A. Kelsey

PAGE 44 LEFT Steamer ANODYNE; courtesy Nobleboro Historical Society, Ivan Flye Collection.

PAGE 44 RIGHT Advertisement from the *Boothbay Register*, 1893. The pale blue glass bottles that the liniment came in still turn up with some frequency in local flea markets and antique shops. The two-ounce size is most common, though occasionally you'll see a large seven-ounce bottle. Although I've never seen one with a paper label on it, the words "Johnson's American Anodyne Liniment" always appear in raised letters spaced vertically around the sides.

PAGE 44 BOTTOM Courtesy George King III.

PAGE 45 LEFT Damariscotta Steamboat Company fleet; courtesy Pemaquid Historical Association.

PAGE 45 RIGHT 1910 timetable; courtesy Elizabeth Alley House.

PAGE 46 The NEWCASTLE crew; courtesy Margaret Farrin House.

PAGE 47 LEFT A Pullman Company train ticket, c. 1915; author's collection. The month, day, fare, number of passengers, and berth are all punched on the ticket. A smaller chit, identified on the reverse side as the passenger's check, was also given to the ticketholder "To be retained by passenger to identify accommodations indicated on the accompanying ticket. Property taken into car will be entirely at owner's risk. Subject to all other conditions stated on ticket. Rate: 45 cts."

PAGE 47 RIGHT Elliott Gamage and Randall Poole; courtesy Margaret Farrin House.

PAGE 48 The steamer TOURIST at the South Bristol wharf, 1914; courtesy Elizabeth Alley House. Ed Gamage's drugstore, Merritt Thompson's grocery, and the two dry-goods stores, all fronting on the main street, are in the background; just behind TOURIST is a wooden walkway that ran behind the grocery store from the steamer wharf to an open space south of Gamage's. Taking that route, passengers could reach the main street without having to negotiate the steep hill up from the wharf. Worn holes in the corners of this rare image show that it was nailed or tacked to a wall for quite some time.

PAGE 49 The wrecked TOURIST, 1918; courtesy Catherine Jordon Walker. "The Last Trip," was written for the Sept. 5, 1918 issue of the *Damariscotta Herald* by Dan Chittenden. "Uncle Dan" lived in the village and was considered quite a character, but it was his brother Larry who was well known for this type of verse. The poem appeared in the same issue of the *Herald* that headlined South Bristol's patriotic incorporation day celebration; courtesy Eugenie Woodward Cole.

The Last Trip

To Everett Spear, drowned in the Wreck.

He dided [sic] at the post of duty,
In his prime, with heart so brave;
No thought in youth's ambition
Of how near he was to the grave.
To the call of the bell made answer
With a torn and bleeding arm;
His nerveless hand was palsied
'Mid the panic of wild alarm.
In the angry swirl of the pitiless wave
Crunching and grinding his youthful form
He dashed for life to find a grave
Out of all trouble, out of all storm.
The tangled seaweed in his hair
On the muddy bank gleamed in the sun,
A requiem whispered in the summer air
For a pale-faced boy whose task was done.

PAGE 50 LEFT Christmas Cove postcard, 1908; courtesy William A. Kelsey. The printed postcard text is in error: the view is northeast, looking across Birch Island to John's Bay. Another postcard from Christmas Cove in Mr. Kelsey's collection is dated 1906 and reads, "*Arrived 4 hours late had four cat naps and wasn't seasick....*"

PAGE 50 RIGHT Advertisement from the *Boothbay Register*, February 1889.

PAGE 51 Steamer WIWURNA in Christmas Cove; courtesy Pemaquid Historical Association.

PAGE 52 LEFT Steamer NEWCASTLE at the wharf in South Bristol; courtesy Catherine Jordon Walker.

PAGE 52 RIGHT Young woman on the South Bristol steamer wharf, 1921; courtesy Marian Coughlin. From the snapshot album of Goldwin Gilbert, who lived at the corner of what is now the West Side Road and Rte. 129, just up the Main Street hill from the wharf.

PAGE 52 BOTTOM Horse and buggy in Christmas Cove; courtesy William A. Kelsey.

PAGE 53 LEFT Captain Frank Y. McFarland; courtesy Frank Y. "Pete" McFarland, Jr.

PAGE 53 RIGHT George Kelsey; courtesy grandson Charles Kelsey.

PAGE 53 BOTTOM: Schedule card for the launch NELL MARIE; courtesy George Kelsey.

PAGE 54 LEFT Captain Ambrose Alley; courtesy granddaughter Elizabeth Alley House.

PAGE 54 RIGHT Captain Mark Thompson on one of his launches; courtesy J. Douglas Thompson. Captain Thompson was a man of many capabilities. In addition to his talents on the water and in boatbuilding, he also built piers at Heron Island and Pemaquid Point, and constructed the Tracy family's log cabin on little Turnip Island.

PAGE 54 BOTTOM Damariscotta River Line card; courtesy J. Douglas Thompson.

PAGE 55 LEFT The J. DOUGLAS; courtesy Nobleboro Historical Society, Ivan Flye Collection.

PAGE 55 RIGHT Excerpt from *Atlantic Fisherman* magazine, March 1924; author's collection. This excerpt comes from the magazine's column, "News of the Boatyards," a new feature that began with that issue.

PAGE 55 BOTTOM The BARBARA J II; courtesy Catherine Jordon Walker.

PAGE 56 The PILGRIM; courtesy J. Douglas Thompson.

BOATBUILDING

PAGE 57 William Addison McFarland; courtesy William A. Kelsey. The notion that Samuel Kelsey may have taught him the craft of boatbuilding is given credence by the fact that William's elder brother Leander is listed with Samuel's family in the 1850 census, two years after their father's death.

PAGE 58 LEFT Excerpt from the *Pemaquid Messenger*, December 1887.

PAGE 58 RIGHT The McFarlands in their Christmas Cove shop; courtesy Frank Y. "Pete" McFarland, Jr. Eldest brother Winthrop, fondly known as "Wink," and Frank Y., Sr., are no doubt dressed to captain one of their launches.

PAGE 58 BOTTOM McFarland's Cove, about 1910; courtesy Cassie H. Manchester Trust.

PAGE 59 TOP DAUNTLESS II; courtesy Frank Y. "Pete" McFarland, Jr. Brightwork is wood—most commonly mahogany or teak—that is varnished with a clear finish rather than painted. DAUNTLESS's bright hull is so highly finished that the shop doors are reflected in its surface.

PAGE 59 BOTTOM Sumner McFarland and Phil Page; courtesy Nobleboro Historical Society, Ivan Flye Collection.

PAGE 60 Horace Kelsey, left, and Will Alley with a client; courtesy Margaret Farrin House. The boatshop and erstwhile grocery store is on the right, with open rolling doors; Ed Gamage's drugstore is in the center background.

PAGE 60 BOTTOM Willard "Bill" Thorpe, with his wife Kathleen and their son John; courtesy Arletta Thorpe Rice.

PAGE 61 LEFT Clifton Poole, 1959; courtesy Katherine Poole Norwood.

PAGE 61 RIGHT Don Stanley, caulking the HERO; courtesy Maine Maritime Museum, Bath, Maine. Stanley writes that he worked at Gamage's yard for a few months after his release from active duty as a Marine.

PAGE 62 TOP Les Thompson; collection of Robert K. Woodward. Photograph from a promotional booklet of the S. D. Warren Company.

PAGE 62 BOTTOM The ARWILDA MORSE; courtesy Margaret Farrin House. An absolute in this image is that the vessel is being built in the A & M Gamage yard; other information about it is conflicting. The local cabinet print of this image is hand-dated 1871 and labels the vessel as the ARWILDA MORSE, which Sidelinger lists as having been launched in 1873. However, research indicates that the Merritt Thompson grocery store, clearly seen in the background of the photograph, wasn't built until the 1880s.

PAGE 63 LEFT Harvey L. Gamage; collection of Robert K. Woodward. Photograph from a promotional booklet of the S. D. Warren Company.

PAGE 63 RIGHT Merton Stapels and Clifton Poole; courtesy Maine Maritime Museum, Bath, Maine.

PAGE 65 Miles Plummer; courtesy Elizabeth Alley House. This is a detail from a larger picture of the partygoers that included the guest of honor, Mrs. Atwood Plummer, as well as Captain Ambrose and Agnes Alley.

PAGE 66 The FLORENCE, 1894; courtesy Pemaquid Historical Association. According to Lowell Sidelinger's "Vessels Built in Bristol with Historical Sketches of Old Vessels and Builders," the FLORENCE was built by Gifford Gamage. The building seen behind her still stands on the Eastern Gut, directly north of the swing bridge; it was once Charles, and then Irving, Clifford's fish market, and later belonged to Polly Lauder, Gene Tunney's mother-in-law.

PAGE 67 The dragger WAWENOCK; courtesy Pemaquid Historical Association.

PAGE 68 Launching of the HERO; courtesy Maine Maritime Museum, Bath, Maine.

PAGE 69 LEFT Pete Seeger and some of the Gamage work crew; photo © Dan Budnik 2003, courtesy Peter and Toshi Seeger. These photographs are from a series of original color slides by Dan Budnik documenting the launching of CLEARWATER.

PAGE 69 RIGHT Pete Seeger at the launching of CLEARWATER; photo © Dan Budnik 2003, courtesy Peter and Toshi Seeger. The CLEARWATER's then-first mate offers a somewhat different account of the mess on the shoreline the next morning: in his version, CLEARWATER supporters conscientiously picked up all of the litter and placed it into a big hopper on the wharf. "... and when most of the crowd had gone, one of Harvey Gamage's men pulled the lever and we heard a great roar, and all the bottles and cans went into the river. I thought Peter was going to puke. And out they went with the tide...."

PAGE 70 TOP Roy Rice, Wink, Pete, and Addison McFarland after the launching of OSPREY; courtesy Frank Y. "Pete" McFarland, Jr. Adele McFarland, Pete's wife, calls this picture "the happy launchers."

PAGE 70 BOTTOM Vessel sliding down Route 129; courtesy Arletta Thorpe Rice. This image was a small snapshot in "The Whoopie Book," a photo album Arletta Thorpe (Rice) had when she was a schoolgirl in Christmas Cove. The technique of sliding a boat from workshop to water on greased boards was essentially the same method that their grandfather used to launch his McFarland's Cove vessels back in the 1800s.

ENTERTAINMENT

PAGE 71 South Bristol Town Hall, 1936; courtesy Eugenie Woodward Cole.

PAGE 72 LEFT Postcard to Goldwin Gilbert, postmarked 1916 or 1918; courtesy Marian Coughlin. This card was probably from Alice Gamage, who lived at the head of Long Cove, down the hill and around the bend from Goldwin. The two girls remained friends even after Goldwin's father, Captain Frank Gilbert, moved his family to Portland.

PAGE 72 RIGHT Entrance to Union Hall; author photo, 1997.

PAGE 73 Class play in the Union Hall; courtesy Margaret Farrin House. Standing, from left: unidentified, Ronnie House, Bruce Hassan, Donna Farrin, Marilyn Knight, David Seiders. Seated, from left: Charlie Frey, Gloria House, Jean Frey, Daniel C. Seiders III, Mary Lou Farrin.

PAGE 74 LEFT Fraternal Order of Redmen postcard; courtesy William A. Kelsey. Office holders were given titles that are native American words for chiefs: Sagamore, and from the Algonquian language, Sachem. The former Redman's Hall stands in its original location on what the natives still refer to as "Kid Hill." The hill on either side of Route 129, sloping up to the north from Shipyard and Thompson Inn Roads, was home to several large families—lots of "kids."

PAGE 74 RIGHT Excerpts from the *Lincoln County News*, 1930s; courtesy Mervin Rice. The clippings are snippets of Walpole news columns from the scrapbooks of Lura Holman, who lived for a time on Clark's Cove Road.

PAGE 75 LEFT The former Hacienda Hall; author's photograph, 1997. Lura Holman, who lived for a time on Clark's Cove Road, kept scrapbooks that included many clippings from the 1930s *Lincoln County News*. Scrapbook excerpts courtesy Mervin Rice.

PAGE 75 RIGHT Cavis Cove dance hall; author's photograph, 1997.

PAGE 76 Lincoln County Fair, c. 1920s; courtesy Nobleboro Historical Society, Ivan Flye Collection.

PAGE 77 Postcard to Winnie Jordon, 1912; courtesy Catherine Jordon Walker. This card was written in a time when there were two mail deliveries a day, and penny postcards were used almost as we would use a telephone now.

Holidays

PAGE 78 Rocking duck, Christmas morning; courtesy Margaret Farrin House.

PAGE PAGE 79 "Home Made Gifts," *Pemaquid Messenger*, December 8, 1886.

PAGE 80 Irving Clifford; courtesy Catherine Jordon Walker.

Childhood

PAGE 81 Tobogganing on the Thompson Inn Road; courtesy Margaret Farrin House.

PAGE 82 LEFT Snowy view of South Bristol village; courtesy Pemaquid Historical Association.

PAGE 82 RIGHT Margaret Farrin and snowshoes, c. 1930s; courtesy Margaret Farrin House.

PAGE 83 TOP Skaters on Nellie's Pond, c. 1930s; courtesy Margaret Farrin House.

PAGE 83 BOTTOM View across Wawenock Golf Course; author's photograph, 1997.

PAGE 84 LEFT Teenagers in bathing costumes, c. 1914; courtesy Margaret Farrin House. This is a small snapshot from the album of Alice Gamage. The girls are sitting on a wooden handrail that ran along the edge of West Side Road where it curved around Long Cove. The end of Long Cove Point can be seen in the upper left background.

PAGE 84 RIGHT Farrin boys in a sailing skiff; courtesy Margaret Farrin House.

PAGE 84 BOTTOM Alice Gamage rowing, 1914; courtesy Margaret Farrin House. The rounded shapes at the bottom of the picture are probably the knees of the photographer, sitting in the stern.

PAGE 85 LEFT Wallace "Foggy" Bridges; courtesy Mervin Rice. Detail from a posed photograph of the 1931 Lincoln High School boys basketball team.

PAGE 85 RIGHT Brooks McFarland and a friend shooting rifles; courtesy Margaret Farrin House.

PAGE 86 LEFT Undated photograph of Babe Ruth; Library of Congress.

PAGE 86 RIGHT Carroll and Mervin Rice; courtesy Mervin Rice.

PAGE 87 LEFT South Bristol High School girls' basketball team, 1934; courtesy Margaret Farrin House.

PAGE 87 RIGHT Lincoln High School's championship basketball team, 1931; courtesy Mervin Rice.

PAGE 88 Everett Gamage's store; courtesy William A. Kelsey.

PAGE 89 TOP Boys' baseball game; courtesy Margaret Farrin House.

PAGE 89 MIDDLE The Tick Tock Toilers in front of Everett Gamage's store; courtesy Margaret Farrin House.

PAGE 89 BOTTOM The Handy Home Helpers, c. 1940s; courtesy Margaret Farrin House. Some of the other South Bristol clubs were the Helpful Handy Home Hustlers, the Lively Little Ladies, and the Merry Maids.

PAGE 90 LEFT Excerpt from the *Lincoln County News*, mid 1930s; courtesy Mervin Rice.

PAGE 90 RIGHT May basket; author's photograph. Sometimes the May basket would actually be hung on a doorknob, as the name of the ritual implies; more often it was just set on the porch or front stoop.

PAGE 91 TOP Viola Gamage and doll, 1909; courtesy Margaret Farrin House.

PAGE 91 BOTTOM Annie and Ruth Farrin, with their cousin Virginia Gamage; courtesy Margaret Farrin House. Everett Gamage and J. R. Little's stores are the buildings on the right; the bridgetender's house can just be seen above Ruth's head, center.

PAGE 92 Riding tricycles on the Thompson Inn Road; courtesy Margaret Farrin House.

PAGE 93 LEFT Organ grinder and monkey, c. 1892; photograph by Hamilton Overspeck, courtesy Library of Congress.

PAGE 93 RIGHT Paper dolls, c. 1915-20.

PAGE 94 Old Orchard Beach roller coaster, 1917; courtesy Marian Coughlin. Snapshot from the photo album of teenager Goldwin Gilbert.

Schools and Teachers

PAGE 95 Clugston's Barn; author's photograph, 1997. A souvenir booklet from the school's 1900 fall term lists the names of its forty pupils, many of whom appear repeatedly in the town's history: Willard Thorpe, Alva Gamage, Angie Kelsey, Dorothy and Arthur Wells, Myra Clifford, Winnifred and Wellingon Jordon, Annie May Gamage, Garrie Young, Arthur and Harry House, Ada Sykes, and the original owner of the souvenir, Henry McFarland. The booklet was quite elaborate, with gilded edges, a silky blue tie cord, and a cover of fancy crinkled paper. The other pages of the booklet had a poem entitled "Some Vacation Thoughts," and another, "One By One":

One by one the sands are flowing,
one by one the moments fall:
Some are coming, some are going,
Do not strive to grasp them all.
One by one thy duties wait thee;
Let thy whole strength go to each;
Let no future dreams elate thee.
Learn thou first what these can teach.

PAGE 96 LEFT Arletta M. Thorp's Certificate of Merit; author's collection. Arletta, or Arlitta, Thorp was the daughter of John and Harriet (Pierce) Thorpe of Christmas Cove. These small certificates came to me from her grandniece Arletta Thorpe Rice, whose father was raised by the elder Arletta.

PAGE 96 RIGHT The original structure of the Lincoln School; courtesy Margaret Farrin House.

PAGE 97 TOP The scholars of the island school, about 1922; courtesy Margaret Farrin House. The children are roughly in order of age, with the youngest children in the front row—except for three-year-old Margaret Farrin, next to her big sister Charlotte in the second row. Too little to be a student yet, she was probably being looked after by her sister that day.

PAGE 97 LEFT Poem by Walter Burnham, 1915; courtesy Margaret Farrin House.

PAGE 97 RIGHT Elmer Gamage with a string of flounder, 1911; courtesy Margaret Farrin House, from a small snapshot in a family album. Elmer, born in 1902, was nine years old in this picture.

PAGE 98 LEFT Lincoln School on Rutherford Island; courtesy William A. Kelsey. Although somewhat altered by its conversion into living quarters, the school building is still recognizable in its original location near the Union Church.

PAGE 98 RIGHT Lincoln School class picture, early 1950s; courtesy Nellie McFarland Frey.

PAGE 99 LEFT The Randall Rice house; author's photograph, 1997. I had been living in this house for nearly three months when I came across the old *Lincoln County News* clipping that identified it as the site of the June 1935 graduation:

> ... due to a few very light cases of scarlet fever the school could not have the exercises in the church and somebody suggested having it out of doors. First thought was the school yard, but Saturday's rain made the grounds muddy, so Mr. and Mrs. Randall Rice kindly offered their home and grounds.
>
> Hasty preparations were made. Porch boxes were filled with flowers donated by

town people, and the porch trellises were artistically arranged with large wild ferns.

Promptly at one o'clock the exercises were held. The young men of the class, Charles E. Frey, Ralph C. Farrin, Robert Farrin, Lamar Seiders, and his twin brother, Claude Seiders, looked very smart in navy suits, and to carry out the class colors, they wore gray ties, and rose carnation boutonnieres. Verna McFarland and Cleo Gamage were very charmingly gowned in white organdy and carried bouquets of rose carnations.

The school program was very entertaining and the young people did exceptionally well....

PAGE 99 RIGHT Page from "The Schoolboy's Magazine," 1914; courtesy Margaret Farrin House.

PAGE 100 LEFT A page from *The Island News*, December 1951; courtesy Margaret Farrin House. It's noteworthy in the other article, "Basketball Season Opens," that the school population was so small three junior high girls had to be recruited to make up a basketball squad of just seven players.

PAGE 100 RIGHT *Collier's Magazine* photograph of the fishing class, 1951; courtesy Elizabeth Alley House.

PAGE 101 The S Road School; author's photograph, 1993.

PAGE 102 LEFT The Gladstone School; author's photograph, 1997. The Supervisor of Schools' report of March 1861 gives a somewhat different spin to the tale of mass exodus to the war; after all, seventeen was nearly half the total of all volunteers from Bristol in that first call.

> Before my last visit I had heard a rumor of trouble in the school, but nothing reliable. When I called I found a difficulty had arisen between the teacher and some of the large boys; but that the teacher had enforced discipline, and the boys had voluntarily withdrawn themselves from the school. I was very sorry to hear this; for, from all that I could learn, I was forced to the conclusion that the boys were in the wrong: and I think when they reflect, they will come to the same conclusion.

PAGE 102 RIGHT Gladstone School scholars, c.1915; courtesy Eugenie Woodward Cole. First row, left to right: Robert Woodward, Doris Goudy, Ruth Feltis. Middle row: Sumner Curtis, Carl Feltis, Clifton Sproul, Percy Brown, Scott Cramer, Paul Goudy, Carolyn Feltis. Back row: Louis Cramer, Doris Mank, Florence Hatch, Marie Brown, Irvine Hatch, Alice Kelsey, Albert Kelsey, Mildred Bowman (teacher), Marguerite Feltis.

PAGE 102 BOTTOM The Four Corners School; author's photograph, 1997. Now located north of Ridge Road, it has been converted to a private residence.

PAGE 103 The Upper School; author's photograph, 1997.

PAGE 104 Miss Sarah Emery and her scholars at the S Road School; courtesy Katherine Poole Norwood. Back row, left to right: Jennie Plummer, Alys Poole, Doris Thompson, Clifton Poole, Minnie Foster, Bill Foster, Marjorie Andrews. First row, standing: Jim Plummer, Mary Farrin, Beulah Plummer, Stella Thompson, Alice Busten. Seated: Alton Farrin, Miles Plummer, Sr., and Herbert Thompson.

PAGE 105 Afton Farrin, 1885–1948. Courtesy of Margaret Farrin House. This is a Bowdoin fraternity picture, taken in 1910, which appeared in a school newspaper tribute at the time of his death:

> To no one's memory could we more fittingly dedicate this edition of "The Islander" than to our friend and former Principal, Mr. Afton H. Farrin, Sr. He devoted his life to his town, its people, and the school. We are grateful to him for being a staunch friend and defender of our school and we hope that our future endeavors will be like a candle burning in his memory.

PAGE 106 TOP Afton Farrin with scholars at the S Road School; courtesy Margaret Farrin House.

PAGE 106 BOTTOM Afton Farrin with Lincoln school students; Courtesy Katherine Poole Norwood. Identified students include Arthur Gamage, Mildred Foster, Jennie Plummer, Doris Sproul, Clifton Poole, Stanley Alley, Harvey Gamage, and Bill McFarland. Mildred Foster later became a teacher at the same school and taught Afton Farrin's children.

Libraries and Books

PAGE 107 Union Church Parsonage; author's photograph, 1997. Like the Rutherford Island church, Walpole Union Church had a community library, started in 1938. An excerpt from the January 20 issue of the *Lincoln County News* announced:

> Books may be taken out before and after Sunday School on Sunday afternoon. It is requested that these books be returned at the end of two weeks. Mrs. Marion Mank and Mrs. Elizabeth Newcomb are the librarians. This new project already has a loan of fifty books from the Sewall Library at Bristol Mills, but it is in need of many more books if it is to adequately serve the church, Sunday School and community. Those who have good books, of any type, that are not in use and who would be willing to donate them to the library, are asked to see that they get to Mrs. Mank or Mrs. Newcomb for cataloguing....

PAGE 108 Title page, *A Child's Garden of Verses*, by Robert Louis Stevenson; author's collection. This 1913 edition is of about the same vintage that Catherine Jordon, born in 1910, would have read with her sisters.

PAGE 109 TOP Postcard with Larry Chittenden's Christmas Cove poem; courtesy David W. Andrews. Like his library bookplates, this card features photographs of Christmas Cove—two of which are pictures of the Autograph Library.

PAGE 109 LEFT Bookplate from the Autograph Library; courtesy William A. Kelsey. The original bookplate was printed on pale green paper.

PAGE 109 RIGHT "Texas Corner," one of the rooms in the Autograph Library; courtesy William A. Kelsey. Fond as he was of signing himself as the "Poet Ranchman of Texas," Chittenden was actually from the East. He had been a reporter for the *New York Times* before he traveled through Texas working as a dry-goods salesman and correspondent; his uncle was a congressman from Brooklyn. In 1885 he visited Anson City, in West Texas, where he attended the Christmas Eve dance that he later immortalized in the ballad, "The Cowboys' Christmas Ball." Two years after the ball he returned to Anson and took up ranching for a time, but soon returned to the East. He may have come to South Bristol because his brother, Dan, had moved there after purchasing Witch Island in 1887.

Memorable Individuals

PAGE 110 Herman W. Kelsey; courtesy William A. Kelsey.

PAGE 111 LEFT George Will McFarland; courtesy Margaret Farrin House.

PAGE 111 RIGHT Letter from Harold McFarland to his sister Christine; courtesy Margaret Farrin House. Harlan and Ava are Harold and Christine's brother and sister.

PAGE 112 Hilda Hamlin, June 1963; courtesy Norman Hamlin. The original color photograph from which this is reproduced shows the lupines flourishing in a multitude of hues, as they still do today at Juniper Knoll.

PAGE 114 LEFT Woodchuck Corner; author's photo, 1997.

PAGE 114 RIGHT Milton D. Thompson; courtesy Katherine Poole Norwood. In the early days of the U.S. Patent Office, prototypes or scale models were submitted as part of the patent application. Like many a South Bristol native who moved away to seek his fortune, Milton Thompson never ceased to think fondly of his home. At the end of his life he returned to South Bristol, and now lies buried among Thompsons in the Main cemetery. He wrote the following in 1920:

Me. for the State of Maine

I was born in the town of Bristol
twelve miles from a railroad train
With my address always written
Me. for the State of Maine
But I, like many others,
heeded the city call,
And moved away from the country,
my birthplace, friends, and all

Large cities pay higher wages
but expenses are much more,
Where lights burn bright at midnight,
and sleeping barred til four.
So stop and think it over
before you leave old Maine,
For I can see by figures
there's nothing you can gain.

You can roam the country over
from north to the sunny south.
From Eastport on the Atlantic
to the Columbia river mouth
There's no place anywhere fairer
in sunshine or in rain,
Than the lakes and ponds and harbors
in the Good Old State of Maine.

This is not the story of one man,
or even the tale of two,
But the talk of the general public
who travel about with you.
If you write to a friend in the city
from Portland or Bangor the same,
You will always end up by writing
Me. for the State of Maine.

PAGE 114 BOTTOM Engineering drawing for the feathering propeller; courtesy Donald M. Thompson, Milton Thompson's grandson. Feathering props are a highly efficient means of providing auxiliary power to sailboats. Once the vessel is under sail and the engine has been shut down, the folded-back blades eliminate unnecessary drag.

PAGE 115 LEFT Elliot Brewer; courtesy Arletta Thorpe Rice.

PAGE 115 RIGHT Charlotte Young Emery, c.1957; courtesy Katherine Poole Norwood.

PAGE 116 LEFT Samuel A. Miles, courtesy Nobleboro Historical Society, Ivan Flye Collection. The Depression-era fence project that Doug Thompson described is still quite evident along State Route 129. Although some of the distinctive metal caps have disappeared, and a few of the posts have fallen, the majority of the fence still lines the east side of the road on the way to Christmas Cove.

PAGE 116 RIGHT The Miles "Fresh Air Camp"; courtesy William A. Kelsey.

PAGE 117 Damariscotta River lumber scow; courtesy Nobleboro Historical Society, Ivan Flye Collection.

PAGE 119 LEFT Willard Metcalf's studio, c. 1930s; courtesy Eugenie Woodward Cole.

PAGE 119 RIGHT *Spring on the River*, by Willard Metcalf, 1904. Private collection, photo courtesy Spanierman Gallery, LLC.

PAGE 120 TOP *The White Mantle*, by Willard Metcalf, 1906. Private collection. Photograph courtesy of Hirschl & Adler Galleries, New York.

PAGE 120 BOTTOM The stone bridge at Clark's Cove; courtesy David W. Andrews.

Staying Healthy

PAGE 121 Dr. Henry Fernald; courtesy Boothbay Region Historical Society.

PAGE 122 Home remedy recipe and an old ledger page; courtesy Laleah Condon Kennedy, Eugene B. Sproul Farm. Note that the accounts on the ledger page are for an A. P. Gamage, who appears to be buying some twelve pounds of butter a week. The only A. P. Gamage listed in the *Vital Records* of Bristol is Albion P., proprietor of the Russell House hotel in Christmas Cove.

Families

PAGE 124 LEFT William and Loletta Jordon; courtesy Catherine Jordon Walker. The original of this image is a small tintype with hand-tinted skin tones, typical of the period.

PAGE 124 MIDDLE Will Jordon; courtesy Catherine Jordon Walker.

PAGE 124 RIGHT Helen Russell Jordon; courtesy Catherine Jordon Walker.

PAGE 125 Frank Jordon; courtesy Catherine Jordon Walker.

PAGE 126 TOP Wellington and Winnifred Jordon; courtesy Catherine Jordon Walker.

PAGE 126 BOTTOM Wellie Jordon on Heron Island; courtesy Catherine Jordon Walker. Reproduced from a small snapshot in a family album.

PAGE 127 The Mary Norwood Gamage house; author's photo, 1997.

PAGE 128 TOP The children of Thomas and Waitstill Thompson Gamage; courtesy Margaret Farrin House. The disparity of the siblings' ages is evident when you look at the eldest, Thomas, born in 1818, and at the youngest, Nelson, born in 1843. When Nelson was born he already had a year-old nephew, Tom's son Llewelyn.

PAGE 128 BOTTOM "Skipper Tom" Gamage; courtesy Margaret Farrin House.

PAGE 129 LEFT Margaret Gamage Norwood; courtesy Margaret Farrin House.

PAGE 129 RIGHT Jonathan Norwood; courtesy Margaret Farrin House.

PAGE 130 TOP Ebenezer Cleveland Poole; courtesy Katherine Poole Norwood.

PAGE 130 BOTTOM Samuel Poole; courtesy Katherine Poole Norwood.

PAGE 131 LEFT South Bristol Town Report cover, 1937; courtesy South Bristol Historical Society. Many in South Bristol fondly remember this design, which for years graced the covers of the town report. By 1937, Everett Poole had been South Bristol's town clerk for twenty-two years, the only clerk since the town's incorporation in 1915.

PAGE 131 RIGHT Marriage certificate of Everett Poole and Katie Cudworth, 1882; courtesy Katherine Poole Norwood. The pictures of Katie Cudworth and Everett Poole are tintypes, slipped into paper pockets on the back of the certificate and revealed through oval openings cut into the paper.

PAGE 132 LEFT Orris McFarland; courtesy Nellie McFarland Frey. He is also listed as a carpenter in the 1906 Bristol Town Register, and in his *History of the Families and their Houses South Bristol Maine 1730-1915*, H. Landon Warner notes that Orris McFarland built the village store north of Alice Pierce's which later became a grocery that operated under various owners until 1970. Most probably he himself was the first proprietor. Yearly editions of the *Maine Register* list him as having a fish market from 1897 until at least 1915. This is true Maine self-reliance and versatility: catch the fish, build the store, run the market.

PAGE 132 RIGHT Henry and Elsie McFarland; courtesy Nellie McFarland Frey. One hundred and ten years later, his little great-great-grandson looks remarkably like this picture of Henry.

PAGE 133 TOP Alice Dodge McFarland; courtesy Nellie McFarland Frey.

PAGE 133 BOTTOM Henry McFarland; courtesy Nellie McFarland Frey.

PAGE 134 TOP Letter from William McFarland, Jr. to his wife Caroline Foster; courtesy Margaret Farrin House. After William's death, Caroline married his brother Pratt.

PAGE 134 BOTTOM William Addison and Annie Young McFarland; courtesy Cassie H. Manchester Trust.

PAGE 135 TOP Rock Ridge and Salana, in Christmas Cove; courtesy J. Douglas Thompson. Reproduced from a photo booklet that shows many of the named South Bristol boardinghouses and lists their proprietors.

PAGE 135 BOTTOM Medora Clifford Thorp; courtesy Arletta Thorpe Rice.

PAGE 136 TOP Arletta, or Arlitta, Thorp with her nephew Willard and his cousin Arthur Wells; courtesy Arletta Thorpe Rice. Arthur's father, Frank, was married to Arletta's niece Rachel Thorp; they lived directly across the road from Arletta and young Willard. The house where they sit is still in the Thorpe family.

PAGE 136 BOTTOM Willard N. Thorpe and Kathleen Geyer; courtesy Arletta Thorpe Rice.

PAGE 137 Albert C. and Emily Hatch Thorpe; courtesy Arletta Thorpe Rice. Arletta Rice remembers Uncle Dud clearly from when she was a little girl; he and Empy lived in his father Eliphalet's house, next door to the house Arletta where grew up.

PAGE 138 Jonathan P. Thorp; courtesy Arletta Thorpe Rice. Reproduced from a hand-tinted tintype.

WAR

PAGE 139 LEFT Nathan C. Hodgdon; courtesy Eugenie Woodward Cole. From the collection of his great-great-great-granddaughter, who still lives in Walpole.

PAGE 139 RIGHT Oliver B. Spear; Courtesy Marian Coughlin. Oliver Spear, a fisherman, was born in Rockland but later settled in South Bristol. By the time this picture was taken in 1909, he lived in a house built by his son Pearl on the grounds of the Virginia Guano Company's pogey factory, on what is now the Thompson Inn Road.

PAGE 140 Albert Hatch; courtesy Phillip Hatch. Although it clearly was taken some years after the close of the Civil War, Albert Hatch proudly wears his uniform for this portrait. Reproduced from a photograph belonging to his great-grandson, Phillip Hatch of Damariscotta.

PAGES 140–42 "Letters from Camp," courtesy Bristol Area Library, Pemaquid, Maine.

PAGE 143 LEFT Frank Farrin, 2nd Regiment, Maine Cavalry; courtesy Lynne Drisko. According to his granddaughter he was stationed in Mobile, Alabama, and his brother Charles, who was on a coaster, found him there. "He was always funny after the war—he would just go away...." Among other adventures, Frank Farrin laid track for the Trans-Pacific Railroad and homesteaded in Nebraska. Later, he owned the Strawberry Inn in Pemaquid.

PAGE 143 RIGHT Civil War monument, West Bristol cemetery; author's photograph, 1998. An excerpt from the *Pemaquid Messenger*, December 18, 1887, describes the effort to raise private funds for the monument: "We understand Mr. John Goudy was out Monday soliciting subscriptions for a soldiers monument to be placed in the new cemetery in this place. Report says he was very successful, $80.00 being subscribed in one day."

PAGE 144 "It has passed away like a dream"; author's photograph, 1997. "Winter Thoughts," an essay that appeared in the *Pemaquid Messenger* January 5, 1887, was an affecting evocation of the emotions felt by the families of the soldiers who served in the Civil War, and it inspired me to take this photograph in the Rutherford Island cemetery one snowy afternoon....

> Yet but a few years elapsed since the clangor of the war trumpets echoed the blast of Old Boreas. We remember those war winters with shuddering. How we lay awake in the nighttime, and thought, and thought, wondering whether those we loved were lying out in the cold night air, or shivering under their shelter-tents, or whether they were hot and fierce in the fire of battle, or whether, perchance, they might not lie, colder than ice, with calm faces set for eternity, under the snow. No human imagination can estimate the agonies of those four winters. In all the catalogue of wars sufferings, there is no such account as this of a vast people, of whom nearly every household was in mourning, or else fearing the wind of the winter lest it might bring as its cold burden the last sigh of someone beloved....
>
> *It has passed away like a dream.* The silver-toned trumpets of peace have sounded...yet it will be many winters before the fireside ceases to be surrounded by saddened faces, and the conversation changes from the sorrowful stories of those four years...it is pleasant, however, to see that as the first snows of winter whiten the graves of those who wore the blue and those who wore the gray, the nation is evincing a disposition to bury in those graves all the bitterness of the past, and cover it out of sight forever. So doing, it will hereafter seem not so sad to have lost those who sleep under the snow..... If we cultivate sympathy and sorrow for every household in the land which mourns one fallen...if the sentiment of common affliction, and therefore of common humanity and suffering, should outgrow the animosities of the struggle, and pity overpower anger, then it will not be so very sad to sit down by the winter fireside and think of what might have been....

PAGE 145 LEFT Wellington Jordon; courtesy Catherine Jordon Walker.

PAGE 145 RIGHT Lewis Stanley Alley, Jr.; courtesy Elizabeth Alley House.

PAGE 146 "War Time Song of 1916," from the notebook of Lura Holman; courtesy Mervin Rice. The notebook contains many lines of verse, both humorous and serious, written by Lura Holman over a period of several years.

PAGE 147 Spotting tower, Rutherford Island; courtesy Margaret Farrin House.

PAGE 148 World War II ration book; author's collection.

Buildings

PAGE 149 Artist's rendering of the Wawenock Clubhouse; courtesy William A. Kelsey. According to their daughter, Robert and Eugenie Woodward's house on Ridge Road had been part of the "golf course house," moved to its present location by the Creamers.

PAGE 150 LEFT The Solomon Cavis house, Rutherford Island; author's photograph, 1997.

PAGE 150 RIGHT The Cornell art colony building; courtesy J. Douglas Thompson.

PAGE 151 LEFT The Davis house; courtesy Margaret Farrin House.

PAGE 151 RIGHT Robert Merrill's Federal house; author's photograph, 1993.

PAGE 152 The Poor Farm manse; author's photograph, 1997.

PAGE 153 *Bristol Town Report for Year Ending February 20th, 1895*, pages 9 and 10: *Selectman's Account*; courtesy Laleah Condon Kennedy, Eugene B. Sproul Farm.

Churches

PAGE 154 Walpole Meeting House; courtesy Catherine Jordon Walker.

PAGE 155 Interior of the Walpole Meeting House; courtesy Catherine Jordon Walker. Reproduced from a card postmarked 1910.

PAGE 157 LEFT The 1687 pewter communion set; courtesy Trustees of the Old Walpole Meeting House.

PAGE 157 RIGHT The Reverend Lewis Evans; courtesy Eugenie Woodward Cole. Photographs of the bride and groom were inserted into pockets in the upper right and left corners of the marriage certificate; the Reverend Evans's photograph was in a pocket centered near the bottom, between the lines of signatures.

PAGE 158 LEFT Walpole Union Church; author's photograph, 1996.

PAGE 159 Newspaper excerpt from the *Pemaquid Messenger*, October 1886. A local column, "Walpole Warblings," reported the following January:

> ... the Sociable at Mrs. William Clark's [was] pronounced a great success. The house was well filled by the young people from all parts of the town, and Mr. and Mrs. Clark with their usual hospitality and genial manner made one and all feel truly welcome. The supper was partaken of by a goodly number,— thus making the gathering a success financially as well as socially. The Chapel Fund was increased to the amount of $13.75.

PAGE 159 RIGHT South Bristol Union Church; courtesy William A. Kelsey.

PAGE 160 Headline from the *Lewiston Evening Journal*, October 21, 1921; courtesy Margaret Farrin House.

LADIES' AID AND EASTERN STAR

PAGE 161 Community House; author's photograph, 1997. This house is still referred to locally as the Clugston House, the name of previous owners. Its garage building, called "Clugston's Barn," was the island school house before the turn of the twentieth century.

PAGE 162 Installation night at the Pogonia Chapter, Order of the Eastern Star; courtesy Margaret Farrin House. Seated, left to right: Lettie Kelsey, Charlotte Farrin Eugley, Lucinda Norwood Gamage, Violet Dunham, Emma Alley, Alice McFarland. Second row: Manley Lane, Hazel Farrin, Annie May Farrin, Helen Jordon, Ella Lane, Helen Seiders, Josephine Gould, Nathalie Seiders Knight. Third row: unidentified, Margaret Farrin House, Nellie McFarland Frey, Eva Farrar. Fourth row: three guest installing officers from other chapters, and Harriet Redonnett, far right.

INCORPORATION AND TOWN MEETINGS

PAGE 163 TOP Second floor of the old South Bristol town hall; author's photograph, 1997.

PAGE 163 BOTTOM Excerpt from the *Lincoln County News*, 1930s.

PAGE 164 TOP The old Clark's Cove wharf; courtesy William A. Kelsey. The steamer NEWCASTLE was the largest vessel in Elliot Gamage's Damariscotta Steamboat Company fleet.

PAGE 164 BOTTOM South Bristol ballot, 1917; courtesy Katherine Poole Norwood. The back of this unused ballot was used by the town clerk, Everett Poole, to list his family members' birth and marriage dates.

PAGE 165 LEFT Banner headline, *Damariscotta Herald*, September 5, 1918; courtesy Eugenie Woodward Cole.

PAGE 165 RIGHT Incorporation Day celebration, August 30, 1918; courtesy Margaret Farrin. House. Reproduced from a small snapshot.

BRIDGES AND MAIN STREET

PAGE 167 Repairing the stone bridge; courtesy William A. Kelsey. This is evidently the "new" bridge, since the photograph of its repair was taken no earlier than 1894, while an excerpt from the *Pemaquid Messenger* dated February 22, 1888 notes that "The Selectmen laid out the new road asked for at South Bristol, last Saturday. This petition was for a new bridge to be built to the westward of the present one." The selectmen referred to would be those of the town of Bristol, since South Bristol was not yet a separate town.

PAGE 168 TOP The stone bridge; courtesy Margaret Farrin House. Although the cyanotype that this was reproduced from is undated, the fact that there is no building on the southwest side of the bridge suggests that it is an earlier image than the bridge repair photograph.

PAGE 168 BOTTOM The first swing bridge; courtesy Margaret Farrin House.

PAGE 169 TOP The counterweight drawbridge, sometime between 1925 and 1930; courtesy David W. Andrews.

PAGE 169 BOTTOM The fixed "little" bridge; courtesy Margaret Farrin House.

PAGE 170 Uphill on the main road, looking north towards the mainland; courtesy Margaret Farrin House.

PAGE 171 Standing in the middle of the road, looking north from the island; courtesy Margaret Farrin House. Annie May Farrin's handwritten list indicates: "1. Bert Thorpe; 2. Nelson Gamage; 3. Merritt; 4. Alice Pierce, Milton Thompson, Chittenden, Pearly Spear."

PAGE 172 LEFT On the main road looking north, some time between 1903 and 1911; courtesy Pemaquid Historical Association.

PAGE 172 RIGHT On the main road, 1914 or 1915; courtesy Catherine Jordon Walker

PAGE 172 BOTTOM On the main road, probably 1930s; courtesy Margaret Farrin House.

Stores

PAGE 173 Ad from the *Pemaquid Messenger*, 1888.

PAGE 174 The Kelsey and Alley grocery store building; courtesy Margaret Farrin House. This snapshot is of the back side of the building; it was taken by someone standing on the steamer wharf, facing eastward toward the main street of the village.

PAGE 175 LEFT Alice Augusta (Gamage) Pierce; courtesy Margaret Farrin House.

PAGE 175 RIGHT Lois R. Otis; courtesy Margaret Farrin House.

PAGE 175 BOTTOM Catherine and Helen Jordon, c. 1918; courtesy Catherine Jordon Walker.

PAGE 176 UPPER LEFT One of the village dry goods stores; author's photograph, 1997.

PAGE 176 RIGHT Advertising card for J. P. Coats thread, c. 1890s; author's collection.

PAGE 176 BOTTOM LEFT Martha Farrin, 1935 or '36; courtesy Margaret Farrin House.

PAGE 177 Village stores, looking south from the bridge; courtesy Catherine Jordon Walker. Even without dating the automobiles, the "L. R. Otis Dry Goods" sign tells us that this is after 1911.

PAGE 178 J. R. Little and his store, 1935 or '36; courtesy J. Douglas Thompson. This is the store, according to H. Landon Warner, that was first built as a fish market by Orris McFarland and subsequently operated as a grocery store by several different proprietors, including J. R. Little, Selden Fuller, Daniel Berry, Nat House, and Ernest Alley.

PAGE 179 UPPER LEFT The back of Farrin's Store; courtesy William A. Kelsey.

PAGE 179 RIGHT Buying lobsters for Farrin's Lobster Pound, 1951; courtesy J. Douglas Thompson.

PAGE 179 BOTTOM LEFT Eliphalet Thompson's gasoline float on the Eastern Gut; courtesy William A. Kelsey. The postmark on the card this image was reproduced from is 1909.

PAGE 180 Chester Clifford and his West Side Road grocery store, Nation Wide Market, c. 1930s; courtesy Margaret Farrin House. On the far end of the porch is a kerosene tank with a hand pump: hard economic times forced many people to buy their fuel in small quantities.

PAGE 181 E. W. Haley's Store, Clark's Cove Road; courtesy Mervin Rice.

Roads and Transportation

PAGE 182 Clark's Cove Road, opposite town hall; author's photograph, 1997. The more often the snowy roads were traveled, the better packed down they were for the sleighs. Excerpts from the *Pemaquid Messenger* in 1889 reported that "the people are improving the good sleighing." and "the farmers in this vicinity have improved the sledding the past few weeks by rushing their lumber to the [Bristol] Mills...."

PAGE 183 Main Street in Damariscotta, with Sam King's first car; courtesy Katherine Poole Norwood. The postcard that this image is reproduced from is addressed to Mrs. E. A. Poole from her daughter Alyce, who was living in Damariscotta while attending Lincoln Academy.

PAGE 184 Mudhole on the causeway; courtesy William A. Kelsey.

PAGE 185 Kelsey's Garage in South Bristol village; courtesy William A. Kelsey.

Mail and the Post Offices

PAGE 186 Robert Hanley Woodward; courtesy Eugenie Woodward Cole. In 1915, Robert H. Woodward was elected to be one of the first three selectmen of the newly incorporated town of South Bristol.

PAGE 187 LEFT William T. Kelsey; courtesy Eugenie Woodward Cole.

PAGE 187 RIGHT Brooks McFarland at the Walpole post office; author's photograph, 1995. Brooks grew up in South Bristol village; he was the son of Eliphalet and Ada McFarland, proprietors of the Thompson Inn. One of the boyhood stories he told me was about riding his little bike around and around the Inn's big porch.

PAGE 188 LEFT Excerpt from *The Clamdigger*, probably 1917; courtesy Arletta Thorpe Rice. The story was transcribed from a 1972 tape recording of Kathleen Geyer Thorpe being an interviewed by her granddaughter Becky Rice.

PAGE 188 RIGHT Albert T. Thorpe on the porch of the Christmas Post Office; courtesy Arletta Thorpe Rice. This is the same Albert Thorpe who was the proprietor of the three Holly Inns. Without the large influx of summer visitors to the Holly Inn, Christmas Cove probably wouldn't have needed its own post office.

PAGE 189 LEFT Early Walpole post office; courtesy Phillip Hatch.

PAGE 189 RIGHT The Rapelye farmhouse post office; courtesy Mervin Rice. This snapshot was taken when Mervin Rice owned the house.

PAGE 190 LEFT Farrin's Store and Ship's Lantern Gift Shop, about 1951; courtesy J. Douglas Thompson.

PAGE 190 RIGHT Building that housed the last village post office; author's photograph, 1997.

Hotels and Boardinghouses

PAGE 191 "Greetings from South Bristol," courtesy William A. Kelsey.

PAGE 192 LEFT Passage from *Ten Years at Pemaquid*, J. Henry Cartland, 1899, page 10.

PAGE 192 RIGHT Holly Inn postcard, postmarked 1906; courtesy William A. Kelsey. I've seen several copies of this postcard; it's the inscription on this particular one that makes it noteworthy.

PAGE 193 LEFT The second Holly Inn burns; courtesy William A. Kelsey. One of the men on the roof is Henry McFarland who ran—literally—down to the Cove to volunteer his help.

PAGE 193 RIGHT The town firetruck; courtesy William A. Kelsey. The Marden house stands behind the pumper; the Holly Inn can be seen through the smoke, up on the high ledge above the Bar.

PAGE 194 The second Inn succumbs to the fire, 1923; courtesy Pemaquid Historical Association.

PAGE 195 LEFT Russell House; courtesy Catherine Jordon Walker.

PAGE 195 RIGHT Summer visitors to the Summit House, 1908; courtesy William A. Kelsey.

PAGE 196 TOP Postcard of Thompson Inn, addressed to Helen Russell; courtesy Catherine Jordon Walker. At the time of this correspondence Helen was working at the Echo House hotel in New Harbor, while Winnie remained in South Bristol to work. Helen later married Frank Jordon, Winnie's older brother.

PAGE 196 MIDDLE Postcard of the "New Holly Inn" dining room, addressed to Ella Burton, 1903; courtesy William A. Kelsey. Walpole girls who worked on Heron Island or in South Bristol village lived too far away to travel back and forth to work each day. 1930s Walpole and Wawenock Ridge local columns in the *Lincoln County News* announced their returns home at the end of the summer: "Miss Catherine Goudy returned home from Thompson Inn, Monday, where she has been employed as waitress...." "Miss Dorothy Brown has completed her summer's work on Heron Island and returned home Thursday...." "Mrs. Will Feltis who has had employment at Thompson Inn, So. Bristol, for several weeks returned home Sunday." Excerpts from the scrapbooks of Lura Holman; courtesy Mervin Rice.

PAGE 196 BOTTOM Postcard of Summit House, 1915, addressed to Mrs. W. H. Wotton in Friendship, Maine, 1915, from "Olivia" in South Bristol; collection of author.

PAGE 197 "Fête Day" at the Christmas Cove Improvement Association, 1913; courtesy Catherine Jordon Walker.

PAGE 198 LEFT Yacht club at anchor in Christmas Cove Harbor; courtesy William A. Kelsey.

PAGE 198 RIGHT Christmas Cove Casino, probably about 1916; courtesy Marian Coughlin. Reproduced from a small snapshot in Goldwin Gilbert's photo album.

PAGE 198 BOTTOM Tennis courts at the CCIA; courtesy William A. Kelsey. The handwritten message reads, "Please send me a leather postcard for my pillow."

PAGE 199 Christmas Cove Land Company plat map and prospectus, 1894; courtesy Catherine Jordon Walker. The development scheme failed because of a lack of funds, and probably because William Nash had no shorefront sites to offer for sale. Born in 1844, William was the eldest child of Tobias and Eleanor Gamage Nash. Nellie Frey recalls "Billy" Nash as the elderly gentleman her grandmother cared for in his home on what is now Coveside Road. He was reputed to be deaf from Civil War cannon fire.

PAGE 200 Birch Island and the Christmas Cove bar; courtesy William A. Kelsey.

Islands

PAGE 201 Catherine Jordon by the Heron Island steamer wharf, c. 1914; courtesy Catherine Jordon Walker. Little Catherine is about four years old in this picture.

PAGE 202 LEFT The Heron Island store and post office; courtesy Catherine Jordon Walker. The back addition and the well house have been torn down, but this building can still be seen from Rutherford Island.

PAGE 202 RIGHT Steamer ENTERPRISE at the Heron Island wharf; courtesy William A. Kelsey.

PAGE 203 LEFT The footbridge from Davis Point to Gem Island; courtesy J. Douglas Thompson. This image is from a commercially printed photo booklet published in 1904 by the Lakeside Press of Portland, Maine. When J. Henry Cartland published *Ten Years at Pemaquid* in 1899, Thomas Gamage was eighty-one and still owned Gem Island. Cartland referred to him as "'Uncle Tommie' Gamage, so well known to commercial and summer visitors whom he so often carries about in his little boat from place to place...."

PAGE 203 RIGHT Postcard of Witch Island, postmarked 1910; courtesy William A. Kelsey. In 1986, Jane Sewall deeded Witch Island to the Maine Audubon Society.

PAGE 204 Gene and Polly Lauder Tunney's house on John's Island; courtesy William A. Kelsey.

PAGE 205 LEFT Passage from *Ten Years at Pemaquid*, J. Henry Cartland, 1899, pages 10-11. An excerpt from the October 5, 1887 *Pemaquid Messenger* marks the date of Edward Holmes's purchase of Thrumbcap Island: "South Bristol. Mr. Holmes of Boston, Mass., has bought Thumbcap [*sic*] Island of Mr. Tobias Nash and is going to ship the shell sand thereon...."

PAGE 205 RIGHT Steamer going through the Thread of Life; author's collection. The message on the front reads, "*Thursday* A.M. *Pa thinks I can't come Sat., as he hasn't his boat in and several things I must help about. I will write again Sat. or Monday Love from Mother.*

PAGE 206 LEFT Passage from *Ten Years at Pemaquid*, J. Henry Cartland, 1899, page 11.

PAGE 206 RIGHT The TOURIST steams through the Thread of Life; courtesy William A. Kelsey. Verso: postmark, 1911, Christmas; addressed to Mrs. L. L. Poland in New Harbor: "*Will come home on the Tourist tomorrow. It leaves here at 9.00 o'clock. I shall get off at the Point.*"

Women's Work

PAGE 207 Martha Marden King; courtesy Arletta Thorpe Rice.

PAGE 208 Recipe page and poem from the 1930 *Rutherford Cook Book*.

PAGE 209 LEFT Elliot Gamage Leeman, about 1889; courtesy Margaret Farrin House.

PAGE 209 RIGHT An 1803 sampler by Jane Sproul; courtesy Eugenie Woodward Cole. Although it has passed through many generations of family hands, the sampler is in remarkably good condition, and some of the colors are still quite vivid. The different lines of letters are worked in a grayish blue, black, dark green, and brown; the leaves and flowers are ochre, and the stems dark green.

PAGE 210 TOP Lucinda Norwood Gamage, 1863–1958; courtesy Margaret Farrin House.

PAGE 210 BOTTOM Margaret Russell Thorpe; courtesy Arletta Thorpe Rice.

PAGE 211 LEFT Myra Clifford and a friend, right; courtesy Margaret Farrin House. The friend looks like she's just realized she has a rat on her head.

PAGE 211 RIGHT Alice Dodge McFarland and daughter Nellie, 1919; courtesy Nellie McFarland Frey.

PAGE 212 Shrimp processing at Farrin's; photograph by Red Boutilier, author's collection.

Getting By

PAGE 214 Children mending nets. *Atlantic Fisherman* magazine, June 1929; author's collection

PAGE 215 Works Progress Administration logo, from a poster of the 1930s.

Icehouses and Brickmaking

PAGE 217 Schooner ALICE M. DEERING at the wharf of the Bristol Ice Company; courtesy Margaret Farrin House.

PAGE 218 TOP Bristol Ice Company ice slide; courtesy William A. Kelsey.

PAGE 218 BOTTOM Excerpts from the *Pemaquid Messenger*, 1888 and 1889.

PAGE 219 Former ice crew boardinghouse; author's photograph, 1997.

PAGE 220 LEFT Ice-cutting crew in front of the Thompson Ice House; courtesy Thompson Ice House Preservation Corporation.

PAGE 220 RIGHT Herbert Thompson at the annual ice harvest; courtesy Thompson Ice House Preservation Corporation. It was Herbert Thompson, along with his wife Gwen, who deeded the icehouse to the Preservation Corporation whose efforts have ensured its survival for future generations.

PAGE 221 Two more excerpts from the *Pemaquid Messenger* describe aspects of the brickyard business on the Damariscotta River:

Sch. IVY BELLE, Loud, is in the river loading with brick, at Piper's yard. She will carry about 100,000.... October 1887

A Bristol Vessel Wrecked. Sch. J. P. WALLACE, Bryant, of Bristol, from the Damariscotta river, for Boston, brick-laden, struck on Devil's Back, Boston harbor, Saturday night and sunk. The crew took to the rigging and remained there till daylight Sunday morning, when they were taken off by the crew of a fishing vessel and carried to Boston.... October 1886

Dousing

PAGE 222 Applewood dousing rod; author's photograph.

Farming and Neighbors

PAGE 224 The Robert Sproul farm; author's photograph 1997. Husking bees were noteworthy social events, and farmers took pride in a good harvest, as evidenced in the local columns of the *Pemaquid Messenger:*

Husking-bees seem to be taking the lead again in the way of entertainments. The one at Mr. Robert Sproul's was enjoyed by all. Also the one at George Huston's; the people from 'Scotta especially enjoying their hay-rack ride....

Robert Sproul sent two very handsome ears of corn to the office, Monday. They measured fourteen inches.

PAGE 225 TOP LEFT Austin Sproul's farmhouse; author's photograph, 1997.

PAGE 225 BOTTOM LEFT Excerpts from the South Bristol personals column in the *Lincoln County News*, 1930s; courtesy Mervin Rice.

PAGE 225 RIGHT A 1933 advertisement for Austin Sproul's chicken farm; courtesy of the Bourgoin family.

PAGE 226 Eugene Wylie's barn on the Thompson Inn Road; courtesy William A. Kelsey.

PAGE 227 LEFT Another example of the postcard used for everyday communications; courtesy William A. Kelsey.

PAGE 227 TOP RIGHT Ernest Gamage in his village blacksmith shop; courtesy Wayne and Amy McFarland. The photograph is undated, but E. E. Gamage is listed as a South Bristol smith in the *Maine Register* only one year: 1896. An article in the *Pemaquid Messenger* dated January 22, 1888 reported the circumstances of his father's death:

The telegraph wires bear many sad messages, but no sadder one have they borne to this town for years than the one received Saturday night telling that Capt. Davis Gamage of South Bristol, commanding the lobster sloop SUPERIOR, had been accidentally knocked over by the boom while getting his vessel underway at Seal Harbor, Saturday morning, and drowned. His son, Ernest, sixteen years old, was with him, but being alone was unable to save him, coming near being swamped himself in his attempt to do so. Capt. Gamage leaves a widow and five children to whom the sympathy of all our people are extended. He was a member of Sea Side Lodge of Masons and was, we hear, a member of Mechanic Falls Relief from which his family will receive $1,000. No higher tribute can be paid to the deceased than to say that he was an honest man,—"The noblest work of God"—and a good and upright citizen.

PAGE 227 BOTTOM RIGHT Cliff on Seal Cove; author's photograph, 1997.

PAGE 228 TOP Draft horses Duke and Bud; courtesy Mervin Rice.

PAGE 228 BOTTOM Orville Clark; courtesy Pemaquid Historical Association. Orville Clark was the great-grandson of George Clark, who came to Walpole sometime before 1751, and from whom Clark's Cove got its name. The house that Orville inherited in 1866, still extant though much altered, was the original one that George built in the first half of the eighteenth century.

PAGE 229 TOP George Atkinson with his team of oxen; courtesy Margaret Farrin House.

PAGE 229 BOTTOM Clifton Poole on his father's hayrake; courtesy Katherine Poole Norwood.

PAGE 230 The Poole farm hayrack; courtesy Katherine Poole Norwood.

PAGES 232–35 Photographs of "The Voices" are by the author.

Bibliography

Books, Articles, and Papers

Abstracts of U.S. Customs Documents, compiled by Robert Applebee. Maine Maritime Museum research collection.

Annual Register of Maine: State Year-Book and Legislative Manual, 1860, 1873-1941 editions

Annual Report of the Municipal Officers of the Town of Bristol, Maine, for the year ending February 20th, 1895.

Atlantic Fisherman magazine, miscellaneous editions, 1921–1929.

Bangor Daily News, March 5, 1970.

Boutilier, Everett "Building Wooden Dory Skiffs Keeps Clif Poole's Hand In," *National Fisherman Magazine*, July 1970.

Bristol Town Register, 1906.

Bruce, Bob "At the Cowboys' Christmas Ball," *Texas Highways* magazine,vol. 38, no. 12, December 1991.

Cartland, Henry, *Ten Years at Pemaquid.* Pemaquid Beach, Maine 1899.

Castner, Harold. "The Castner Papers." Collection of unpublished manuscripts and clippings. Damariscotta, Maine: Skidompha Public Library.

Damariscotta Herald, September 5, 1918.

deVeers, Elizabeth and Richard J. Boyle. *Sunlight and Shadow: The Life and Art of Willard L. Metcalf.* New York: Boston University/Abbeville Press, 1987.

Dodge, Christine Huston, ed.*Vital Records of Old Bristol and Nobleboro in the County of Lincoln, Maine*. Reprinted by the Pemaquid Historical Association under authority of the Maine Historical Society. Damariscotta, Maine: Lincoln County Publishing Co. 1988

Gamage, Nelson W. *A Short History of South Bristol, Maine*. South Bristol, Maine: South Bristol Union Church, 1953; reprinted by the Rutherford Library Association, 1990.

Hanna, Joshua. "The Pemaquid Peninsula of Maine: A Study of Economic and Community Development, 1815–1915." Hanover, New Hampshire: Dartmouth College, 1994. Undergraduate honors thesis.

Howland, John. "Heron Island Memories, 1914–1995." Unpublished memoirs.

Humphries, Floyd. "Boyhood on a Maine Island, 1904-1916." Unpublished memoirs.

Humphries, Romilly. "Summer's End," *Cruising the Maine Coast* magazine, March/April 1996.

Johnston, John, LL.D. *A History of Bristol and Bremen Including the Pemaquid Settlement*. Albany, New York: Joel Munsell, 1873; reprinted by the Bremen Library Association Bremen, Maine 1988.

Lee, W. Storrs "Hilda 'Lupina's' Beautiful Crusade," *Yankee Magazine*, June 1971.

Lewiston Evening Journal, "Some South Bristol People Declare It's Only a Tempest in a Teapot," October 21, 1921.

Lewiston Journal, January 13, 1917.

Lincoln County News, c. 1930s. Clippings in scrapbooks of Lura E. Holman, collection of Mervin Rice.

McLane, Charles B. and Carol E. McLane. *Islands of the Mid-Maine Coast, Volume IV: Pemaquid Point to the Kennebec River.* Gardiner, Maine: Tilbury House, Publishers, 1994.

The Menhaden Fishery of Maine. Association of Menhaden Oil and Guano Manufacturers, 1878.

The Pemaquid Messenger, miscellaneous editions, 1886–89.

Portland Evening Express, "Two Fishermen Lose Gamble With Storm," March 3, 1947; "Fisherman Found," March 5, 1947.

Report of the Supervisor of Schools of the Town of Bristol for the Year Ending March 11, 1861.

Rowe, William Hutchinson. *The Maritime History of Maine: Three Centuries of Shipbuilding and Seafaring*. New York, New York: W. W. Norton & Co., 1948.

Seaver, Henry. "Old Days at Heron Island: Absorbing Story of Early Visits to Heron Island Told in Letter Form to His Nephew," *Lincoln County News*, July 29, 1934.

Sewell, John "Steam Boat Days at the CCIA," *CCIA Notes*, Summer 1966. Newsletter of the Christmas Cove Improvement Association.

Sidelinger, Lowell. "Vessels Built in Bristol with Historical Sketches of Old Vessels and Builders," 1896.

Smith, Kenneth E. "Outsiders and Natives: An Ethno-Historical Account of Fishing and Fishermen Along the Pemaquid Peninsula of Maine." Henniker, New Hampshire: New England College.

Warner, H. Landon. "History of the Families and Their Houses, South Bristol, Maine 1730-1915." Unpublished manuscript, 1986. South Bristol Historical Society.

Archived Interview Tapes and Transcriptions

Curtis, Mertie Knipe. "Shipwreck of 1903," Heritage Tapes interview by Gladys Lewis, 1974. Bristol American Bicentennial Committee Collection of Bristol Area Library, Pemaquid, Maine.

Emery, Sarah. Interview by Richard Hawkins, 1975. Collection of the South Bristol Historical Society.

Thorpe, Kathleen Geyer. Interview by Rebecca Rice, 1972. Collection of Arletta Thorpe Rice.

Additional Interviews by Author

Everett "Red" Boutilier, Bremen, Maine, 1999.

Debbie Hunter, Walpole, Maine, 1999.

Adele McFarland, Christmas Cove, Maine, 1997.

Edward Myers, Walpole, Maine, 1998.

Written Memories Contributed at the Round Top Center for the Arts Exhibition, 1998

Phyllis Bryant Charette
Annie Louise Alley Farrin
Alfred Harrington
Phil Hatch
Carolyn Edna Kelsey
Claire Curtis McNamara
Janice O'Brien
Gina Riddiford
A. Stanton Wells

Ellen Vincent

Ellen Vincent is an award-winning photographer and sculptor whose numerous solo and group exhibitions in venues nationwide include showings at the Chrysler Museum, Baltimore Museum of Art, and the Corcoran Gallery. Her photographs have been cover art for magazines and record albums, and her writing credits include photo essays and critical reviews for *Country Magazine* and *The Washington Post*. A native of Maryland, she currently lives in Wisconsin where she is Professor of Art at the Milwaukee Institute of Art and Design. She visits South Bristol whenever she can.

South Bristol Historical Society

The South Bristol Historical Society was organized in 1998 by a number of individuals who cared deeply about the town's history and wanted to encourage broad participation in the preservation and enjoyment of the rich heritage of the area. The Society set as its goals the collection and preservation of historical memorabilia and important records, promotion of interest in local history among school children and the general public, and the operation of an historical and genealogical reference center for the public.

The publication of *Down on the Island, Up on the Main* represents both a significant step towards achieving a number of Society goals and a major opportunity for the SBHS to help awaken an appreciation for local history in other small towns in Maine and elsewhere in New England. Throughout each year, the Society works toward its goals in many ways: holding meetings open to the public featuring a guest lecturer or demonstration; interviewing townspeople to augment an already significant collection of oral histories; writing articles on local history for the SBHS newsletter and local newspapers; and supporting the Thompson Ice House Preservation Corporation each July by presenting demonstrations of historical interest at the Ice Cream Festival and Fair.

The Society has created a small museum and research center in the former town library building at 2124 State Route 129, a simple one-room building renovated and equipped by member volunteers. In addition to extensive genealogical records, the collection includes published and unpublished local histories, oral history tapes, photographs, paintings, postcards, daybooks and ledgers from local stores, signs from early businesses, as well as numerous and varied family heirlooms and household artifacts. Member volunteers keep the building open for visitors one to three days a week, depending on the season, and by appointment.